Spring 2009

SYMBOLIC LIFE
2009

A JOURNAL OF
ARCHETYPE
AND
CULTURE

Fall 2009

SPRING JOURNAL
New Orleans, Louisiana

CONTENTS

INTERVIEW

CURRENT CONTROVERSIES

BOOK REVIEW

GUEST EDITOR'S FOREWORD

It has been seventy years since Jung spoke about "the symbolic life" to the Guild of Pastoral Psychology in London.[1] In the intervening years, the cultural trends that he commented on there have only deepened and broadened; they have not ameliorated. The secular world is even more rational and technological today in 2009 than it was in 1939, and the deep cleavages and splits in our contemporary culture have not been bridged or healed to any significant extent since Jung's day.

On the other hand, the surprising resurgence of fundamentalist forms of religion worldwide in the last half century offers a dramatically contrasting alternative to the modern worldview. Their current power and ubiquity were unimaginable in Jung's lifetime. One could look on them as a compensatory impulse from the collective psyche meant to restore the symbolic to its proper role in human life, individual and communal—a cry of the human soul for a home in a cold, impersonal, and fragmentary universe. More accurately, however, they are a regressive, angry protest to the globalization of modernity and its secular values. Traditional and fundamentalist religions provide a safe harbor for anxious souls who are threatened by the increasingly prevalent meaninglessness and spiritual emptiness of modernity.

The standoff between a rational secular worldview and a traditional religious one was of course extremely familiar to Jung. While he lamented the loss of religious belief and conviction in the modern world around him, as he made clear in his talk to the Guild in 1939, he also recognized its inevitability in the evolution of human consciousness. "We cannot turn the wheel backwards; we cannot go back to the symbolism that is gone. No sooner do you know that this thing is symbolic than you say, 'Oh, well, it presumably means something else.' Doubt has killed it, has devoured it. So you cannot go back."[2] Jung was no happier or more content with modernity than we are today, since it offers so little in the way of a sense of personal meaning in a mechanistic universe and blocks all routes of access to the transcendent. The so-called postmodern world of 2009 is not much less modern than what it grew out of, in the sense that the prospects for meaning, personal and communal, remain negligible. In some views, the present world has only increased in spiritual vacuity and offers nothing more or less for the soul than the Void, the sheer absence of the possibility of personal meaning.

To live a symbolic life outside of the containment provided by a religious tradition, and actively so, even within the present cultural world, despite its aridity, is what Jung sought out. His way was one of profound introversion and engagement with the images that emerged spontaneously into consciousness. His famous "Red Book," which is now in 2009 being published and made available for public inspection and scholarly review, is a testament to this dedication and to what can come of it. No doubt Jung found a way to the symbolic life for himself, and in 1939 he could speak about it with confidence and conviction. For him this was not something grandiose. Rather, in his talk to the members of the Guild, he stressed the importance of full acceptance of the shadow and of taking responsibility for one's psyche and its enactments: "[T]he argument is that it is immoral to allow Christ to suffer for us, that he has suffered enough, that we should carry our own sins for once and not shift them off on to Christ—that we should carry them all."[3]

Is Jung's path into a symbolic life still viable in 2009? I believe that many people who have been influenced by Jung's ideas and methods, whether only intellectually or also through the experience of a personal analysis, continue to attempt a symbolic life along similar but usually much less intense lines than Jung himself managed. What this way entails is a specific attitude toward the psyche, especially toward the unconscious. For it is to the unconscious that one looks for hints and cues toward the symbolic, if one follows the classic methods described by Jung. The religious traditions may also offer useful images and motifs, since they are ultimately products of the psyche as are all human constructions. Such images may suggest possible hints of transcendence, as do numinous images from other sources such as dreams, personal visions and intuitions, and synchronistic experiences. This way means opening the door to a vast array of personal and traditional manifestations of the spirit and the human soul.

It is the process of receiving and reflecting on such images that one would today designate as "a symbolic life." This means living reflectively with numinous symbols that crop up spontaneously, that capture the feeling of meaning and offer a sense of direction. Much of this way is based on feeling and on the feeling function, but there is also the requirement to think about the symbols given, to use them as metaphors that may unfold further thinking, and also eventually to discover their limitations as guiding images.

The essays in this volume come at the issues involved in living a life with symbolic consciousness from a variety of directions. The authors— all are analysts or students associated with The International School of Analytical Psychology in Zurich (ISAPZurich)—rely on many sources for their reflections on symbolic representations of psychic reality and processes. The thematic contents of these essays circle around several foci—transformations in consciousness, the deepening of meaning for individuals and communities, psychic survival after suffering severe stress and trauma, and cultural evolution. Some are concerned primarily with the individual, others more with communal and cultural issues.

What is a "symbolic life" like in 2009? Traditionally, it meant partaking fully of religious symbolic systems, not necessarily in a fundamentalist mode but certainly in a non-ironic, believing mode that would be called faith. In the psychological approach, individual symbols are held and reflected in another way. They are regarded as impermanent images of the Divine that can be used for guidance and orientation and can also be set aside or discarded when they no longer serve cognitive and emotional needs. The human factor is in charge of the symbolic, rather than the other way around, as it is in traditional religions. If a particular symbol loses its power and numinosity for a time, it does not mean that one cannot return to it later and ask more questions, gather further enriching associations, and regroup one's energy and orientation from it. Once an image establishes itself as a symbol for a person, it occupies a more permanent place in consciousness than a momentary flicker of an image, as from a quickly forgotten dream or an experience at the movies. A symbol holds a place of privilege and may be active and effective over long periods of time—years and even decades. An attitude of respect for the numinous presence of the Divine, akin to worship, belongs inherently to the symbolic life. To live with a symbol means to come back to it often and, in this return, to renew its energy and to be renewed by its profound connections to the Source, the Self.

For myself, I prefer to think of "living with symbols" rather than being contained within "a symbolic life." The symbols one finds oneself living with are not usually chosen by a free will, out of interest or fascination, or for aesthetic reasons. They are rather given, even imposed, by the will of the Self, and the role they play in a person's psychological and emotional life lasts for a time and then may fade in importance or be replaced by other symbols. In this sense, the symbolic life is a process constantly in motion, momentarily fixed on certain specific images, then unfolding and evolving with others.

Symbolic life 2009 is process. To be engaged in such an enterprise is to step into the stream of psychic life as it flows into conscious life and offers channels of expression and directions for movement that cannot be predicted. It is to be part of an eternal process of creation, destruction, re-creation.

—Murray Stein, Goldiwil (Thun), May 2009

NOTES

1. C. G. Jung, "The Symbolic Life," in *The Collected Works of C. G. Jung* (Princeton, NJ: Princeton University Press, 1939/1976), vol. 18.

2. *Ibid.*, § 632.

3. *Ibid.*, § 638.

SYMBOLIC LIFE 2009

Symbol as Psychic Transformer

MURRAY STEIN

My personal physician in Thun recently complained about the many patients he sees who are perfectly healthy but come to him doubled over in pain and complaining about their illusory symptoms. "They are crazy," he said, throwing up his hands in frustration. "Perfectly healthy people, but not able to live with their health! On the other side I have patients who feel as healthy as can be, and I have to tell them they have six months to live because of a recently discovered lymphoma. I'd like to send the healthy ones to the moon! They're nuts!"

His complaint reminded me of the opening pages in Jung's 1936 Terry Lectures at Yale University, entitled "Psychology and Religion." There he is telling the audience about the power that a neurosis can have over patients' lives. For instance, he says, a man imagines he has cancer, but there is no physical evidence of cancer in his body. He then feels at a complete loss and becomes convinced that he is crazy. So he consults Jung, a psychiatrist. "Help me, doctor. I think I'm dying from cancer but this is nonsense, yet I can't stop it!" What does the psychiatrist Jung do with this imaginary cancer?

Murray Stein is currently president of The International School of Analytical Psychology in Zurich. He is the author of *Transformation—Emergence of the Self* and *The Principle of Individuation*, among other books, and the editor of *Jungian Psychoanalysis*. He lives in Goldiwil (Thun), Switzerland.

> I told him that it would be better to take his obsession seri-
> ously instead of reviling it as pathological nonsense. But to
> take it seriously would mean acknowledging it as a sort of di-
> agnostic statement of the fact that, in a psyche which really ex-
> isted, trouble had arisen in the form of a cancer-like growth.
> "But," he will certainly ask, "what could that growth be?" And
> I shall answer: "I do not know," as indeed I do not. Although
> …it is surely a compensatory or complementary unconscious
> formation, nothing is yet known about its specific nature or
> about its content. It is a spontaneous manifestation of the un-
> conscious, based on contents which are not to be found in
> consciousness….I then inform him…that his dreams will
> provide us with all the necessary information. We will take
> them as if they issued from an intelligent, purposive, and, as it
> were, personal source….The symptom is like the shoot above
> ground, yet the main plant is an extended rhizome under-
> ground. The rhizome represents the content of a neurosis; it is
> the matrix of complexes, of symptoms, and of dreams. We
> have every reason to believe that dreams mirror exactly the un-
> derground processes of the psyche. And if we get there, we lit-
> erally get at the "roots" of the disease.[1]

The delusional idea of a cancerous growth in a healthy body, then, is a *symbol*, which can provide a point of entry into the unconscious realm of complexes, processes, and hidden conflicts. And just as a physical cancer will suck the life out of a living organism if it is allowed to grow and remains unchecked, a psychic cancer too will drain a person's life of psychic energy and produce a state of hopeless stagnation and eventually even psychic death. Symbols have the power to do just that. They collect, hold, and channel psychic energy, for good or ill.

In one sense, this psychic symptom is a metaphor, in that it is borrow-ing the language of physicality (cancer, illness) and applying it to the psychic domain. This transfer of language from one domain to another is what poets do when they employ metaphors. The psyche is involuntarily acting in a poetic fashion by stating, "I am sick with cancer," when the person, were he more conscious of his psychic suffering, would say, "I am in profound despair," or "I have no energy," or "I am in hopeless conflict and it's eating me alive!" But this patient cannot say that. He can only say: "I am convinced I have cancer, and I can't get this irrational idea out of my head!" He is an unwilling poet. He has not chosen this symbol con-sciously or voluntarily; it has chosen him. He is unfree to dismiss it and unable to interpret it. So he goes to the analyst, and he confesses that he is possessed by a symbol and doesn't know what it means. Understandably, he is humiliated by the stupid symptom and its unyielding grip on him. Jung says that such morbidity is usually shameful, and the patient is embarrassed to admit this weakness. He is in the grip of a complex, and this psychic factor—powerful, autonomous, and unconscious—is symbolized as a cancer. It must be analyzed and made conscious so that the very real suffering caused by the symptom-symbol can be transformed into psychic suffering. Perhaps other psychic resources can thus also be constellated, which will assist in bringing about the free flow of energy (libido) into more life-enhancing tasks and goals.

What Is a Symbol?

As Jung understands and employs the term *symbol*, it is different from a metaphor in that what it is communicating or presenting to consciousness is utterly untranslatable into any other terms, at least for the time being. Symbols are opaque and often bring thinking to a standstill. Metaphors are transparent and must be so if they are to do their job. They help us think in creative ways "outside the box." If a poet writes, for instance, that a bridge leaps ("vaulting the sea") and addresses it as a "harp" and an "altar," as the American poet Hart Crane does in his famous poem, "To Brooklyn Bridge," the reader can with diligence puzzle out a sense of what the poet means to communicate. We know what a bridge is, and we know what "vaulting" signifies and what "altars" and "harps" are, and we can think along with the poet and appreciate what he is getting at with these metaphors. The images all refer to sense data in the material world, and reflection will yield interesting ideas about how they belong together and what this unique concatenation signifies. But if a patient says, "I am convinced that I have a cancerous tumor in my body but there is no evidence—what does this mean?" the psychotherapist must confess, with Jung: "I have no idea what it means, but we can explore the image. By looking at your life, your history, your dreams and fantasies, we may be able to discover something that at this moment is locked out of consciousness and is analogous to a cancer." It is an important difference. The link between signifier and signified is totally opaque in the case of symbols; with metaphors, on the contrary, this link is evident even if often very complicated and at first glance puzzling.

Jung relates the symbol to an understanding of psychological dynamics, and this sets his view apart from other definitions of symbol and the symbolic, such as philosophical or literary ones. His is a psychological definition and is meant to serve the purposes of grasping the meaning of symptoms and images as they appear irrationally in the experience of patients in particular, but also in people the world over generally. He defines the symbol as follows: "The symbol is not a sign that disguises something generally known (a disguise, that is, for the basic drive or elementary intention). Its meaning resides in the fact that it is an attempt to elucidate, by a more or less apt analogy, something that is still entirely unknown or still in the process of formation."[2] A symbol presents an unconscious content making its way towards consciousness. As an analogy, it presents something that is otherwise completely unconscious.

The patient with the delusional idea of having a cancerous growth in his body cannot at the moment express his suffering in any other or better way, or in a more accurate and psychologically descriptive way. He is therefore speaking in symbols and without any conscious understanding whatever of what the symbol might be saying. His judgment is that it is simply a delusional idea, a crazy thought that he can't shake. Nor does the doctor know what it means. With symbols one knows only that they are presenting something by analogy, that there is much more here than one can readily grasp consciously, and that there is something deeply hidden and obscure. The Jungian psychoanalyst will have faith that there is something meaningful in the symbol, but for the moment that is all.

Once a symbol is understood cognitively—be it as an expression of an outgrowth of childhood trauma, as an image of intrapsychic or interpersonal conflicts, as a block to creative potential, or whatever else the meaning may turn out to be—it can be put aside as a symbol. Here is a statement of Jung's hermeneutic:

> A view which interprets the symbolic expression as the best possible formulation of a relatively *unknown* thing...is *symbolic*. So long as a symbol is a living thing, it is an expression for something that cannot be characterized in any other or better way. The symbol is alive only so long as it is pregnant with meaning. But once its meaning has been born out of it, once that expression is found which formulates the thing sought, expected, or divined even better than the hitherto accepted symbol, then the symbol is *dead*, i.e., it possesses only

> an historical significance....An expression that stands for a
> known thing remains a mere sign and is never a symbol.[3]

Thereafter the symbol becomes a sign, and signifier and signified are then both out in the open and clearly linked. It becomes an historical marker: "I used to think I had cancer, but what I found out was that my libido was blocked because of trauma, childhood conflicts, and consequent lack of self confidence," the hypothetical patient might declare. Once the necessary *psychic* suffering has been discovered and made conscious, the symbol becomes a "sign" and can be used then as a metaphor by consciousness if the patient chooses to be poetic.

One chief therapeutic goal of analysis is to convert symbols into signs and possibly into metaphors and so to free the patient's consciousness from the grip of the autonomous complexes and to unblock the flow of libido into more satisfying channels of living, loving, and creating. So my physician in Thun should, instead of sending those crazy patients to the moon, send them to a good psychotherapist!

So far so good, but is this enough? Jung and most Jungians today too would, I venture to say, object to stopping at this good but rather limited goal for analysis. To find this sufficient would mean being satisfied with turning unconscious suffering into conscious suffering and achieving what the American psychoanalyst Elizabeth Zetzel defined as psychic health: "Psychic health demands successful initiation and later integration of those capacities which will facilitate throughout life, first, passive recognition and tolerance of limitations, losses and threats, and equally, active efforts towards finding and obtaining available objects and personal goals which permit both passive gratification and active achievement."[4] This is, of course, a highly desirable outcome for a therapeutic analysis, but it stops short of what Jung saw as the full potential for the psychic development that analysis is intended to foster.

SOME DIFFERENCES BETWEEN JUNG AND FREUD

I will speak now briefly of some differences between Jung and Freud and how they led to significant differences between the two fields they engendered, psychoanalysis and analytical psychology.

With regard first to the term "libido," the chief difference was that Jung chose to use the term in the more general sense of "psychic energy," and did not limit its meaning, as Freud did, to sexual desire or sexual impulse/instinct exclusively. For Jung, libido became a generic term cov-

ering all specific types of psychic energy manifestations. At first this may
have seemed like a small difference, but in time it really did make a big
difference in their theories about the psychic economy, about motivation, and for the practical application of these theories in clinical work.
As Jung continued his explorations of the personal and collective unconscious in the years following the break with Freud, he picked up on an
early intuition he had had already in his pre-Freud period and evidenced
in his book on schizophrenia, *The Psychology of Dementia Praecox*. He
elaborated the idea that the psyche has a forward-moving and creative
function, and that when symbols become activated they serve to organize
the structures and patterns that libido follows. In this view, symbols play a
dynamic role in potentially moving the psyche *forward* in a development
toward greater wholeness, rather than holding it *back*.

The most immediate cause of the sharp and decisive break between
Jung and Freud was Jung's work *Symbole und Wandlungen der Libido*
(1912-1913), and of course Freud's cool reception of the revisionist ideas
that Jung was putting forward there. Already at that time Jung was using
the term libido in the more general sense of psychic energy or simply
"interest," rather than as sexual energy or desire specifically. Going further, he interpreted the incest wish and the incest taboo as the wish to
remain infantile (a kind of wish for paradise), and the prohibition against
fulfilling this wish as a psychic imperative toward development and
maturity. In this work, Jung was groping toward a formulation of the psyche as a self-regulating system and one aimed toward the goal of full development of potentials. That is, he regarded the psyche as purposive and
goal-oriented toward development. Hence the title *Wandlungen der
Libido* (Transformations of Libido). The transformations of libido he was
speaking of here had, in his view, a purpose and a goal, and symbols played
the leading role in this process. At that time, Jung had not yet sufficiently
worked out what would become the theory of archetypes to explain this
teleological feature of the psyche's life. He was groping in the dark, hence
the rather chaotic nature of the text. However, when he revised this book
for publication in 1952 and gave it a new title, *Symbols of Transformation*,
he added extensive passages that explained and grounded the work in
archetypal theory. Thus, in a new passage he writes of symbols as follows:

> The symbols it [i.e., the psyche] creates are always grounded
> in the unconscious archetype....The symbols act as *transform-*
> *ers*, their function being to convert libido from a "lower" into

a "higher" form. This function is so important that feeling accords it the highest values. The symbol works by suggestion; that is to say, it carries conviction and at the same time expresses the content of that conviction. It is able to do this because of the numen, the specific energy stored up in the archetype. Experience of the archetype is not only impressive, it seizes and possesses the whole personality....[T]he prime task of the psychotherapist must be to understand the symbols anew, and thus to understand the unconscious, compensatory striving of his patient for an attitude that reflects the totality of the psyche.[5]

Here he proposes the idea that symbols transform libido in an "upward" direction. This is similar to Freud's "sublimation," but does not indicate a defense mechanism, nor does Jung see this as leaving the famous Freudian residue of "discontent." One could say that symbols are the means by which psychic energy is sublimated because they can mold and channel libido and send it surging into pathways that result in "higher"—i.e., more complex and filled-out—motivations, activities, attitudes, and states of consciousness. Without the symbolic capacity, humans would be much simpler creatures and devoid of mind and culture. For Jung, the human capacity to receive symbols and to do something with them belongs to the very definition of what it means to be human. Symbols shape and reshape matter![6]

In this passage (and in many others as well), Jung links symbol closely to archetype. This is extremely important in Jungian theory. Archetypes are archaic and deeply unconscious potential patterns of psychic functioning. Unconstellated, they are extremely diffuse and vague. They become more chiseled and precise as they emerge into psychic life as patterns of perception, behavior, motivation, and attitude. Archetypes are innate in the sense that they are sourced in psychic regions that are prior to and much more general than the individual's precise personal experiences and acquisitions. They belong to the collective unconscious, which is not personal, just as culture is not personal. One is born into it. Archetypes are not inherited memories or ideas but rather potential patterns of motivation, action, and reaction (defense), which emerge in a variety of human situations as responses to challenges and to environmental fields that call for adaptation—the mother/infant and other family relationships, the call to heroic action in peer groups and society, the chance for love, the threat of death, etc.

Archetypes can look much like "instincts" in a biological matrix, waiting to be "triggered." Sometimes Jung will speak of them this way, as "innate patterns of behavior," and many Jungians have followed this model. The danger in this view is, however, that symbols then become reduced to mere representations of specific unconscious structures that exist somewhere in the biological substructure (e.g., in the brain). This reductionism is not so different from Freud's well-known biological reductionism. The contemporary Jungian analyst Jean Knox has written:

> In this sense, both psychoanalysis and analytical psychol-
> ogy…can actually therefore be seen to be reductionistic, in so
> far as psychic life is reduced and objectified by attempts to ex-
> plain its functioning in terms of bodily processes. So this simi-
> larity between Freud and Jung is one which contemporary
> psychoanalysts and analytical psychologists should join to-
> gether in rejecting, which I think would re-vitalize both our
> disciplines.[7]

Knox goes on to advocate "a view that a stream of current experience con-stantly re-shapes and guides the development of the human mind and brain….[I]nfant studies…demonstrate the crucial role played by inti-mate relationships in the development of the human psyche."[8]

If we understand archetype in a psychologically dynamic sense, how-ever—perhaps as Knox would also advocate—it can be conceived as a broadly flexible potential pattern of motivation, attitude, action, and reaction to critical human situations, or, as Jung defined the term in a let-ter to Wolfgang Pauli, as statistical probability: "the archetype represents nothing else but the probability of psychic events."[9] Archetypes then are understood as probable emergent modes of psychic operation rather than as fixed and inherited entities waiting to be triggered. Symbols, in this understanding, have two functions in relation to archetypal patterns: (1) to express them in a graphic and succinct way, making them visible, memorable, and imagistically concrete; and (2) to attract libido and fur-ther energize the emergent archetypal patterns and in this way to trans-form and channel libido. Because the archetypal patterns are subject to the rules of emergence, they remain partially or largely unconscious until they become fully operationalized, hence the rationale for the view that symbols are the best possible present expression of a pattern that is still largely unconscious. Symbols therefore anticipate the fully emerged pat-terns. Once the patterns are active and completely unfolded, consciousness can put names and cognitions in place that capture their meaning and interpret them effectively. When this is done, symbols become signs and are emptied of their numinosity and their suggestive, mysterious, and also compulsive quality. Symbols have a sort of midwife role in the psyche.

Symbolic Processes

Let us return now to our hypothetical patient with the delusional idea that he had cancer. Taking this idea as a symbol, we would say that some unconscious content was trying to emerge due to a crisis in the patient's life, and that the symptom was both a cry for help ("Doctor, doctor, I'm dying!") and the psyche's attempt at offering a solution to the crisis in which the patient presently finds himself. A Jungian approach to treatment in this case would be to create as full a picture of the patient's life context to date as possible, including his life history, his major previous developmental deficits and unresolved conflicts, his present conscious situation in life (with respect to intimate relationships, to work, to meaning), and then to add to this consciously established and created context the unconscious material derived from dreams, fantasies, projections, transference, and so forth. Once one had this picture, one would presumably begin to understand the meaning of the symptom, why cancer was chosen as the symbol, why cancer of this organ and not that, why the precise set of symptoms that manifested. However, this would be just the beginning of the analytic process.

What Jung and most Jungians following him and his methods have been most keenly interested in is not primarily getting rid of symptoms or even understanding their symbolic meanings, but rather in the symbolic process that opens up and reveals itself when the unconscious is actively engaged in analysis. What is important here is not just *a* symbol, but a *symbolic process* that reveals an invisible and hard to discern but all-important and life-giving tendency in the psyche that is intent on creating *meaning* in the large spiritual sense of that word. Only symbols can convey this content, only symbols can present it, only symbols can contain it and make it available to consciousness. It is a process that pulls libido powerfully in its train and in the end transforms life radically and decisively.

In the Terry Lectures, where he speaks of a hypothetical patient with this delusional idea of having cancer, Jung unexpectedly drops this figure and turns to another one, now to a real patient whom he knew well and followed over a long period of time. He says:

> I propose to choose another case as an example of how dreams
> reveal the unknown inner facts of the psyche....The dreamer
> was [an] intellectual, of remarkable intelligence and learning.
> He was neurotic and was seeking my help because he felt that
> his neurosis had become overpowering and was slowly but
> surely undermining his morale....I set him the task of observ-
> ing and recording his dreams himself. The dreams were not
> analysed or explained to him and it was only very much later
> that we began their analysis.[10]

This man was a well-known scientist and academic in Zurich who had
landed in a midlife crisis. Today the personal details are quite well known
by scholars, but I will not mention them here. Suffice it to say, he was bril-
liantly successful in his academic life but a miserable failure in his personal
and intimate life and suffered from "anxiety states, psychogenic alcohol-
ism, and general moral dissipation."[11] The dreams he produced after an
initial meeting with Jung and while in treatment with one of Jung's students fascinated Jung because of the suggestions they offered about "possible sources of information about the religious tendencies of the
unconscious."[12] Jung sums up the conscious attitude of the patient toward
religion and the spiritual as follows:

> Religion was of no concern to my patient and he certainly
> never expected that it would concern him in any way. But he
> had come to me because of a very alarming experience. Being
> highly rationalistic and intellectual he had found that his atti-
> tude of mind and his philosophy forsook him completely in
> the face of his neurosis and its demoralizing forces. He found
> nothing in his whole *Weltanschauung* that would help him to
> gain sufficient control of himself.[13]

What the dreams brought to the patient's attention was, in Jung's view,
"the problem of a religious attitude,"[14] which in effect meant the problem
of meaning on a more than simply personal level.

Jung goes on to offer a glimpse into the symbolic process that unfolds
in this patient's extensive dream series. About a dream series as such, he
says: "[T]here is probably...a continuity of unconscious processes—perhaps even more than with the events of consciousness....If we want to
shed any light on the deeper reasons for the dream, we must go back to the
series and find out where it is located in the long chain of...dreams."[15]
The idea here is that there is a symbolic process at work in the uncon-

scious, which if understood and correctly interpreted will reveal the deepest and most hidden intentions of the human psyche. What are they?

In breaking with Freud, Jung disputed the prime, even exclusive, centrality of sexuality and the sexual drive in psychic life. In fact, he concluded that for Freud the theme of sexuality itself was a symbol, a numinous power based on archetypal energies and patterning, which had grasped Freud's consciousness and controlled it. For Freud, he felt, sexuality was a religion. And like all religions, it gave his life direction and meaning. As a symbol, it offered meaning and an infinite prospect for further elucidation. In the symbolic process that Jung was studying in the dream series of the Zurich intellectual, the creation of symbols that would offer meaning also seemed to be the goal. The symbolic process is aimed at creating images and themes that give ultimate meaning to the individual's life. That is why he thought of this process as spiritual development, as a kind of sacred pilgrimage. His difference with Freud was based on an understanding of sexuality as a symbol (Eros), not as only a physical and biological pressure or drive. But he considered this but one symbol among many possibilities, not necessarily for everyone the most important one. In that sense, he was not a monotheist but rather a polytheist. As there are many myths, many gods and goddesses, each with its own sacrality and numinous drawing power, so there are many symbols and symbolic processes. For the Zurich intellectual, meaning would be presented in quite a different symbolic statement, not in images of sexual union as the final fulfillment and satisfaction, but in images of complex harmony that united rhythms in three grand movements, as presented in the "world clock" image he discovered in a vision: "There is a vertical and a horizontal circle, having a common centre. This is the world clock."[16] The clock moves in three great rhythms or pulses: a small pulse, a middle pulse, and a great pulse. Jung comments on this as follows:

> All these dreams lead up to one image which came to the patient in the form of a sudden visual impression. He had had such glimpses or visualizations on several occasions before, but this time it was a most impressive experience. As he himself says: "It was an impression of the most sublime harmony."…The vision was a turning point in the patient's psychological development. It was what one would call—in the language of religion—a conversion.[17]

Such is the transformative power of the symbol.

NOTES

1. C. G. Jung, *Psychology and Religion*, vol. 11 of *The Collected Works of C. G. Jung,* trans. R. F. C. Hull, ed. H. Read, M. Fordham, G. Adler, Wm. McGuire, 20 vols. (Princeton, NJ: Princeton University Press, 1953-1979)(hereafter *CW*), § 35-37.

2. Jung, "The Structure of the Unconscious," in *CW* 7, § 492.

3. Jung, *Psychological Types*, *CW* 6, § 815-817.

4. Elizabeth Zetzel, *The Capacity for Emotional Growth* (London: Maresfield Library, 1970), pp. 283-284.

5. Jung, *Symbols of Transformation, CW* 5, § 344-346.

6. In a letter to Kurt Plachte, 10 January 1929, Jung writes: "A religious experience strives for expression and can be expressed only 'symbolically' because it transcends understanding. It *must* be expressed one way or another, for therein is revealed its immanent vital force. It wants to step over, as it were, into visible life, to take concrete shape. (The spirit shows its effective power only in the reshaping of matter.)" C. G. Jung, *Letters*, vol. 1, selected and edited by Gerhard Adler (Princeton, NJ: Princeton University Press, 1973), p. 59.

7. Jean Knox, "Who's Afraid of Sexuality? Self, Object, Drive and Desire—A Contemporary Jungian View" (unpublished paper), p. 4.

8. *Ibid.*, pp. 4-5.

9. C. G. Jung, Letter to Wolfgang Pauli, 13 January 1951, in *The Jung-Pauli Letters*, ed. C. A. Meier (Princeton, NJ: Princeton University Press, 2002), p. 69.

10. Jung, *Psychology and Religion*, *CW* 11, § 38.

11. *Ibid.*, § 55.

12. *Ibid.*, § 39.

13. *Ibid.*, § 51.

14. *Ibid.*, § 53.

15. *Ibid.*

16. *Ibid.*, § 111.

17. *Ibid.*, § 110.

IMAGINATION AND SPIRITUALITY

ROBERT M. MERCURIO

What better way to start off than with a dream? "I'm in a very beautiful English Gothic cathedral, together with my mother. As we walk around, we admire all the various details in the architecture and in the decorations. When it's time for us to leave, we stop at the door and start to compare notes as to what we liked best about the church. My mother says that she liked the stone columns—I disagree. She says that the frescoes and the stone carvings were beautiful—again, I disagree. Finally she says that she liked the altar, but I disagree once again. The only things I liked about this glorious cathedral were the stained glass windows, and not even all of them! I only liked the ones that were pastel-colored because they allowed a lot of light to shine through."

Naturally, the dream needs to be placed in its proper context. In a study group in Rome on the relationship between Jungian psychology and spirituality, it had been decided that we would all reflect on the rela-

A graduate of the Jung Institute in Zurich (1989), Robert Mercurio is a member of the Centro Italiana di Psicologia Analitica (CIPA), where he teaches courses on the process of individuation, active imagination, and on the relation between analytical psychology and spirituality. He also teaches at the Libera Scuola per lo Studio della Terapia Analitica (LISTA), has offered courses on active imagination at ISAP in Zurich, and collaborates with the Istituto di Ortofonologia in Rome, where he conducts courses on myth and fairy tales. He lives and works in Rome, Italy.

tionship between traditional religious forms, on the one hand, and direct
experience of the "great mystery" within each one of us, through dreams
for example, on the other hand. The dream seems to offer a direction to
be followed in working on this problem, and may even contain an answer.
As far as my mother is concerned, suffice it to say that she was a very sin-
cere, believing woman, even if her brand of faith might be considered
"traditional." The obvious linguistic connection between *mater* and *materia* might suggest here that she stands for a form of the *Anima,* for a sort of
religious sensitivity that risks being overly concrete and literal, one that
could get lost in the forms as such. The preference for the pastel windows
seems to point to the fact that the forms make sense and have value insofar
as they allow something greater than themselves to shine through, insofar
as they enhance the greater mystery and point to something above and
beyond themselves. They have to be translucent, and we have to be able to
see and experience them as translucent or transparent. T. S. Eliot's *Cho-
ruses from the Rock*[1] speaks of the various decorative elements in a newly
constructed cathedral; he pauses when speaking of the windows and the
light they filter into the church. That light, he tells us, is but a reminder of
the true light, which is invisible.

Recently, a colleague in Rome shared with us an experience she had
had in her work with a nine-year-old boy of Jewish origin. This ethnic
and religious element was important in the family dynamic, as the boy's
father wanted his children to grow up in the Jewish faith even though he
himself felt no real emotional attachment to it, but had a purely formal
type of connection. At one point during the play therapy sessions, the
young client used the clay he was playing with to fashion a Star of David.
Not content with it, though, he used his finger to make a hole in the center and then held the star under the faucet in the room *so that the running
water could flow through it.* Again, a sacred form needed to be seen not as
an end in itself but rather as something capable of channeling a greater
energy.

No doubt we all remember how often the image of running water
comes up in fairy tales as a symbol of the dynamic life of the imagination,[2]
as the life of the psyche as it creates images, both personal and transpersonal ones. In the Grail myth, once Parsifal manages to dissolve the frozen, sterile state of affairs in which the Fisher King is languishing, the
water in the rivers and the streams begins to flow again. The beautiful
"Alchemical Allegory" interpreted in Jung's *Mysterium Coniunctionis* also

points to the water flowing from a fountain as the life of the imagination, which restores fertility to the arid land.[3] Our symbols become dead, cease to be real religious symbols, when they are stopped up and the water of the imagination no longer flows through them, or when they become opaque and are unable to channel the greater light. The religious and spiritual situation that corresponds to this is one of dogmatism and rigidity, if not indeed fundamentalism. It is a spiritual situation in which what ought to be the highest expression of our own personally experienced relationship to the numinous is sadly cut off from immediate experience. It is a situation in which people can do little more than accept codified forms and profess belief in them instead of looking into themselves in search of new, more meaningful ones.

IMAGINATION AS EXPERIENCE

The alchemists, says Marie-Louise von Franz, who were so in touch with and so open to the symbol-making function of the imagination, were *empirical explorers* of the numinous because of their direct and immediate experience of it.[4] Jung was so interested in the whole phenomenon of Gnosticism for the same reason, for the emphasis it laid on individual experience and on the knowledge or *gnosis* that comes from that, and which had precedence over dogmatism and systems of belief. Jung himself emphasizes how, for modern man, belief in what has not been experienced becomes harder and harder, and how we can really only accept systems whose contents reflect our own psychic experience.[5] Admittedly this gave rise, in Gnosticism, to a myriad of systems, at times bizarre and complex. But the Gnostic writers continued to underscore the importance of individual involvement and experience, to the extent that Gilles Quispel has described Gnosticism as the mythic expression of a Self experience.[6]

Einstein once called for imagination rather than intellectualism and rationalism. We are all familiar with his own powerful fantasy experience on that day when he just let go and "followed a sunbeam" with his imagination. As he "watched" it, he saw that it ran clear round the world, curving as it did so, and it was from this that he got the original inspiration for the space-time curvature in his theory of relativity. The history of science, at least the official one, tends to downplay the role of the imagination, but there are a great number of discoveries that have come about thanks to *rêverie* or to the imagination, such as Kekulé's discovery of the benzene ring or Poincaré's discovery of the automorphic functions.[7] Traditional schooling has made it extremely hard for us to get beyond the left-brain, logical approach that it placed such a premium on. Imagination and fantasy would never have been accepted as the basis for a point of view or a theory. Logic and facts were what was called for, especially when dealing with the natural, "precise" sciences.

In one of his letters, Jung writes that the creative imagination is the real ground of the psyche and "the only primordial phenomenon accessible to us."[8] The creative imagination, at the moment in which it is genuinely creative, is the one thing that takes us beyond what the Orientals call the "Web of Maya" or the illusions we have of how things *really* are. It breaks through the web of projections that we live in. And it is here that real, living religious symbols are born. The collective church, as it strived to find a sense of identity and to strengthen its own organization, understandably frowned upon individual recourse to one's immediate religious imagination, but this is exactly what we desperately need to recover today, if we hope to avoid throwing out our whole religious heritage as something bogged down in the past that no longer speaks to modern-day people.

IMAGINATION AND MIRRORING

Jung positions the role of the imagination within a much broader framework: the fourfold mirroring relationship between the ego and the unconscious, and then between the collective unconscious and the natural material world.[9] In the first instance, the unconscious acts as a mirror to and for ego consciousness, sending back to it, chiefly through dreams, images of something the ego sees only partially or one-sidedly. Our very sense of identity stands before that mirror in every dream, and what we see reflected there is rarely flattering, at times may be downright shocking, and occasionally is even humorous. Likewise, our ego consciousness seems to be a sort of mirror to and for the unconscious, more specifically for the Self. It would seem that the Self, that virtual center of completeness and totality, "needs" to see in the ego just how it is emerging and what form it is taking in the context of an individual's life. The way a person lives, how he or she works or loves, the products of one's own ingenuity and creativity are all images that consciousness, as mirror, holds up to the Self, which then reflects back other images of its own.

Jung suggests a further step, which von Franz has developed at length.[10] The collective unconscious would be a mirror in which the natural world "looks at itself"; it then sends back to us images of the physical world (think of the images of the atom, for instance, or of the formulas—images!—used in quantum physics). And it might just be, so Jung hypothesizes, that the physical world in its various manifestations is a mirroring image of the collective unconscious. Nature as we see it around us would then be the result of the mirroring imagination of the *anima mundi* or the living "reflecting" soul of nature. Edward Edinger, for example, saw flowers as the mandalas of the natural, organic world,[11] as mirror images of the ordering function of the Self in the collective unconscious. And as the great scholar of Islamic traditions, Henri Corbin, has shown, for the mystical Arab schools of thought the various flowers in nature corresponded to and were the expression of various divine powers that came to life and expressed themselves by means of meditation or imagination on and around them.[12] That fascinating collection of old alchemical texts, the *Corpus Hermeticum,* states, "God created the world *through imagination* and manifests Himself in everything. Thus the creative fantasy of God is contained in the visible world."[13]

From this point of view, the old alchemical idea that the imagination could actually activate the healing potentials of plants and herbs makes eminent sense. Imagination means that we meet the image for what it is, as image on the imaginal plane, and instead of simply manipulating it in a cold and technical way (guided imagination, for example) we enter into dialogue and interact with it so that something can happen. This wonderful world of imaging and mirroring is at the very basis of the production of our symbols and religious imagery. As the ego approaches the numinous, or as it bumps into the mysterious and the sacred, the unconscious reflects back the image that, from its point of view (so to speak), corresponds to and encapsulates the experiential moment.

THE SUBSTANCE OF IMAGINATION

Barbara Hannah suggests in one of her essays that many of the Old Testament exchanges between Yahweh and the prophets should be seen as examples of what Jung called *active imagination,* i.e., a voluntary lowering of the level of vigilance on the part of the ego so as to be able to actually converse with an activated image arising out of the unconscious.[14] Likewise, Edinger refers to the book of Job as an example of active imagination,[15] and Jung, in a particularly interesting letter, describes the encounter of Christ and Satan in the desert in a way that clearly qualifies it as a form of active imagination.[16] A sort of "power devil" in the shadow of Jesus tempts him with the prospects of possessing an earthly kingdom; Jesus, on the other hand, is identified with his role as "Suffering Servant" but actively engages and confronts this personification of an unconscious power drive. In the end, this experience produces the reconciling symbol of a kingdom, but of an inner spiritual kingdom "not of this world."

Thomas Moore's book *The Soul's Religion* contains a fascinating chapter entitled "Jesus, the Imagination." It captures the original, gripping way he, Jesus, used the power of the imagination: he meets a woman at a well, and as he speaks with her the well water becomes alive and vivifying; he challenges us to stretch our imagination and see our enemies as brothers and sisters. He takes bread and wine and looks through them imaginatively enough to be able to say, in all sincerity, that they are his body and his blood. All the philosophical and theological speculation in the Middle Ages on the question of transubstantiation are examples of that materialistic, concretistic mentality that loses sight of the fact that *it all makes sense and works because of the power of the imagination*. Naturally all of this implies that our definition of the imagination be anything but minimalistic and reductive. It implies an outlook that recognizes that imagination has body and is of consequence.

Many years ago, as a high school student, I read a book of poetry entitled *Something Solid as a Spirit*. I honestly cannot remember anything about those poems, and I even suspect they may have been of somewhat dubious quality. But the oxymoron in the title struck me then, and now, a good forty years later, I still remember it. It struck me because it contained something of what I was much later to find in the whole symbolism of glass as developed by the alchemists—something that is transparent and *apparently* without solidity, but that does in fact have body and substance. The alchemists termed this the *corpus vitreo*, and it is not so far from what Paracelsus called the *subtle body*—again, something that might seem to be exclusively ethereal, but that nevertheless is *body*. The alchemists were referring to a dimension of spirit that needs to be taken with the utmost seriousness, to the extent that it becomes as real as a rock or a chair. It is a way of looking at and experiencing spirit that implies a form of solidity. In short, what they were hinting at was the ancient idea of the *unus mundus*, a unitary vision of reality in which categories such as "matter" and "spirit" stand for *points of view* that consciousness needs but that ultimately separate aspects of a primordial unified reality. For Paracelsus, this *subtle body* is the *imaginatio vera*:[17] imagination not in the sense of passive fantasy, but rather a committed attention to the images that arise from the deep within us, and a willingness to take them seriously, to acknowledge the body they have. It is a sort of middle realm where the very terms "matter" and "spirit" actually point towards the central indivisible reality. Barbara Hannah once said that within the context of active imagination the images of things are so real that you could actually trip over them![18] It is a definite point of contact with the unified spirit/matter reality.

The whole question of the imagination is extremely important not only for our own inner lives, but also for the clinical issues we find ourselves facing day after day. It helps to give us a wider, religious context for what we sometimes tend to call, all too flippantly, "pathology." We know that many phenomena become pathological because the imaginative context in which they are lived is too limited and limiting. Compulsion is a driving force that is lived in a context that is too limited and totally neglects the god behind it. The divine drive wants to go somewhere, but the ego, not being able to really make space for it, becomes trapped in repetitive behavior. Paranoia is what it is because the imagination has dried up and can't break through the literalism.[19] The greater Self within, the mirroring Self of which we spoke earlier, which observes us, is not recognized as being within at all; the observing faculty is projected outside, where every sort of person and situation becomes a judgmental persecutory mirror.

In a letter from 1945, Jung writes as follows about the phenomenon of *fear*:

> [A]s a psychotherapist I do not by any means try to deliver my patients from fear. Rather, I lead them to the reason for their fear, and then it becomes clear that it is justified. (I could tell you a few instructive stories in this respect!) If my patient understands religious language, I say to him: Well, don't try to escape this fear which God has given you, but try to endure it to the end—*sine poena nulla gratia!* I can say this because I believe I am a religious man and because I know with scientific certainty that my patient hasn't invented his fear but that it is preordained. By whom or what? *By the unknown.* The religious man calls this *absconditum* "God," the scientific intellect calls it the unconscious. Deriving fear from repression is

neurotic speculation, an apotropaism invented for cowards; a
pseudo-scientific myth in so far as it declares a basic biological
instinct unreal and twists it into an *Ersatz*-formation. One
could just as well explain life as a flight from death or love as
an evasion of the hate which one hasn't the courage to muster.
They are neurotic artifices with which one diddles hysterics
out of the only meaning they have (which lies precisely in
their neurosis), naturally with the best but unendurably shal-
low intentions.[20]

It is striking the way Jung refuses to give a superficial imaginative
framework to psychological phenomena, and how he insists that the sort
of imagination needed is one that takes the phenomena seriously and
positions them within an equally serious context, i.e., one that recognizes
and appreciates their depth and searches for the meaning in them. In
another letter, Jung stresses that the main direction of his work was aimed
not at resolving neuroses but rather at adopting the right attitude towards
the numinous, which is, in the end, the real cure. What he calls "an archetypal experience," a direct encounter with the deeper layers of the psyche
from which a disturbance arises, and which often manifests itself in the
metaphor of myth or religion, is the ultimate healing experience. A limited or limiting way of imagining, "neurotic imagination," as Jung calls it,
desecrates our world and all of our human phenomena.

THE RISKS OF IMAGINATION

Naturally, spirituality, or what passes for spirituality, can also represent a form of escape. In his treatment of schizoid personality disorders,
Donald Kalsched warns the therapist about how this type of client may at
times display a penchant for spiritual themes in order to avoid really
touching his or her own intense suffering,[21] while Nathan Schwartz-
Salant provides useful guidelines for dealing with the question of spirituality when working with borderline clients.[22] A neurotic use of spirituality
is a defensive way of flying up and above the real questions that need to be
faced and addressed. Genuine spirituality urges us to pay close attention
to the images that reveal the deepest dimensions of what afflicts us. We
might "test" the authenticity of our own spirituality (and that of a client)
by asking ourselves if that spirituality really helps keep the transcendent
and the immanent in touch with one another; if it connects spirit with
earth, and earth with spirit.

In his essay "On the Nature of the Psyche," Jung uses the metaphor of the light spectrum in an attempt to explain the gradient along which this energy travels.[23] He suggests that where we would find the infrared extremity of the spectrum, we could place our drives, instincts, appetites—in short, our biology. At the ultraviolet end, he would have us place meaning, archetypes—in short, spirit. What mediates between these two realities is the world of the imagination. Images mediate between instinct and spirit, and between immanence and transcendence. And here what Jung calls *active imagination* and what the alchemists, both Western and Arab, refer to as *imaginatio vera* comes into play in the elaboration of a real spirituality that we can live. It is a spirituality that doesn't aim to reach or be absorbed in the spirit; it is not a "mystical spirituality," but rather one that could be described as a continual *tending towards spirit*. In active imagination, the ego defends its position and situation in the world, defends its bodily and biological reality, but it opens itself up and lowers the intensity of its own light so that it can meet halfway the images that come up from the unconscious. This encounter is imaginative in the sense Jung and Barbara Hannah spoke of. It is an encounter with the images behind the deepest and often most problematic sides of ourselves—our own "psychotic corners," those impenetrable and apparently unshakeable nuclei that resist all our attempts to normalize them or to adapt them to conventionality. To see the God in the disease and not simply let the divine sink down into and hide in our disease, we need the imagination.

Our task *vis-à-vis* God, Jung tells us, is not to blindly obey him nor to childishly plead for what we need.[24] What we are called to do is to collaborate with the divine (the alchemists went so far as to say that they were perfecting what God had left imperfect in his first act of creation!). We can help the divine in us become conscious of itself and of its own conflicts, and search for a symbolic solution to them. Any personal search that goes into depth, says Jung in one of his letters, will sooner or later come up against not-yet-transformed aspects of the Godhead. These, no doubt, have to do with aspects of the Self that are far removed from the light of consciousness and far away from a sense of relationship with consciousness. Through the imagination—*active imagination*—these deep contents start to unravel the knots they are tied up in, to differentiate as they come into contact with a form of consciousness delicate and strong enough to open itself up to this meeting, to stand its ground while accepting changes in itself.

In his 1925 seminars,[25] Jung describes his own deep experience of active imagination. He calls it an encounter with "the dark basis of ourselves," which sooner or later we must come into contact with; this contact with the divine (or diabolic) element (what Jung calls "deification" in the seminar) gives lasting value to life and, as Jung himself emphasizes, allows many to survive and go on living.

I began with a dream, and now I would like to close with one. This is a dream from a good twenty-five years ago, but I still remember it as if I had had it last night. At the time of the dream, I had not as yet met Marie-Louise von Franz, but I had read and studied a number of her books. The dream goes as follows:

> Von Franz and I are on a beach, similar to the one on the Italian island of Ponza. A terrible storm is raging with flashes of lightning, thunder, and an enormously strong wind blowing in off the sea. Huge waves come crashing onto the shore. Von Franz and I are huddled behind a huge rock standing there on the beach, facing the sea. Suddenly, she raises a hand and worriedly exclaims, "I wonder what Yahweh has up his sleeve for us…this time?!"

As I said, I hadn't yet met Dr. von Franz, but on the suggestion of my own analyst, Dr. Dieter Baumann, I sent the text of the dream to her, and she immediately responded with a short but pointed message. She emphasized how we do indeed live in dangerous times, with new things such as collective phenomena and pathologies arising from the unconscious. We may not know how to approach or deal with these things. For this reason, she added, it is vitally important for us to be closely aware of the dreams and images that visit us.

Our spirituality, our careful contact with the world within, is also a vantage point from which to observe not only what happens in our own hearts and souls, but one from which we can at times catch a glimpse of developments taking form within the collective, objective psyche at large.

NOTES

1. T. S. Eliot, *The Complete Poems and Prose of T. S. Eliot* (London: Faber & Faber, 2004).

2. Marie-Louise von Franz, *Alchemical Active Imagination* (Dallas: Spring Publications, 1979), p. 39.

3. C. G. Jung, *Mysterium Coniunctionis*, vol. 14 of *The Collected Works of C. G. Jung,* trans. R. F. C. Hull, ed. H. Read, M. Fordham, G. Adler, Wm. McGuire, 20 vols. (Princeton, NJ: Princeton University Press, 1953-1979)(hereafter *CW*), § 189ff.

4. Marie-Louise von Franz, *C. G. Jung: His Myth in Our Time* (New York: G. P. Putnam's Sons, 1975), p. 203.

5. Jung, *Psychology and Religion, CW* 11, § 142.

6. Gilles Quispel, "Gnosis and Psychology," in *The Allure of Gnosticism*, ed. Robert Segal (Chicago: Open Court, 1995), p. 16.

7. Marie-Louise von Franz, *Projection and Re-Collection in Jungian Psychology: Reflections of the Soul* (Chicago: Open Court, 1980), pp. 69ff. and pp. 88ff.

8. C. G. Jung, *Letters*, 2 vols., selected and edited by Gerhard Adler (Princeton, NJ: Princeton University Press, 1973), 1:60.

9. C. G. Jung to Wolfgang Pauli, August 1957, in *Atom and Archetype: The Pauli/Jung Letters 1932-1958*, ed. C. A. Meier (Princeton, NJ: Princeton University Press, 2001), p. 167.

10. Von Franz, *Projection and Re-Collection.*

11. Edward Edinger, *The Mysterium Lectures: A Journey through C. G. Jung's* Mysterium Coniunctionis (Toronto: Inner City Books, 1995), p. 290.

12. Henri Corbin, *Spiritual Body and Celestial Earth (*Princeton, NJ: Princeton University Press, 1977), p. 32.

13. Marie-Louise von Franz, trans. and commentary, *Aurora Consurgens: A Document Attributed to Thomas Aquinas on the Problem of Opposites in Alchemy* (Toronto: Inner City Books, 1964/2000), p. 186.

14. Barbara Hannah, *The Inner Journey: Lectures and Essays on Jungian Psychology* (Toronto: Inner City Books, 1967/2000).

15. Edward Edinger, *Transformation of the God Image: An Elucidation of Jung's Answer to Job* (Toronto: Inner City Books, 1992).

16. Jung, *Letters*, 1:267 ff.

17. For more, see Jung, *CW* 13, § 173, and Marie-Louise von Franz, *On Dreams and Death: A Jungian Interpretation* (Chicago: Open Court, 1997), pp. 139-140.

18. Hannah, *The Inner Journey.*

19. See James Hillman, *On Paranoia: The Eranos Lecture Series, 8* (Dallas: Spring Publications, 1986).

20. Jung, *Letters*, 1:400.

21. Donald Kalsched, *The Inner World of Trauma: Archetypal Defenses of the Personal Spirit* (London: Routledge, 1996).

22. Nathan Schwartz-Salant, *The Borderline Personality: Vision and Healing* (Wilmette, IL: Chiron, 1989).

23. Jung, "On the Nature of the Psyche," *CW* 8, § 420ff.

24. Jung, *Letters*, 2:312ff.

25. C. G. Jung, *Analytical Psychology: Notes on the Seminar Given in 1925* (Princeton, NJ: Princeton University Press, 1989).

LIVING WITH SYMBOLS

HEIKE WEIS

"God exists! This story is true!"

The deep meaning and function of symbols was once again brought home to me through the encounter with an African patient from Rwanda who was deeply traumatized during the genocide in 1994. This man's story is a moving testament to the human spirit and to how it gets support from the "transcendent" in moments of real danger and in the face of immense loss. His experience and the therapeutic process bear witness that behind chaos and destruction there seems to be a "generator" for the reconstruction and evolution of the psyche. The value of understanding archetypal energies and symbols unfolds in the progressive discovery of the psyche's strength to reconnect with life.

An important precondition for this type of healing is that patient and therapist undergo together a process of confrontation and acceptance of the different aspects of the soul, accompanied by a deep transformation and differentiation of the feeling function. The analytical process I will describe briefly, ongoing for six years, demonstrates through life events and dreams that the methods outlined by Jung can provide an "instru-

Heike Weis, M.D., trained as a psychiatrist in Belgium and as an analyst at the C. G. Jung Institute in Zurich. She is a participant member of ISAPZurich, and has a private analytic practice in Zurich.

ment" for dialogue with a complete stranger. The main bridge-building elements in this dialogue are symbols and the consideration of them in the vessel of the therapeutic relationship. Important psychodynamic movements in the individual are expressed through symbols. They indicate the possible support from information implicit in the brain in moments of total stress, and they represent the actual transforming energy, status, and direction of development.

PIERRE'S STORY

Pierre was born in 1958 in Kigali, the capital of Rwanda. He grew up as a Hutu in a situation of emotional and financial security. Besides being a car technician, he loved to play guitar, and he composed music. In his twenties, he married and had a daughter and a son. The family lived in their own house in the neighborhood of his parents. His father was a catholic priest and very respected among his people. His relationship with the members of his family was relatively good. He lived a "normal life," without being very religious, until the ethnic turmoil and genocide in 1994.

Pierre's life changed suddenly when he saw his parents, sisters, and brothers decapitated by Hutu extremists because his family was not supporting them against the Tutsis. He was able to escape, along with two of his brothers, but he lost track of them and of his wife and children. In this chaos, there was no chance of discovering their whereabouts. In July 1994, former musician friends of his helped Pierre to make his way to Geneva. Nearly one and a half years after his arrival in Switzerland, he happened to see his son on TV news in a refugee camp. He was so moved by this that he decided to go back to Rwanda in spite of the life-threatening situation in his home country. In September 1995, he was back in Rwanda and was there immediately imprisoned because of being suspected of carrying on espionage activities. Over several months, he was tortured, at times nearly to death.

During the hours of physical torture, he had for the first time in his life visions of the Virgin. She spoke to him of hope and peace, and her presence helped him to endure the pain and fear he was experiencing. Within himself, he witnessed the beginnings of a process of forgiveness towards the murderers of his family. These visions and dreams opened a new state of mind in him, and he was profoundly touched by their content. Moreover, it helped him to accept the idea that he would probably be killed in these extremely brutal circumstances. After a profound vision of Maria, he was suddenly and surprisingly liberated from his fear of death and suffering. Physically he was very weak, but mentally he was strengthened through the symbolic experience.

In fact, he did not die from the torture inflicted upon him. He was released from prison, and after some months of searching he first found his son in a camp and later also his wife with their daughter. They were reunited in a refugee camp and deeply grateful finally to be together again. The conditions in this camp became so miserable, however, that they decided to leave it, together with more than a hundred other refugees. This band of refugees walked for more than seven months through the jungle. On the third day of this trek, his seven-year-old son was bitten by a snake and died shortly thereafter. Pierre could mentally bear this tragedy because of the dreams and visions of the Virgin and Christ that had sustained him in prison. He often visualized a blue light, which gave him the feeling of divine presence and consolation. After the death of his son, he and the remainder of the group continued wandering through the forest and were exposed to extreme human traumas. When finally they emerged from the jungle, there were left only around thirty people from the hundred who had begun.

Now they were located in a military camp with better conditions than the refugee camp had offered. But political changes intervened, and Pierre was about to be forced to fight in a war beside child soldiers. He spoke to his wife, and they decided to flee from this camp. This was at the end of 1999. They were able to hide in a friend's house. Finally, they decided that Pierre would go back to Switzerland and organize from there the transfer for his wife and daughter. At the end of January 2000, he arrived in Zurich, now ill with malaria and psychologically frail. For the second time, he asked for the right of sanctuary. In the first weeks after his arrival, he was quite optimistic about bringing his family along to Switzerland. It turned out differently, however. Suddenly Pierre had to confront another drama: his wife and daughter were abducted by the military. The family they had been living with had no idea where they had been taken or indeed if they had been killed. In the first months after receiving this news, Pierre began an intense effort to find them through official organizations. All traces of them had been lost. The failure to locate them provoked a dangerous decline of Pierre's health. He stayed alone in his dark, one-room apartment for days and weeks. Panic attacks and severe anxiety states increased to an unsupportable degree. He developed acoustic and optical hallucinations, along with horrible nightmares, for the first time. Socially he was totally isolated. Frequently he was invaded by memories of earlier traumatic experiences and with survivor guilt. Pierre became highly suicidal at this time.

PIERRE IN THERAPY

In this condition, Pierre was sent to me for therapy because I am a psychiatrist and I speak French. I listened to his story, which touched me deeply, and at the same time I asked myself how I could ever help him. It seemed that he felt my impotence, because he told me simply that I would be a last witness of his destiny and that he was grateful for that. A profound humility was unfolding in me, and I think between us. It was the beginning of our intense human interaction.

Until our meeting, he had tried to survive through regular visits to a church. Once he asked the priest to come to his home to give it a blessing, because of the overwhelming voices he experienced there during his hallucinations. With a big smile, Pierre told me that afterwards the voices were even more intense. This was the first flicker of a new resource: humor! He was sure that I could help him more than the priest could. I wasn't so convinced, to tell the truth. Suddenly I had the idea of asking him what his mother would have done against bad spirits. She was initiated in local folk medicine and voodoo practices. Pierre remembered that she used to place salt in the corners of the house. I advised him to do the same. The voices disappeared in one week.

At this moment in therapy, Pierre spoke the sentence quoted above: "God exists! This story is true."

I was more than a little surprised, but we were both happy with the result. The voices of his torturers never did come back, but the nightmares increased for several months. A depressive syndrome was strongly present, but in the transference Pierre could endure it. He began to record his dreams and found that it was very helpful to do so and to share them with me. He recognized the compensatory function of the psyche in the helpful symbols that had appeared during his imprisonment and helped him to survive. Now, his life being physically safe in Switzerland, nightmares were coming into awareness: dreams of genocide and the brutal loss of his family, images of a sea of blood with dead human bodies floating in it. There were many repetitive elements in these nightmares. I invited

Pierre to be attentive to the details. Courageously, he noted all the parts of every dream and wrote them down.

The veil of his depression lifted after he had a dream in which some marvellous blue birds rose in flight out of the sea of blood and flew upwards towards the sun. Pierre felt that this was a symbol of "going home" for the souls of his dead loved ones.

His feeling of guilt began diminishing at this time. In the period following, Pierre had a "banal" dream, as he called it at first. In this dream, he was following his wife in the jungle when suddenly she disappeared. In her place appeared an exceptionally large blue butterfly. Pierre felt very attracted by the butterfly and was profoundly moved by this winged creature. The butterfly perched on his left hand. Pierre felt a deep connection with it. After this dream, we realized that he was beginning to better connect to life around him in Switzerland. Further, he was caring much better for himself, and progressively he increased contact with people from Rwanda in Geneva.

The therapeutic process as a whole has been rich with symbolic material and life experiences, which cannot be exposed here in detail. The therapy sessions also have had the additional pedagogical function of helping Pierre to adapt more fully to life in Europe.

The sharing, mirroring, and symbolizing experiences in therapy seem to be repairing the psychological damage incurred through the traumatic years in Pierre's life during the war and genocide in his homeland. In the last year, it has become evident that a new kind of consciousness is unfolding. Pierre is experiencing a state of being like a "newborn." He feels strength for living and connecting with people such as he never had felt before. The religious function of his psyche seems to be the most powerful aspect in the symbolic expressions that come into awareness. Deep emotions are triggered by these symbols in both of us, and they push the feeling function in us to differentiate further. The symbols indicate that the Self is conducting post-traumatic repair work, and at the same time they bring up new information that is received in a strongly felt sense. The symbols rearrange and re-associate seeds of future growth that had emerged even before the therapy began, and this movement is greatly strengthened and reinforced through our conscious work with the dreams in and through the transference as it has appeared in the therapeutic relationship.

A very special discovery for Pierre was the insight that symbols of the

Self, as they appeared in visions of Christ and the Virgin, actually had the effect of initiating the process of forgiveness. Pierre was able truly to forgive the murderers of his family. Forgiveness and humility have become integrated aspects of his psyche, and these give him the power to confront everyday life with good energy and to feel liberated from the past. Pierre himself says: "I entered therapy KO'd. I leave each time more OK."

The careful and respectful work with symbols as they appear in dreams, in visions, and in the container of therapy, plus the constellation of a profound therapeutic relationship, are the two most important factors that bring about change in analysis. The capacity to produce symbols can be blocked through trauma, or it can be triggered in situations of extreme stress. Also, silence can be the stimulus that activates systems of implicit memory in the form of various symbols. Neuroscience has revealed that unsymbolized traumatic experiences—which contain a primitive core of unspeakable terror, intrusive ideation, and somatic sensations, and exist cordoned off within the patient's psyche—are not available to reflective processing and the traditional talking cure. This suffering core of a wounded human being, which is often protected behind the semblance of a well-functioning and interpersonally adapted and related self, can only be reached through the engaged and warmly holding attitude of a therapist with sufficient parenting and reflective capacities. The power of this "holding" is able to promote repeated positive experiences in the neural network over a period of time, which in turn build and rebuild attachments within the patient to the self and other people. This constructive process becomes visible and gains healing power through symbols, which transform the unconscious and raise implicit information into an explicit form. This is experienced together in the analytical dyad. The emotional links and the felt sense that is triggered through symbols and mirrored by the analyst are most effective means for building up the personality and for healing important wounds of the soul. The symbols light up multiple centers in the brain, enabling increased connectivity so that assimilation as a mutual penetration of consciousness and the unconscious can take place. Consciousness itself may be understood as the connectivity established in the individual brain. Symbols and transference experiences are essential for this connection-building process, so that the internalization of space, mobility, separateness, and felt connectivity can occur. This allows persons to participate in their own becoming and their own healing processes.

THE SYMBOLIC DIMENSION IN TRAUMA THERAPY

URSULA WIRTZ

> Truth did not come into this world naked; rather it came in
> prototypes and images.
> —*Gospel of Philip* 67:9-12

This article is concerned with Jung's concept of the "symbolic attitude," a concept he defines as: "a definite view of the world which
assigns meaning to events…and attaches to this meaning a greater
value than to bare facts."[1] I want to explore the deeper implications of the
way the symbolic can be applied in working with survivors of trauma.

Symbolic messages and myth unlock the gates of the unconscious
psyche, create reality, and provide a sense of context and purpose. In a letter to Freud, written in 1909, Jung conveyed his insight that without
mythology the "ultimate secrets of neuroses and psychosis" cannot be
solved.[2] The language of symbols and myth as "the primordial language of
psyche"[3] is particularly necessary when working with human beings who
have been traumatized. The inherently fragmentary character of the trau-

Ursula Wirtz holds a diploma from the C. G. Jung Institute Zurich (1982) and is a
training analyst and supervisor on the faculty of ISAP Zurich. She has taught at various
European universities and published on trauma, ethics, and the spiritual dimension of
analytical psychology. She is involved in the training of developing Jungian groups in
Eastern Europe and a member of the ethics committee of the IAAP.

matic experiences, their discontinuous quality and nonrational and non-linear nature, invites our consciousness beyond the factual and asks for a symbolic, imaginal approach to this descent into Hades with its primitive and chthonic power.

For Jung the acknowledgement of the power of the symbolic perspective led to "living the symbolic life," an attitude considered indispensable for giving meaning and orientation. Jung was deeply convinced that only the symbolic life can satisfy the needs of the soul. He firmly believed in the power of imagination to make meaning: "Image and meaning are identical: and as the first takes shape, so the latter becomes clear."[4]

I want to elaborate on the relevance of symbols, myths, and metaphors for trauma therapy. As the inner world of a traumatized person suffers from fragmentation and fracture, imagination and fantasy are of utmost importance to heal the split and create one's own myth in order to integrate traumatic experience. Kalsched has pointed out that both Freud and Jung had struggled with "the 'mythopoetic' fantasy images that were thrown up by the psyche as the sequel of trauma."[5]

Gripped by the archetypal power of trauma, wounded by the shattering of meaning and values, a symbolic frame is needed to voice what cannot be expressed in rational discourse. Survivors of trauma need to engage actively in imagination and fantasy to overcome fixations of intrusive, repetitive, indelible images and haunting bodily sensations. Traumatic memories are, as Judith Herman[6] described, often characterized by the lack of verbal narrative and context but are encoded in a flood of sensations and images. Traumatic dreams, like nightmares, have a fragmentary character with no imaginative elaboration. Working with the symbolic, engaging in fantasies and using metaphor as a matrix and bridge, fosters the working through of affects and emotions and enables clients to repair their damaged capacity to symbolize. Metaphors provide a way to talk about traumatic experiences that cannot be literally described. Creative metaphoric construction encourages the symbolization of psychic contents; metaphors have an integrative quality, giving form to cognitive processes and presenting possible solutions for unbearable conflicts through a new frame. This quality of metaphor to promote the transition of affect into language makes its use in trauma therapy indispensable.

The use of metaphor and the symbolic perspective in psychoanalytic theory formation and analytic thinking has a long history.[7] Freud is well known for his masterful use of metaphor; in fact he believed that to speak about the psyche one could only use metaphors. The psyche speaks in images, and it is through metaphor and symbols that we connect to the soul. We encounter the subject's relationship with the symbolic also as a central theme in modern psychoanalysis, particularly in Lacanian psycho-analysis. For Lacan, psychoanalysts are essentially "practitioners of the symbolic function."[8] His concept of the "symbolic order" and the imagi-nary order that structures human existence has been very influential in modern psychoanalytic heuristics. Modern and postmodern theories of imagination (Heidegger, Ricoeur, Kristeva) show how visionary Jung's contribution to our understanding of the role of imagination has been, although his contribution has been totally overlooked. Within contem-porary psychoanalytic heuristics, Lachauer emphasizes the integrative function of metaphor and images for focal therapy and asserts that: "You should make a picture,"[9] alluding to the biblical commandment forbid-ding images of God. He refers to modern brain research, where the brain is considered an image-generating organ and life an image-generating process. This primacy of the image can already be found in Hegel, and going even further back, to the Gospel of John, we could translate "in the beginning was the word" as saying that, since language is an act of sym-bolization, "in the beginning was the symbol."

Our thought processes are structured by underlying metaphors; thinking and the symbol originate in bodily experience. Jung states: "The symbol is thus a living body, corpus et anima."[10] Traumatic experiences attack the connection between body and mind, spirit and instinct, with the result that the symbolic meaning-making function is severely impaired and individuals lose a sense of animation, playfulness, and imagination.

As in Jungian understanding transformation of the psyche happens through its inherent unconscious and autonomous symbolizing power, the analytic task in working with trauma cases is to foster a growing abil-ity to symbolize the trauma and its manifold meanings. We need to reconnect to this bodily basis of meaning and imagination that plays such an important role in the analytic imaginal space between analyst and cli-ent. Gustav Bovensiepen describes how the symbolic attitude and symbol formation can be used in the transference-countertransference frame to develop a symbolic space; for him, "analysis in its totality is a symbolic space *par excellence.*"[11]

Jung termed the psychological function of symbol formation *the transcendent function*, a natural, goal-oriented, and prospective process that springs from the tension of opposites and manifests as energy in our dreams and visions.[12] This relational dynamic of integration is a meaning-making process on the individuation path, a process that can also be translated into attachment theory terms as "appraisal," a constant evaluation of the world that is necessary for survival and therefore particularly relevant for trauma survivors. The psyche engages in a constant process of interpretation and re-interpretation of implicit and explicit patterns of symbols and images. Jean Knox[13] has shown how meaningful experience depends on the transcendent function, a process that compares and integrates internal objects and the self, explicit and implicit knowledge, left brain and right brain, cognition and emotion.

The conceptualization of the "transcendent function," manifested as a confrontation of conjoined opposites, provides a healing pattern that offers containment and order in a chaotic and confusing unconscious psychic state.

Although symbol-making is considered a natural activity, we find that traumatized people often are severely damaged in their capacity to symbolize. It seems as if trauma undermines the transcendent function, although this notion of symbol and the workings of the transcendent function was conceived by Jung in his own state of extreme crisis.[14]

THE INTEGRATIVE POWER OF SYMBOLS

The word "symbol" traces its origin to the Greek word "*symbolon*," meaning proof of identification.[15] In ancient Greece, two friends who were parting from each other performed a ritual: they would break a clay tile in two, one piece for each. Anyone who at a later date produced the missing half, be it the friend himself or a member of his family, was entitled to be received as a friend. The clay tile was the visible evidence of the psychic bond between the friends. The etymological background points to a very important property of symbols: the symbol is unitive, it creates relationship, and it originates in duality. A symbol is always relational, and symbolization is an act of translation fostering new connections. The Greek verb *sym-ballein* means "to join, to throw together." It throws together two halves, joins and connects opposing forces, and even suggests something more that cannot be named or fathomed, reaching into spheres beyond speech. Jung stresses the reconciling function of the symbol, its mediatory power, uniting human beings with each other and with what is beyond.

The symbolic offers a holistic approach to the spiritual concerns of our patients, because the symbol "points beyond itself to a meaning that is darkly divined."[16] Symbols reveal the dualism of all that exists, while they also reconnect the poles with each other, building bridges between the conscious and the unconscious. They challenge boundaries, bridge opposites and reconcile them with each other, being both revealing and concealing at the same time, organizing chaotic experience into meaningful structures and a kind of order.

The ability of symbols to provide inner orientation has proved especially valuable in psychotherapy with persons who have been shocked and shattered by traumatic events. Great distress is always an experience of separation, whereas the symbolic dimension unites. This is why it heals.

This function of the symbol is urgently needed in trauma therapy where we have to create a safe symbolic space in which the depth of the traumatic experience can be uncovered and the nameless terror of the void and the abyss, the archetypal experience of abandonment and betrayal, can be symbolized. This quality of symbols to bind together and join dissociated fragments assists us in overcoming dissociation that is caused by traumatic splitting.

Symbols are "pregnant with meaning." They belong to our original, archaic human language. Psychoanalyst Erich Fromm postulated: "Symbolic language is the one foreign language each of us must learn."[17] Symbols span a bridge between the visible and invisible and point the way to a hidden reality, which we experience as meaningful. Emerging from the fertile soil of the unconscious, they bring us in contact with the deeper layer of being, with the ultimate source of our collective basic ground. Symbols connect external objects and events to inner psychic reality, and they apprehend more than cool reason can ever comprehend, a wisdom that Shakespeare has already conveyed to us. As signposts they announce a larger frame of reference, connecting us to the oldest layers of the human mind and mediating between the rational and the irrational. Edward C. Whitmont, in *The Alchemy of Healing*,[18] ranks symbols among the "most potent transmitters of energy, able to move mountains." As transformers of libido and manifestations of archetypal activity with a great liberating and transformative quality, they enhance our awareness.

Symbols as messages of wholeness emerge from the creative potential of the psyche and help us to move beyond our state of isolation and alienation. The potency of symbols is related to this spiritual longing for wholeness. Working with symbols and myth-making is a powerful tool for achieving psychological integration, bringing the fragmented parts of ourselves "home" and helping to achieve a greater sense of continuity in life.[19]

We create symbols in order to recreate ourselves, to create meaning and make sense of the confusing multiplicity of the world. Symbols point to something new. They have a prospective-purposive function, moving us forward and making us permeable for the other, the ultimate, the numinous that we are unable to grasp with our limited consciousness. I agree with George B. Hogenson when he writes: "The process of change in analysis is always oriented to the transcendent nature of the symbolic."[20]

The messages of symbols, pictures, and dreams are always a step ahead of us. They crystallize the focus of our impending psychic development in an image or metaphor. When we are at a dead end, frozen and petrified, when we cannot move forward or back, the unexpected appearance of a symbol may rescue us by setting the psychic process in motion again.

At the very points where the physical and psychic foundations of our existence have been most severely damaged, and where the feeling of being cut off from the rest of the world dominates our psychic landscape, symbols can appear with special poignancy to throw light as through a fissure into the prevailing desolation. When trauma strikes and the ground gives way under our feet, we lose touch with our own center and fall into an altered state of consciousness that precipitates a symbolic quest with a deeply spiritual underpinning.

The Symbol of a Labyrinthine Journey

The labyrinth is an ancient image of order, combining the imagery of the circle and the spiral in a meandering path. It bears great similarity to the nonlinear spiral dynamics that we encounter in working with trauma survivors. It is a symbol of tension and dynamic movement, a metaphor pointing to a difficult, confusing situation. Like analysis, this journey leads repeatedly close to the desired center, but then we are again far away from where we want to go. For me, the symbol of the labyrinth represents a model for the flow of psychic energy and analytical work. This is a centered, nonlinear process where fear of impasse lurks constantly—the dead end—and also fear of being seized by something bigger than the ego and beyond control. But there is also hope of empowerment after reconnecting with the energizing center, the inner sanctum. I consider the labyrinth to be a symbolization of the soul's journey toward transformation. The individuation process of a traumatized person resembles the meandering spiral journey that Jung described: "The way to the goal seems chaotic and indeterminable at first, and only gradually do signs increase that it is leading anywhere. The way is not straight but appears to go around in circles. More accurate knowledge has proved it to go in spirals."[21]

THE ARCHETYPAL BACKGROUND OF TRAUMA

Trauma reaches into an archetypal level of consciousness where the symbolic dimension and imaginal approaches become central for the healing process. Traumatic experiences activate archaic levels of our psyche and constellate an archetypal landscape that is highly charged with affect.

Trauma is existence *in extremis*, a "destroyer of meaning," but also a potential catalyst for a new orientation in life. I view the destruction in the context of the progression of life, just as I envision individuation as a sequence of death and renewal in which disintegration and destruction are opportunities for new creation.

Trauma has been conceptualized in multifaceted ways. Traumatic life events cannot be assimilated with the victim's inner schemata of self in relation to the world (Horowitz);[22] they destroy the victim's fundamental assumptions about the safety of the world, the positive value of the self (Janoff-Bulman),[23] and cause a disturbance of affectivity. Krystal believed that trauma produces a regression in affect, an impoverishment and a deficit of the capacity for symbolic representation and fantasy formation.[24] Winnicott points to the necessity of a good "holding environment"[25] to deal with disintegration anxiety caused by traumatic events, and Kohut[26] refers to the dissolution of a coherent self. Kalsched[27] shows how trauma ruptures transitional processes of human relatedness that constitute meaning.

The experience of archetypal suffering inspires the use of religious and mythological language in order to communicate the unspeakable. We lean on myth to describe what is essentially indescribable. We refer to trauma as an experience of "hell," of "God in exile," of a terrifying encounter with the dark side of God, with "Deus Absconditus," who parades "heaven as an abyss" (Celan) and inflicts the archetypal experience of being cast out and forsaken. We symbolize trauma as a "yawning abyss," the "black hole" (van der Kolk; Farlane), and the "void" (Krystal), an experience of "anti-creation" (Primo Levi), severing "the thread of life" (Asper), creating a "tear in the self" and a rift in the psyche. Trauma victims suffer from impaired human relationships, from "the broken connection," as Robert Jay Lifton[28] has termed this sense of alienation a state of "being outside of culture." He believed that trauma disrupts the capacity to develop images and symbolic forms that provide a sense of continuity, and he states the necessity for transformation and reanimation of these symbols in order to find new meaning.

This archetypal dimension of trauma has a "numinous" (R. Otto) quality, the mesmerizing power to destroy as well as the capacity and the power to give life and to renew. When our worldview falls apart and our whole way of being crumbles, the prison of the ego can break open. This archetypal boundary experience of the black hole that defies description can open into holistic dimensions, to the transformation of consciousness and to individuation. When trauma strikes, our perception of ourselves and the world undergoes a radical reorganization. The meaning of the word "catastrophe" in ancient Greek is "a turning point," and it is precisely at these turning points that an enantiodromia (Heraclitus) can occur. In dynamic systems theory, phase transitions happen when "symbolic density" is heightened, a concept that Jungian analyst George Hogenson has developed.[29] Trauma research refers to the transformational power of trauma as "post-traumatic growth," a new paradigm that describes the process of change in the areas of self-perception, interpersonal relationships, and philosophy of life and spirituality. The wounding and the suffering in traumatic states can be a gateway for the numinous, experienced often as "the dark night of the soul," calling for transformation and growth and possibly leading to the "Dark Light of the Soul."[30] The traumatic experience of our own nothingness and of the insubstantiality of the ego is one such numinous experience.

The archetypal aspects of traumatic experiences connect to a transpersonal dimension in which the issue of meaning and the need to accept the paradoxes of human life are at stake. The symbolic attitude is most essential for traumatized individuals because it reconnects the person with something beyond; it reestablishes a broken connection and facilitates a shift of attitude, a metanoia.

WORKING WITH THE IMAGINAL REALM

Trauma therapy deals with liminal states, where Hermes reigns. This creates a very specific interactive energy field,[31] where the somatic unconscious of the analyst is stimulated. I adopt an imaginative method using metaphoric images, based on an attitude of intuitive receptivity. This establishes a space free of value judgments and open to the emergence of possibilities. This fosters growth and movement toward change. I try to embody a receptive state of awareness, an ability to wait and tune into the "archetypal frequencies" in order to better understand the *interactive field* in which we are moving. Murray Stein has stated, "The interactive field is in between the field of the collective unconscious and the realm of subjectivity, while at the same time including them both."[32]

The healing quality of this interactive field has been described by Jung. By following his hunches and listening to something within himself, he was quite at sea in terms of rational interventions but then came up with irrational, instinctive reactions that were healing, such as singing a lullaby with his mother's voice to a girl who suffered from insomnia. The mysterious healing power of images, words, and songs allows the unconscious to break through and move the individual to change the conscious attitude.

In order to tune into the silence and the body language of my traumatized patients, I need to allow myself to enter into a state of analytic reverie and metaphor, the kind of dreaming state that Bion referred to in his concept of *rêverie*.[33] When I attentively listen to my own experience of resonance, I can use the inner images and metaphors that originate in me from the shared imaginal realm to reflect and organize the patient's experience, reframe the story, and transform the often chaotic, archaic material into conceptual thinking. My own inner images may point to the patient's potential and to their resources and strengths. Cocreating, we develop a symbolic approach that allows us to access latent creative possibilities and that nurtures the process of increasing consciousness. Entering into the patient's pain empathically rather than wanting to cure it requires a joined suffering and mourning of what cannot be repaired.

The reliable presence of the therapist provides a symbolic space where containment can be experienced. In this "enabling space" of the analysis, which is an "incubation chamber" or an "alchemical vessel," mutuality is experienced and traumatizing, emotionally loaded images can be safely embodied and an archetypal healing force constellated. When I engage fully with my traumatized patients, a space for creation unfolds between us, with reciprocal healing images arising in me as part of our joint fantasy and intuitive dialogue. Through this subtle mode of exchange, formerly blocked areas of experience are called back to life and resources accessed. The metaphorical amplifications of the story, the reciprocal transference of moods, and the mutual reflection of feelings are part of an identity-forming process.

It is of course of utmost importance, when working with the imaginal realm, to assess the strength of the ego in order to use the right interventions and to prevent an intrusive flooding of emotional images, a blurring of boundaries, and an inappropriate state of fusion.

The process of transference-countertransference can be viewed as a dialectical relationship in which changes are produced not according to a fixed program, but in a dynamic, systemic, jointly determined process of mutually responsive interaction or "co-evolution." Jung's idea that treatment is the product of reciprocal influence is especially applicable to the relationships we need to establish in trauma therapy: "The encounter of two personalities with each other is like the mixing of two chemical compounds. If they mix at all, both will be altered."[34] The same idea has been expressed by Balint when she refers to the "harmonious (or disharmonious) interpenetrating mix up."[35] Balint also stresses the value of "entering into" the patient's suffering as the key healing factor. The soothing responsiveness presupposes a solid groundedness of the analyst, since trauma can have a poisonous contagious character. The therapist must guard against "psychic infection," which means to literally take over the sufferings of the patients, as Jung postulated.[36] Whitmont describes this deliberate identification with the patient's state as "a vicarious self-offering by virtue of a conscious empathic 'suffering with.' His or her own wounds resonate with the client's in the course of the mutually inductive effects of the therapeutic relationship."[37]

LISTENING WITH THE THIRD EAR

I believe that a particular way of listening is required that is different from Freud's "evenly suspended attention"—a listening with the third ear, as Theodor Reik[38] described it. It works in two ways: it picks up what patients do not say, but only feel and think, and at the same time it is a listening turned inward. In this mode, the therapist listens to an inner voice, a kind of prospective listening to what demands to be born. This mode of listening creates a healing environment in which being is doing. Jungian analyst Kathrin Asper speaks of the "mother specific attitude" that we need when working with severely wounded patients. Like a mother who intuits empathically the unspeakable, we need to adopt this kind of affective attunement, which promotes growth and can gratify needs that cannot yet be articulated.

Listening to people who have been tortured is like listening to voices from the underworld, the land of no return. I was reminded of the mythical underworld, where the whole person is in life but devoid of life, when I encountered the tortured prisoners of war who had survived the camps in Omarska, Manjaca, and Batkovici. They were dead to the world. Although they looked like living human beings, their entire mode of existence had been vaporized. "We only look as if we are alive," they said when I interviewed them a couple of days after their release from the camps, "but the truth is, we are dead." Encountering people whose symbols and values have been destroyed by torture and violence, we are left with the feeling that these are human beings who walk as the dead in the midst of life. If the symbolic function is destroyed, they no longer have any living relationship to their own psychic creativity. This is because symbols transfer libido into activity and ultimately give meaning to life.

Maybe we need to couple our listening with the third ear with cultivating a mode of seeing with the third eye, a deepening perspective that Hillman proposed as "seeing through," looking from the angle of the imaginal: "This is what depth psychology has always insisted upon: look at conscious events and intentions from the unconscious, from below."[39]

I remain alert to archetypical images that may arise in me in response to what I hear. Sometimes the image of the phoenix emerges, a mythological symbol of the process of renewal, since this bird is consumed in the funeral pyre and then arises up out of the ashes; sometimes it is Leviathan, the embodied Chaos monster that inhabits the ocean's depths, with the ability to swallow even the sun. Encountering a chronic state of traumatic fixation, I might experience the person as swallowed up by Leviathan. Myths of Osiris and Dionysos, images from Dante's *Divine Comedy*, narrations of life in hell pass through my mind in working with trauma survivors.

From myths we have become acquainted with processes of dismemberment and of dissolution or disintegration that lead to enlargement rather than to a narrowing of consciousness, to finding rather than losing meaning, and to love rather than hate. When I enter the chambers of evil, I am accompanied from within by these stories of the underworld, and the "consolations" of the stoic philosophical therapeutics help me to do my work in the archetypal field of death and renewal.

Working with traumatized people challenges my ability to act as a container, allowing the somatic transferential and countertransferential symptoms to emerge. I need to attune to what cannot yet be told, to the unknown that might emerge in my own inner space with incoherent, fragmented images and with flooding bodily sensations. The clients' dreams and images unconsciously evoke my own unconscious reactions, and the archetypal pattern within myself responds to what is constellated in the interactive field between us.

With supportive containing and holding, empathically attuned resonance, and the bridge-building of the reflective stance, I try to reconnect these patients through active imagination, art, sand play, and fantasy to their own symbolic capacity. Our circumambulation often dances around the death and rebirth pattern as a core archetypal theme in the process of transforming trauma. These mythic patterns connect traumatized patients with their own pressing existential issues and hence provide a feeling of connectedness, healing the experience of being "outside of culture."

Working in an integrative manner and taking into account contributions from related fields, I weave the process of therapy by exploring the symbol systems of religions, myths, and fairy tales about our age-old human confrontation with the mysteries of life and death, destruction and renewal, dismemberment and reconstitution. I think of Ovid and Heraclitus with their firm belief in change and transformation and that nothing visible keeps its form, and nature, the transformer of all things, creates from the old ever new shapes.

The dynamic development of the symbol assists in the capacity of adaption and facilitates greater self-regulative and meaning-making processes. The trauma-therapeutic process can be seen as a kind of emergence from darkness, deep pain, anguish, and a distorted state of mind to one in which the transformation to a truer and more accurate view of self and world takes place. Lisa McCann and Laurie A. Pearlman refer to the allegory of Plato's cave in describing this as a "gradual process of accommodation as the person moves from blindness to catching a glimpse of the new reality."[40] The wounds are calling out for healing and development after the ego has been forced to give up its central position.

WORKING WITH PICTURES AND GUIDED IMAGINATION

Images touch us at a deeper level than words. Traumatic imagery usually consists in disturbing flashbacks and fragmented vivid images that represent symbolic manifestations of traumatic memory. The chaotic nature of emerging images causes overwhelming affects, which are experienced metaphorically as avalanches, volcanoes, earthquakes, or tsunamis. Transforming these images and encouraging the patient to create healing images that provide safety can be done by guided imagination—facing the danger together with imaginary figures and inner helpers, helpful animals, or the assistance of the analyst. All creative expressions such as drawing, writing poems or fairy tales, or journal writing facilitate the process of revisioning oneself beyond the victim stance and creating a new identity. Pictorial expression may restore the ability to speak and to initiate communication after long periods of dwelling in a silent and bottomless abyss. Creating pictures is a leap forward in the ability to make contact and communicate.

In a picture, clients can discover and envision themselves in a new way as active persons. The value of the picture, like the value of the symbol, consists in the capacity to create a new vision of reality. For traumatized individuals, the attempt to depict their suffering in a picture represents an attempt to master the trauma, to communicate and to get hold of overwhelming affects, and to regain some power. The process of composing a picture can be liberating, giving an image to the monstrosity of the experience without getting drowned in the reexperiencing of the trauma. This creative process is a working-through of the haunting inner representations of traumatic images.

To create a picture is a first step toward recreating oneself. To paint implies relating—to the brush, to the paint, to the paper. This relieves the client's total isolation, the condition of "the broken connection." No matter how hopeless its content might appear to be, or in what deep solitude it might have been painted, every picture is a step out of isolation, because the painter has some awareness that another person may also look at it. Pictures originate in a sense of relationship, including that between the painter and the image. When we create pictures we restructure reality, and in so doing we also restructure ourselves. In symbolic representation we can repossess lost or severed fragments of our identity.

As the trauma itself breached boundaries, so the creation of images in therapy also serves to cross boundaries and is orientated toward transcendence. The process of producing symbols promotes self-regulation and integrative processes. It enables one to encounter oneself and to engage in a dialogue where the archetypal content of the picture can be integrated into the psyche through intrapsychic communication. Painting is a creative act in psychotherapy, an imaginative leap in an effort to create a new identity for oneself. Relegating threatening contents into the framework of a picture creates a feeling of safety and distance from them.

I find art-therapeutic approaches particularly helpful because they strengthen self-confidence and self-worth, assist in gaining psychic stability, lead out of fragmentation, and initiate integration. In giving form to traumatic contents, images make difficult inner processes more transparent and activate hidden creative potential, at the same time strengthening healthy aspects of the personality.

I also include receptive art therapy in my therapeutic work with traumatized clients. Pictures by Hieronymus Bosch, Goya, Picasso, Georg Baselitz, Louise Bourgeois, and Frieda Kahlo help me to symbolize dismemberment, splintering, violence, and psychic fragmentation. I facilitate many varied modes of expression and creation, as I have described in my book *Seelenmord: Inzest und Therapie* (Soulmurder: Incest and Therapy).[41]

Often, significant dreams of the type that Jung called "big dreams," which may be full of daemonic horror or enigmatic wisdom,[42] reveal the transformational energy of the collective unconscious pushing through in traumatic states. Through encountering the dragon, the devil, the Minotaur, the hidden treasure, or the black wise woman, the numinous embedded in our own psyche gets symbolized. Depending on the strength of the ego and the phase of the trauma therapy, engaging in active imagination with these figures can be a path to the exploration of the unknown and uncovering the meaning hidden in these images.

THE RELEVANCE OF RITUALS

Rituals are inherent to the nature of human being, and reflect the autonomous activity of the objective psyche. They have always been used to deal with critical stages of life. Centering on the mystery of life, they deal with the intersection of ego and self. Rituals help to quieten the mind, soothe the soul, and mend the heart. In trauma therapy, they serve as a container for powerful emotions and archetypal forces, mediating between consciousness and the unconscious, fostering the emergence of the transcendent function. The healing energy of sand pictures, as in sand play, makes the unprocessed traumatic experience more amenable to integration. Rituals symbolize the need to defend, protect, and create a safe *temenos*, and to enact processes of death and rebirth. Creating rituals of letting go and mourning also releases energy and is an important stage in the healing process.

Being aware that imagination stimulates more regions of the brain than mere words, trauma therapists focus on a variety of hypnoprojective techniques that help to stabilize, control, and regulate the process. These are well known as screening techniques, such as imaginary videotape, safe place, *trésor* or a treasure chest in which to store traumatic material, or an inner team and inner helpers to assist in gaining mastery over intrusive images. Analysis is a symbolic healing ritual where the traumatic wounds become tolerable and less tormenting. We need to clean the wound, attend to it, get the dirt out, seal it, and give it time to heal.

MYTH AND NARRATIVE IDENTITY IN TRAUMA THERAPY

Identity is an unfolding narrative in which the past is reconstructed, the present perceived and described, and the future anticipated. A meaningful, living myth is made up of the elements that shape one's life. The concept of "narrative identity" goes back to Paul Ricoeur;[43] it refers to the stories people tell about themselves in order to define who they are.

Identity is something dynamic; it confers individuality and continuity and creates a meaningful whole. This is why after the trauma "biographical work"—i.e., the processing of the trauma by telling its story and forging a coherent personal myth that leaves space for ambiguity and paradox—is a way of reconstructing one's identity and making sense of oneself. There is an archetypal need to tell the story and to reclaim one's dignity after the traumatic experience of fragmentation—sometimes a kind of compulsion to bear witness.

Storytelling in narrative psychology is a mode of "self-making and world making,"[44] an attempt to reconstruct a coherent sense of self by transforming life into a narrative. Narration functions to form and to frame the chaos of trauma. Analysis works with these healing narratives to structure subjective experiences and to promote a dialogue between conscious and unconscious material. The trauma narrative can be considered an odyssey of self, an attempt at self-creation. Traumatized human beings are in search of a new concept of themselves and therefore are also in search of a new myth, one that takes account of the trauma they experienced and attempts to decipher the pattern and the meaning of these events.

Jung felt strongly about the mythic nature of personal experience, and repeatedly stated that he felt driven to know his own myth.

In the ritual of analysis, the trauma story is reinterpreted over and over again—meaning ascribed to it, behaviors explained and justified, broken links reestablished. In so doing, the client gradually regains control and unfreezes. These stories are told from different vantage points, in words and in images, to develop meaning, to increase coherence, and to clarify orientation. They are always changing in the course of analysis; they are just as fluid and unstable as the concept of identity is. Just as individuation is an ongoing process, there is also an ongoing process of attribution of meaning to the trauma experienced.

The evolutionary success of the human race is based on its ability to adapt to adverse life conditions, to be flexible, and to create new options for thought and behavior. Trauma survivors must transform and create themselves anew. They must establish themselves as an "evolving identity." When in traumatic shock, when the world as one thought it was is shattered, when one's ego has been toppled from its directing function, one is compelled to reconstruct and recompose one's identity in order to recover a feeling of coherence. To reshape traumatic experiences into a story is a creative act of coping, for in this way the storyteller gains control over the traumatic event, at least in the aftermath. Trauma narratives are, in a certain sense, ways of recovering something lost and attempts to find out how one's personal fate fits into the scheme of things.

The imaginal trauma stories convey how clients emotionally came to grips with the shattering of belief systems and worldviews, and how they ultimately elaborated their personal experiences within a more collective and even spiritual perspective. In analysis, the elaboration of this personal myth in archetypal, symbolic, and imaginal language takes place. The new paradigm in trauma therapy, known as "post-traumatic growth," indicates how personal and collective myths are created in the aftermath of suffering, reflecting also one's relationships to the transpersonal dimension of human existence that was triggered by traumatic experience. The experience of torture, for example, has forced individuals to consider the question of what they are ready to suffer or even die for. In other words, they are forced to deal with the issue of "ultimate concern," a concept developed by the theologian Paul Tillich.[45] The numinosity of trauma may either put the survivor in touch with this ultimate concern that can only be expressed symbolically, or the traumatic experience may lead to the loss of any ultimate concern and throw the individual into existential anxiety or into utter meaninglessness. We must help our clients to connect to the capacity for renewal, applying symbolic and imaginal consciousness in order to decipher the mythic dimension of what has happened to them. We assist them to figure out how their traumatic experience has shaped their awareness of the main concerns in their life, their values, worldview, and their connection to the infinite.

In my practice working with survivors of torture, sexual violence, and war-inflicted traumas, I listen attentively for archetypal patterns that emerge in the stories of violence. In extreme situations in which a client is most vulnerable, archetypal patterns and dynamics are more likely to break through and to take charge in creating a sense of identity and meaning. Roesler[46] has observed that in traumatic situations when the ego is most vulnerable, the psyche tends to find its new orientation in basic archetypal patterns. The modes of experience, behavior patterns, and styles of narration comparable to those in myths, fairy tales, and works of art and poetry appear in the stories. There is a blending of personal and archetypal patterns in these narratives of an emerging self. To pay careful attention to how the stories are being shaped as blueprints of a future life and to the meaning that is attributed to the traumatic event, and to which role the traumatic event is given with respect to the person's feeling about life and his interpretation of himself and the world, helps to identify the basic archetypical pattern that unconsciously casts the traumatized in the role of victim or hero and that directs the process of individuation.

Richard Stromer,[47] in his work on personal mythology as pathway to the sacred, refers to Pieracci,[48] who coined the term "ontic myth" to refer to a set of beliefs dealing with how one should be in this world, how people are or ought to be in order to avoid the repetition of trauma. There is an interdependent relation between how the experience shapes the creation of the myth and how the myth shapes further experience. In listening to such "ontic myths," I focus on the archetypical patterns and combinations of symbols that appear in the images, and I identify the person's resources and any protective factors. I am guided by questions such as: How does the traumatized person describe the struggle for survival after the trauma? Which models are called into play out of the treasury of archetypical wisdom, myths, religions, literature, film and music, in order to find/give meaning? What may I learn about the "miracle" of healing and rescue, about the archetype of the wounded person and that of the wounded healer, about victims and perpetrators, about the child-archetype and that of the hero, about surrender and sacrifice? The manner in which human beings cope with, grow beyond, and overcome their traumatic experiences demonstrates the capacity of the self to create meaning.

STAGES OF THE SYMBOLIC QUEST

In trauma therapy we usually differentiate between various stages of healing. First, safety and stabilization are the primary concern. We need to create a *temenos* with clear boundaries and structure. This establishes an atmosphere of compassion and solidarity. We have to strengthen the capacity to tolerate painful emotions that are connected with intrusive imagery, and we slowly accompany the circuitous descent of our patients into the underworld. As analyst, I provide the link between the two worlds, the Ariadne thread holding the "broken connection" for the wounded person who has descended into the realm of the dead. Timing and pacing are of extreme importance, also patience and persistence. I think of the myths of Demeter and Persephone or of Inanna as images for the process of recovery. There are times in the therapeutic process when the wounded person goes back again and again to the netherworld, to times of feeling dead again. I need to trust the process that this continual dying of countless deaths is a necessary phase of this quest, in order to be reborn.

In the second stage of healing, I help the patient to confront and symbolize the traumatic core through guided imagination. The exploration of the imagery system of memory is a very powerful affective experience that needs to be carefully planned and prepared. Sufficient inner strength to bear the often deeply frightening images and a capacity for self-soothing is a precondition for this phase. Mourning the losses, like Demeter, is a very important step during this stage. With the help of dreams and active imagination, I support the process of weaving a new life myth, and I encourage expressing this narration symbolically. Rituals assist in this process of the newly emerging self. Adopting a state of reverie, I tune into where this person appears to me as most whole, most genuine, most at home, and I encourage the patient to engage in an inner dialogue with this "other being" within. Working with the emerging images and archetypes gradually fosters the process of symbolization and transformation.

In the third stage of the work, there must be a return from the underworld to join the world of humans again and face the task of creating a future. This phase is like a homecoming after a very perilous quest to remake oneself, separating from the old way of life and moving into a new mode of being and relating to oneself and the world. Having reclaimed lost parts of oneself and mended the broken connections may feel like finally having found the hidden treasure, a spiritual experience that paves new paths to intimacy and solidarity with others and often a new relationship with the numinous. The patients have achieved a narrative competence and are able to tell their story of wounding, struggle, descent, and return as their own myth of wholeness. The individuation process, forced upon them through traumatic events, helped them to become who they are and to know themselves on a very deep level. Some of my trauma patients would agree with the insights a former client of Jung wrote to him: "Out of evil, much good has come to me. By keeping quiet, repressing nothing, remaining attentive, and by accepting reality—taking things as they are, and not as I wanted them to be—by doing all this, unusual knowledge has come to me and unusual powers as well, such as I could never have imagined before."[49]

Joining Jung's efforts to rescue the living symbol from annihilation is often a slow, painful process of re-membering what was dis-membered and of retrieving what was lost. I am only too acutely aware of the limitations I encounter in myself as an analyst doing this work, with the burning question Rilke poses in the first Duino Elegy ringing in my ear: "All this was mission—but could you accomplish it?"[50] Then I find Jung's consoling words echoing in my soul: "The serious problems of life…are never fully solved. The meaning and purpose of a problem seem to lie not in its solution but in our working at it incessantly."[51]

Embracing these problems with my whole being is my contribution to the opus.

NOTES

1. C. G. Jung, "Definitions," in *Psychological Types*, vol. 6 of *The Collected Works of C. G. Jung*, trans. R. F. C. Hull, ed. H. Read, M. Fordham,

G. Adler, Wm. McGuire, 20 vols. (Princeton, NJ: Princeton University Press, 1953-1979)(hereafter *CW*), § 819.

2. *The Freud/Jung Letters: The Correspondence between Sigmund Freud and C. G. Jung,* ed. William J. McGuire, Gerhard Adler, and Aniela Jaffé, trans. Ralph Manheim and R. F. C. Hull (Princeton, NJ: Princeton University Press, 1974), p. 279.

3. Jung, *Psychology and Alchemy, CW* 12, § 28.

4. Jung, *The Structure and Dynamics of the Psyche, CW* 8, § 402.

5. Donald Kalsched, *The Inner World of Trauma* (London: Routledge, 1996), p. 2.

6. Judith Herman, *Trauma and Recovery* (New York: Basic Books, 1992), pp. 38 ff.

7. Leon Wurmser, "A Defense of the Use of Metaphor in Analytic Theory Formation," *Psychoanalytic Quarterly* 46 (1977): 466-498; G. Pederson-Krag, "The Use of Metaphor in Analytic Thinking," *Psychoanalytic Quarterly* 25 (1956): 66-71; J. A. Arlow, "Metaphor and the Psychoanalytic Situation," *Psychoanalytic Quarterly* 48 (1979): 363-385.

8. Jacques Lacan, *Écrits: A Selection,* trans. Alan Sheridan (London: Tavistock, 1977), p. 72.

9. Rudolf Lachauer, "Du sollst Dir ein Bildnis machen," *Forum Psychoanalyse* 21 (2005): 14-29.

10. Jung, "The Psychology of the Child Archetype," in *CW* 9/1, § 291.

11. Gustav Bovensiepen, "Symbolic Attitude and Reverie: Problems of Symbolization in Children and Adolescents," *Journal of Analytical Psychology* 47 (2002): 247.

12. Jung, "The Psychology of the Unconscious," in *Two Essays on Analytical Psychology* (1916/1928), *CW* 7, § 121.

13. Jean Knox, "The Analytic Relationship: Integrating Jungian, Attachment Theory and Developmental Perspectives," *British Journal of Psychotherapy* 8 (2009): 5-23.

14. See Hester McFarland Solomon, "The Transcendent Function and Hegel's Dialectical Vision," in *Who Owns Jung?* ed. Anne Casement (London: Karnac, 2007), pp. 265-290.

15. In German: *Erkennungszeichen;* see M. Lurker: *Wörterbuch der Symbolik* (Stuttgart: Kröner, 1979).

16. Jung, *Structure and Dynamics of the Psyche, CW* 8, § 643-644.

17. Erich Fromm, *The Forgotten Language: An Introduction to the*

Understanding of Dreams, Fairy Tales and Myths (New York: Rinehart & Co., 1951).

18. Edward C. Whitmont, *The Alchemy of Healing* (Berkeley: North Atlantic Books, 1993).

19. See also Stanley Krippner, "Personal Mythology: An Introduction to the Concept," *Humanistic Psychologist* 18/2 (1990): 133-142; Ernst Kris, "The Personal Myth," *Journal of the American Psychological Association* 4/4 (1956): 653-681; Daniel Feinstein and Stanley Krippner, *The Mythic Path: Discovering the Guiding Stories of Your Past—Creating a Vision for Your Future* (New York: Tarcher, 1997).

20. George B. Hogenson, "From Moments of Meeting to Archetypal Consciousness: Emergence and the Fractal Structure of Analytic Practice," in Casement, *Who Owns Jung?* p. 311.

21. Jung, *Psychology and Alchemy, CW* 12, § 34.

22. Mardi J. Horowitz, *Stress Response Syndromes* (New York: Jason Aronson, 1976).

23. Ronnie Janoff-Bulman, *Shattered Assumptions* (New York: The Free Press, 1992).

24. Henry Krystal, *Integration and Self-Healing: Affect, Trauma, Alexithymia* (Hillsdale, NJ: The Analytic Press, 1988).

25. Donald W. Winnicott, *The Maturational Process and the Facilitating Environment* (New York: International Universities Press, 1965).

26. Heinz Kohut, *The Restoration of the Self* (New York: International Universities Press, 1977).

27. Kalsched, *The Inner World of Trauma.*

28. Robert Jay Lifton, *The Life of the Self* (New York: Simon and Schuster, 1976); *The Broken Connection* (New York: Simon and Schuster, 1979).

29. George B. Hogenson, "The Self, the Symbolic and Synchronicity: Virtual Realities and the Emergence of the Psyche," *Journal of Analytical Psychology* 50/2 (2005): 271-284.

30. Kathryn Wood Madden, *The Dark Light of the Soul* (Great Barrington, MA: Lindisfarne, 2008).

31. An excellent dissertation on the subject of interactive field is Constance S. Rodriguez, "Dancing in the Thresholds: Exploring the Interactive Field" (PhD diss., Pacifica Graduate Institute, 2001).

32. Murray Stein, ed., *The Interactive Field in Analysis* (Wilmette, IL: Chiron, 1995), p. 1.

33. Wilfred Bion, *Learning from Experience* (London: Karnac, 1984).

34. Jung, *The Practice of Psychotherapy*, *CW* 16, § 358.

35. Enid Balint, "Memory and Consciousness," *International Journal of Psychoanalysis* 68 (1987): 475-483.

36. Jung, *The Practice of Psychotherapy*, *CW* 16, § 358.

37. Whitmont, *The Alchemy of Healing*, p. 152.

38. Theodor Reik, *Listening with the Third Ear* (New York: Grove, 1949).

39. James Hillman, *Re-Visioning Psychology* (New York: Harper, 1975), p. 138.

40. Lisa McCann and Laurie Anne Pearlman, *Psychological Trauma and the Adult Survivor: Theory, Therapy and Transformation* (New York: Brunner/Mazel, 1993), p. 170.

41. Ursula Wirtz, *Seelenmord: Inzest und Therapie* (Stuttgart: Kreuz, 1989).

42. Jung, *Structure and Dynamics of the Psyche*, *CW* 8, § 554, and *The Development of Personality*, *CW* 17, § 209.

43. Paul Ricoeur, *Time and Narrative*, trans. K. Mc Laughlin and D. Pellauer (Chicago: University of Chicago Press, 1988).

44. J. D. Bruner, "Self-Making and World Making," in *Narrative and Identity: Studies in Autobiography, Self and Culture*, ed. J. D. Bruner (Amsterdam: Benjamins, 2001), pp. 25-37.

45. D. Mackenzie Brown, ed., *Ultimate Concern: Tillich in Dialogue* (New York: Harper & Row, 1965).

46. Christian Roesler, "A Narratological Methodology for Identifying Archetypal Story Patterns in Autobiographical Narratives," *Journal of Analytical Psychology* 51/4 (2006): 574-586.

47. Richard Stromer, "Faith in the Journey: Personal Mythology as Pathway to the Sacred" (PhD diss., accessed at http:/www.personalmyths.com).

48. Michael Pieracci, "The Mythopoesis of Psychotherapy," *Humanistic Psychologist* 18/2 (1990): 208-223.

49. Jung, "Commentary on 'The Secret of the Golden Flower,'" in *CW* 13, § 70.

50. Rainer Maria Rilke, *Duino Elegies*, trans. Stephen Mitchell (Boston: Shambhala, 1992).

51. Jung, *CW* 8, § 771.

The Odyssey as a Symbol for Jungian Analysis—The Limits of Symbolization

Doris Lier

The Historical Distance of *The Odyssey*

The story of *The Odyssey* as a symbol for psychoanalysis, especially as a symbol for Jungian analysis, seems at first view to be obviously correct.[1] The image of the sea voyage has been a metaphor for human existence since time immemorial, and psychoanalysis is an adventurous voyage, full of perils and the dangers of running aground on reefs and rocks. To compare psychoanalysis and *The Odyssey* seems to be obvious. But this initial impression should be carefully reconsidered. What at first view makes sense does not always stand up to critical investigation. There are two problems that arise from the attempt to take *The Odyssey* as a symbol for analysis: the date of its composition, i.e., its historical distance from us, and the limits of symbolization in general. First I will discuss the problem of historical distance.

The epic poem *The Odyssey* describes human experiences that are far away from our contemporary way of life. It was written down in the

Doris Lier holds a Diploma in Analytical Psychology from the C. G. Jung Institute Zurich. Since 1988 she has had a private practice in Zurich and is currently a training analyst, supervisor, and lecturer at ISAPZURICH. She has published articles about analytical psychology, history of symbols, and epistemology.

eighth century B.C. and refers to experiences that date back to events centuries earlier. Sailing at that time was a life-and-death struggle. The dangers—such as storms, cliffs, and rocks—were incalculable. In addition to this, the ancient Greeks often did not know what problems they would face when riding at anchor. The one-eyed Polypheme, the Amazons, Circe, and many other images are representations of what Greek seafarers had to endure.

No doubt, in our days as well as in former times, curiosity, adventurous desires, necessity, or even misery may initiate a sea voyage. The words curiosity and misery, however, have changed their meanings over the centuries: When the ancient Greeks set sail to the coast of Asia Minor, or when they passed the Dardanelles and traveled across the Bosporus into the Dead Sea, or headed westwards to Italy, Sicily, and to the northern coast of Africa, they never knew if they would ever reach home again. Storms made sailing so dangerous that any rescue could become impossible.

In the centuries between then and now, the world has been measured and contemporary technology can make of seafaring a comfortable voyage in a five-star hotel. There are detailed maps and navigation systems, satellite-generated weather forecasts, and ingenious ship construction. There are multiple possibilities for conserving food and carrying medical equipment. Only people seeking asylum, crowded together on little, poorly-equipped ships, might experience something similar to the experiences of the ancient Greeks. They are endangered, but even they have a good chance of being spotted by the harbor's surveillance and rescued.

So much for the dangers coming from outside. Inner experiences, too, have been fundamentally transformed over the centuries. Homer's Greeks lived in mythological times. They did not deify psychic phenomena, they deified natural powers. They tried to humanize and domesticate overpowering natural forces by transforming them into gods and demons. The gods they worshipped behaved more or less like human beings, i.e., like themselves. Instead of being exposed to dangers coming from uncontrollable outer powers, the Greeks could debate with figures behaving similarly to themselves and enter into contracts with them. Personal interactions between human and superhuman beings were admitted realities.

The psychological digestion of dangerous situations was fundamentally altered over the centuries. In a first step, mythological thinking was replaced by a metaphorical approach. The Greek philosophers became aware that we human beings are the creators of the gods. Since the beginning of the Modern Age, the triumphant advances of the natural sciences and technology have progressively transformed all human problems into scientific questions that could from then on be managed by finding technological solutions. Natural catastrophes were and are no longer seen as the revenge of insulted gods. On the individual level, one still might believe in something like gods, but if someone said that Poseidon had prevented him from coming home from a holiday in the Maldive Islands, we would think he suffered from a psychiatric disease and would consult a diagnostic manual. Nowadays there are mental structures other than deities that give us the tools to cope with the world and its dangers. These structures belong to the scientific world or to the humanities, especially to hermeneutical methods. One-eyed giants and sea monsters can of course still be found in contemporary fairy tales and maybe also in dreams, but we know that they are mankind's creations and must be understood through interpretation.

There is the possibility of arguing, in the frame of reference of archetypal concepts, that imaginative figures such as Circe, Poseidon, Zeus, or Hera are psychic manifestations, representations of ubiquitous inner experiences. This view allows us to hold on to these figures and to interpret them in the context of depth psychology, especially in the Jungian context. It was C. G. Jung who proposed such a transfer by taking the old gods and demons as psychic components:

> For thousands of years the mind of man has worried about the sick soul, perhaps even earlier than it did about the sick body. The propitiation of gods, the perils of the soul and its salvation, these are not yesterday's problems. Religions are psychotherapeutic systems in the truest sense of the word, and on the grandest scale. They express the whole range of the psychic problem in mighty images.[2]

There is no doubt that the creation of narratives about gods and demons was an attempt to master anxiety. But, as I already mentioned, the ancient Greeks' superhuman figures were located in the outer world—in rivers, seas, and mountains, in rain and storms. The ancient Greeks did not think in terms of integration, of individuation and self-reflection. In mythological times, the world was full of threatening events of a miraculous nature, and the mythological narratives were recited in the context of ritual celebrations. They were performed in order to worship and to recreate the outer world and at the same time to ground and consolidate the Pan-Hellenic community.

Jung's idea that "there are peoples and epochs" where the psyche "is found outside" belongs to contemporary understanding.[3] It would not have been understood by the ancient Greeks, for whom the narratives were not a mirror of inner psychological phenomena but rather described the actual world with which they had to cope. In ancient Greece, people did not know about an internal psychic realm and introspection. In other words, for them there was no difference between the world as it is and the world as we human beings interpret it.

The Odyssey can only be taken as a symbol for psychoanalysis within a psychoanalytical vocabulary.[4] We cannot say that *in fact* or *in reality* the Hellenic gods were internal figures. It is only the contemporary language-game that leads us to interpret these figures in a psychoanalytical sense. It is not the truth of the way of life 2,800 years ago. Precisely said, our psychoanalytical view is anchored in the way of life as it has been experienced since the middle of the nineteenth and the beginning of the twentieth century.

THE PROBLEM OF IMAGINATION

(a) Metaphors for Existence

Whenever we speak of metaphors or symbols, we have left the mythological worldview and proceeded to the differentiation between the world as it may be and our human reflections and ideas. This change was already recognized by the Greek philosophers, especially by Aristotle. It went underground during the Middle Ages and was rediscovered in the Renaissance.

Before beginning with the interpretation of *The Odyssey*, it is important to emphasize that there are some metaphors that stay in use over centuries. Hans Blumenberg has called them "metaphors for existence."[5] Seafaring is one of these metaphors. Even nowadays in the twenty-first century, we still use the metaphors of sailing and shipwreck to grasp the movement of our being. This is amazing because contemporary metaphors for human existence could be taken from what the natural sciences have now revealed, from the much enlarged universe and the microcosm of the virtual world. Science fiction films, which are contemporary fairy tales, offer a wide range of new symbolizations. In spite of the fact that nowadays there are many new and maybe more adequate possibilities to symbolize our psychic realms, we are still holding on to nautical metaphors. This fact can be seen as a kind of psychic traditionalism. All these new metaphors and symbols might not yet be well enough anchored in our souls. Our personal experiences do not yet sufficiently include the science fiction world. Our dreams are still equipped with traditional symbolism. The width and depth of the seas can still be compared with the immensity and incalculability of the human soul. To integrate the realm of science fiction will be a task of the near future. It will become inevitable as soon as we are confronted with it in our own and our analysands' dreams.

(b) The Image of the Journey Back

Homer was not a poet in our contemporary sense. He only collected the stories of the oral tradition and united them within two epic poems, in *The Iliad* and *The Odyssey*. *The Iliad* is about the ninth year of the Trojan war, and *The Odyssey* tells us of Odysseus's travel homeward from Troy to Ithaca. But what happened on the journey out? Neither in *The Iliad* nor in *The Odyssey* is this journey mentioned. The story of Odysseus's journey home, however, consists of some 12,000 verses.[6] The fact that Homer described the journey back at such great length but disregarded the journey out can be taken as a psychological phenomenon that deserves our reflection. Certainly, some other authors of antiquity gave several hints about the drama of setting sail for Troy. They tell us about the sacrifice of Iphigenia in order to appease Artemis's anger against the Greeks and gain her blessing for the journey. But the journey itself is nowhere precisely accounted for. Only one minor incident is described: It is said that Philoctetes, Heracles' battle friend, was bitten by a snake and had to be left on the Chrysian Isle. Other adventures were not considered worthy of mention.[7]

How can we explain that the ancient Greeks reached the coast of Asia Minor without notable incident, whereas Odysseus's journey home became the paradigm for the dangerous voyage as such? How can we understand the fact that the other famous Greek epic journey poem, the *Argonautica*, also describes the journey home as an "odyssey"? The *Argonautica* was written down in Hellenistic times, in the third century B.C.E. It describes setting sail for Colchis, to the outermost place of the Dead

Seas (euphemistically called Pontos Euxeinos, the Happy Seas, at that time). No doubt, the Argonauts had to overcome many obstacles on their journey out. But the sailing back was an odyssey full of mostly threatening experiences, not comparable with what they faced on the voyage to Colchis. The Argonauts not only had to cross over the dangerous Happy Seas, they lost their way on the rivers that led them far into Celtic territory and from there along the west coast of Italy, then to the south, down to Northern Egypt, to Libya, and finally from there back to Thessaly.[8]

Why is the way back so much more difficult than the way out? What does it mean psychologically to be on the way home? To be retracing the very same path that has already been traveled and should be well known? Why is Odysseus constantly dogged by ill fortune, followed by Zeus's anger and Poseidon's vengeance, to the end that he is forced to abandon the familiar sea route?

To answer this question, let me first digress a bit. C. G. Jung pointed out that Jungian analysis should rather be done in the second half of life than in the first.[9] In the first part, we are forced to enter the world, to explore the outer life, and to establish a position in society. The second part is intended for the exploration of the so-called inner world. I am not sure if this still holds true nowadays, but the idea brings us closer to what the journey back could mean.

Every new start dealing with outer or inner departures is accompanied by fear, great expectations, and hope for success. It is accompanied by the vision of finding a treasure and bringing it back home. In spite of the fact that we do not know whether we will safely reach harbor again or get lost in the attempt, we are embarking under full sail. The hopeful mood gives us the courage to start any adventure. Focusing on the goal, we do not let anything stop us. Moreover, the fear of being shipwrecked often intensifies the initiative.

On the journey, we expose ourselves to danger. There are rocky coasts, and on the high seas the ship has to negotiate various kinds of obstacles. It can easily happen that unforeseen developments force us to change course and to look for new harbors. We try to survive, we suffer from our failings, and we enjoy our successes. We are completely employed and full of expectations of what will happen and what may be discovered.

Only little by little, and sometimes still during the journey out, does a new development begin. We gradually become aware of our thoughts, feelings, wishes, and actions. Questions come up: What am I doing here? What intentions led me to undertake this voyage? How do I react to the various dangers? Self-reflection often begins even before any destination or goal is reached. This beginning of self-reflection is the beginning of the journey back in a psychological sense. By engaging in self-reflection, we become aware of our desires and limitations. Unconscious aspects come to light.

Thus, every life journey can at the same time be seen as a journey out and a journey back, with the journey out being realized as the outer experience, and the journey back as the process of becoming conscious of the meaning in one's actions. In this regard, we can even say that, viewed psychologically, human beings are often on the way back before they even depart. This is true whenever we are planning a journey and trying to discern the unconscious wishes and desires that led to the idea of venturing out to begin with. In other words, the image of successive acts of setting sail and putting into harbor are two movements that play in close dialectical relationship.

Our focus thus far, i.e., the dawning of consciousness—not yet in analysis, but still in everyday life—is an integration process that begins to take shape and evolve even as it initially remains hidden. It is the navigation of life, in which unconscious wishes always play the main role, but have not yet become visible or understood.

By comparison, psychoanalysis offers a vessel in which our anxieties and desires can become conscious. The psychoanalytical setting offers the possibility of thinking carefully through the wishes that are hidden behind our outer adventures. In this sense, psychoanalysis is at first sight the consideration of the voyage of outer life; it is a review of that life from a psychological standpoint. However, this thinking through or review is a voyage in itself. We can call it an artificial voyage or a voyage in the narrow psychological sense. On this new voyage, even those ventures that were not experienced as having been difficult in outer life can turn out to have new and problematic dimensions. Somebody might be convinced that he or she married because of love and the wish to found a family, but later in analysis it may become clear that other desires were forcing this step, e.g., the desire to be rescued from depressing circumstances such as the cramped conditions of a former life or a blocked capacity for inward development.

At this point in my reflection, I would like to recall Freud's well-known description of psychoanalysis. He summed it up in three expressions—*remembering, repeating, working through*: Analysands remember life's rocky cliffs and storms, the departures and sailing out and the shipwrecks. During analysis, they repeat these experiences in the relationship with the analyst, who is sitting in the same boat with them, in the analytical setting. This repetition—called transference and countertransference—is at the same time and with the analyst's help the psychological working through. C. G. Jung considered even another aspect; he did not stay with the personal unconscious but went on to what he called the collective unconscious, the high seas of the soul of humankind as a whole. According to Jung, this realm needs to be integrated as well.

This is quite demanding. Exploring the unconscious in the course of analysis may be the most complicated and most uncharted odyssey ever invented by humankind. Psychoanalysis contains not only the inner world of analysands, it also includes their previous journeys and their present and future journeys, and it is a journey in itself as well. We have yet not included the analyst's journeys, which are also in the boat heading home. All these different journeys, which are blended together, have to be figured out—separated, sorted, understood, perhaps then put back together. Even now, trying to imagine what psychoanalysis implies, we get into rapids and find ourselves struggling to stay above water.

Undoubtedly, "journey back" is an image that captures the act of self-reflection, of diving into internal realms. But even this image does not come close to embracing the complexity of psychological self-relatedness or introspection. The common notion that psychoanalysis is a navigation of the inner world and a voyage into the unconscious is a rational idea, and still far away from psyche's own logic. To draw closer to psyche, we must take care not to reduce the journey, out of rational impulse, to a concrete undertaking split in two directions, of which we are forced to choose one after the other. It is far more complex than that. Even if we try to differentiate things by stating that in analysis we have to face reciprocal movements, the problem is not solved. Movements that simultaneously oppose themselves cannot be represented by an image. As soon as we try to imagine how this might work, we get entangled in a web of confusions.

Strictly speaking, the movement of self-reflection cannot be pictured. Self-reflection belongs to what Blumenberg has called an "absolute metaphor."[10] We lack the space here to debate the adequacy of this term or under which preconditions it may suffice, so I will stay with the expression. Absolute metaphors are metaphors of abstract mental notions and logical "movements" that in fact are not at the imagination's disposal. They are not accessible to perception. All the "metaphors for existence" belong to this category. The original source of this statement is Immanuel Kant, who distinguished between notions that refer to perception and notions of pure reason. According to Kant, these latter notions lead us to the storm-tossed seas where we lose orientation.[11] All the terms that refer to a totality, to the world or humanity as a whole, or of course also to God, are terms of this kind. They are not open to theories in a strict sense, but they also cannot be pictured because they are imperceptible.

Psychology is full of such notions, because psychological phenomena and movements, in spite of the fact that psychological stirrings are due to emotion, are themselves actually beyond sensation. In our psychoanalytical everyday life, however, and even in theoretical investigations, this amazing and uncomfortable fact is seldom considered. We easily forget that we constantly imagine what is beyond imagination. In fact, self-reflection, introspection, individuation, and similar notions speak of something that cannot be compared with any concrete phenomenon or direction.

Having arrived at this aporetic point of reflection, the question arises: How can this problem be solved? In his book *The Soul's Logical Life*, Wolfgang Giegerich proposes to overcome imaginal psychology. He wants Jungian psychology to go on to be a psychology that transgresses the positivism of our worldview and redeems it from its concretistic prejudices.[12]

In my interpretation, this appeal cannot mean that analytical psychologists should totally abandon images and the imaginal realm. Psychology speaks of the soul's life, which we can only grasp by perception, affectivity, and imagination. Giegerich's appeal rather means to teach us how not to get caught in the trap of staying on the imaginal level but instead to transcend the imaginal by "thinking the images."[13] "Thinking the images" in this sense does not mean to use a function. It "is not exhausted by the capacity of discursive reasoning....Thinking has do with having been reached by and being committed by one thought."[14] Similar proposals are also offered by theoreticians of metaphor, for example, among many others, Max Black, David Davidson, Nelson Goodman, George Lakoff, Mark Johnson, and Hans Blumenberg. I would like to give some hints about such a task on the basis of the correlation of harbor and high seas.

(c) The Correlation of Harbor and High Seas

In Jungian psychology, individuation and self-realization have a high value. Individuation is taken as a journey back in the sense of coming home to oneself, to one's own harbor. Self-realization is often not only understood in the sense of learning more about one's reactions, not only of reaching the whole of the personality, but even in the sense of obtaining spiritual experience. This is normally expressed by the experience of being held and led by the Self, an entity conceived to be larger than and transcending the little ego or even the sense of "I." Such an idea of self-reflection is also inspired by the mazes of ancient times, with their center in the middle. But, as was already shown, the image of the maze or voyage back does not sufficiently represent what happens in analysis. The sea journey in general and the travel back home in particular can only be understood by recognizing the co-relatedness of harbor and high seas.

Correlation means that both poles—harbor and high seas—are states of the soul that are determined by each other. The idea or experience of reaching harbor is due to the idea of transcending or violating the border. The other way round: The sea voyage can only be an experience of violating the border in contradistinction to the harbor. This means that in psychology reaching harbor can never mean coming home in the sense of reaching the goal of the soul's journey. "Home," in the sense of undoubting trust, belongs to humanity's unattainable wishes. This is also shown in the Old Icelandic saga summarized by Giegerich in the above-mentioned book. The saga is about a young man who was a stay-at-home. His mother could not stand this and forced him to leave her house. He finally got up and left home. He "threw his spear as far as he could, then ran up to the place where it had landed in order to retrieve it. At this point he again threw the spear as far ahead as possible and then followed it, and so on."[15] Giegerich interprets the text in terms of projection. According to the above-mentioned correlation between harbor and high seas, I read the text as a correlation that begins after having left home: The young man left home, and as a consequence "home" in the former sense could not be regained anymore. Before having left his mother's house, he was sitting behind the stove, i.e., he wanted to stay in the psychological status of doubtless trust (symbiosis) and experienced the outer world as being only dangerous. After having left home, he achieved a new understanding of the notions home and outer world. He learned that "home" does not

mean to regain the former security. "Home" in the sense of being in symbiosis was definitely lost. There was no way back home, but only the possibility of having a rest at the places where the spear was landing. These
places can be seen as images for the harbors that, after one has started the
sea voyage, can be reached from time to time.

"Harbor" and "high seas" are mental distinctions that enable us to
register our experiences as adult persons. Of course we can, constantly or
temporarily, be more attracted by one pole or the other. Yet we have to
keep in mind that, like the pair of notions anima and animus, one pole
never exists without the other. If somebody thinks that psychoanalysis is
solely about coming home, then he or she loses consciousness of psychoanalysis as continuous seafaring. On the other hand, one who pursues
only adventure loses touch with the meaning of harbor.

Harbor and high seas are contradictions, but at the same time they
contain each other and build a unity without giving up their respective
differences. This makes psychic experiences attractive and repulsive at the
same time. In other words, there may be a certain allure or clarity in experiencing one pole, but it can be most discomforting to experience the
whole, which comes when we begin to acknowledge the play of the contradictory counterpart. Giegerich has found a formula for this soul's logic:
the unity of the unity and contradiction of the contradictions. With this
formula he wants to emphasize that in the soul's logical life there are
opposites but there is no simple "*coniunctio oppositorum.*" As an example:
anima and animus are in some sense opposites but can never build a simple wholeness; they can build a certain unity but in this unity the differences can never be eliminated. We can easily understand that a logic like
this cannot be adequately pictured. At best, images can concretize this
complicated psychic status and bring some of its aspects into light. When
we, for example, speak of analysis as a Sea Voyage or even as a Night Sea
Journey, we only grasp one aspect of something that is far beyond imagination. The image cannot visualize the fundamental self-contradiction in
the psychic state.

Psychoanalysis can help clients, but it can never salvage them from
their contradictions, especially not from their self-contradictions. Psychoanalysis can only show people how to live with the human condition of
being dissociated. It can make clear that those of us who arrive home per-
manently or reach home in the sense of a basic trust are psychologically
dead.

This contradictory logic of the psyche becomes visible in human behaviors. We travel across the seas, climb the highest mountains, or conquer the microcosm and a part of the universe, and yet we build our houses on secure ground and protect ourselves against natural catastrophes, against wind and rain, tidal waves, volcanic eruptions, landslides, and the like. We make every effort to tame a terrifying nature, and yet we construct the worst possible horror, the atomic bomb. The history of mankind has always been the history of surviving natural disasters and yet risking life and limb.

ANALYST AND ANALYSAND AS CO-DETERMINERS OF THE DAWNING OF CONSCIOUSNESS

In the previous section, I explored the co-relatedness of harbor and high seas. I pointed out that the two poles comprise mental distinctions that enable human beings to register and orient themselves to their experiences.

In psychoanalysis we always have to deal with such distinctions, determinants, or dissimilarities. The dawning of consciousness comes about through the experience of differing determinants that have to be put into correlation. Our contemporary consciousness cannot only be described as inhering in a more or less strong "I" and its capacities to look back at itself and forward at the world. "Inside" and "outside" are also mental distinctions and phenomena that lie outside of space and time. They point to the self-contradictory nature of the human being. As already mentioned, whatever we experience is a correlation of an historically influenced personal view and an outer world that is mirrored in this view. This is why we do not only interpret the world's phenomena, but we create our experiences by interpreting what we encounter.

In psychoanalysis, this correlation of experiencing and interpreting transpires between two persons: the analyst and the analysand. At first glance, the analysand appears to experience the world and to rely on the analyst's help to become conscious of what he or she experiences. But as I said above, the movement is much more complicated, because the analysand's experiences are already interpreted experiences. On the basis of Richard Rorty's concept,[16] we could say that analysands use their "vocabulary" to tell the analyst what happens to them. The analyst's task is to find a new vocabulary that gives analysands the possibility of having new experiences. Communicating in this way, the two individuals mutually create a new and common vocabulary that correlates with their experience in analysis and in the world.

C. G. Jung, too, recognized that psychoanalysis contains such correlations. He described it not by using the metaphor of sailing nor by using another metaphor, but by reaching to a more abstract level:

> The tragic thing is that psychology has no self-consistent mathematics at its disposal, but only a calculus of subjective prejudices. Also, it lacks the immense advantage of an Archimedean point such as physics enjoys. The latter observes the physical world from the psychic standpoint and can translate it into psychic terms. The psyche, on the other hand, observes itself and can only translate the psychic back into the psychic.... There is no medium for psychology to reflect itself in: it can only portray itself in itself, and describe itself. That, logically, is also the principle of my own method: it is, at bottom, a purely experiential process in which hit and miss, interpretation and error, theory and speculation, doctor and patient, form a *symptosis* (σύμπτωσις) or a *symptoma* (σύμπτωμα)—a coming together—and at the same time are symptoms of a certain process or run of events.[17]

In this paragraph, C. G. Jung demonstrated his awareness of the complications contained in analysis. Here, too, he implicitly acknowledged the limits of symbolization as I have tried to explore them in this paper.

To summarize my thoughts: whenever we understand an image to picture a psychological phenomenon or movement, we must bear in mind that this can only be an initial approach, which then enables us to delve into the determinants and explore their dialectics.

NOTES

1. In this paper, the term psychoanalysis is used as a generic term for analytical work in the context of depth psychology.

2. C. G. Jung, "The State of Psychotherapy Today," in *Civilization in Transition*, vol. 10 of *The Collected Works of C. G. Jung* (hereafter *CW*), trans. R. F. C. Hull (London: Routledge & Kegan Paul, 1928/1964), § 367.

3. Jung, "The Spiritual Problem of Modern Man," in *Civilization in Transition*, *CW* 10 (1934/1964), § 158-159.

4. Concerning my use of the term "vocabulary" in this paper, see

Richard Rorty, *Contingency, Irony and Solidarity* (Cambridge: Cambridge University Press, 1989); German version: *Kontingenz, Ironie und Solidarität*, übers. von Christa Krüger (Frankfurt am Main: Suhrkamp, 1989), esp. pp. 21-51.

5. Hans Blumenberg, *Shipwreck with Spectator, Paradigm of a Metaphor for Existence*, trans. Steven Rendall (Cambridge, MA: MIT Press, 1996).

6. Homer, *Ilias/Odyssee*, in der übertragung von Johann Heinrich Voss (München: Winkler, [1974]).

7. *Der neue Pauly - Enzyklopädie der Antike*, hsg. v. Hubert Cancik und Helmut Schneider (Stuttgart; Weimar: J. B. Metzler, 2000/2002), s.v. *Odysseus*, Spalten 1110-1116; s.v. *Troia*, Spalten 852-865.

8. Apollonios Rhodos, *Die Fahrt der Argonauten*, Griechisch/ Deutsch, herausgegeben, übersetzt, und kommentiert von Paul Dräger (Stuttgart: Reclam, 2002).

9. Jung, *The Practice of Psychotherapy*, *CW* 16 (1935/1954), § 110f., § 474. See also Jung, "On the Psychology of the Unconscious," in *Two Essays on Analytical Psychology*, *CW* 7 (1942/1953), § 114f.; *The Structure and Dynamics of the Psyche*, *CW* 8 (1948, 1931, 1934/1960), § 112f., § 749-795, § 796-815.

10. Hans Blumenberg, *Paradigmen zu einer Metaphorologie* (Frankfurt am Main: Suhrkamp, 1998), esp. p. 10. See also Hans Blumenberg, *Work on Myth*, trans. Robert M. Wallace (Cambridge, MA: MIT Press, 1985).

11. Immanuel Kant, *Critique of Pure Reason*, trans. and ed. Paul Guyer and Allen W. Wood (Cambridge: Cambridge University Press, 1998), A 235-237.

12. Wolfgang Giegerich, *The Soul's Logical Life: Towards a Rigorous Notion of Psychology* (Frankfurt am Main: Peter Lang, 1998).

13. *Ibid.*, esp. p. 44f. and p. 203.

14. *Ibid.*, pp. 44-45.

15. *Ibid.*, p. 9.

16. Rorty, *Contingency, Irony and Solidarity*, esp. pp. 21-123 and pp. 127-161.

17. Jung, "The Structure of the Psyche," in *The Structure and Dynamics of the Psyche*, *CW* 8 (1927/1960), § 421.

The Golden Fish

NATHALIE BARATOFF

O ne of the more archetypal manifestations of the negative mother complex in a man is a certain lassitude and lethargy, which results in a general passivity towards life. It is as when Demeter withdraws her fruitful influence from the earth or when Isis places the poisonous snake at Ra's feet, or, yet again, when the Sirens enchant seamen with their song and keep them from proceeding on their journey.

Grimm's tale of "The Golden Children" presents an image of such an archetypal constellation and shows us what is needed for its resolution. Here is a brief synopsis of the tale:

There once lived a fisherman and his wife, so poor they could barely keep themselves alive. Their life suddenly changes after the fisherman catches a golden fish that is ready to pay for its life with a castle and a cupboard full of food. This gift comes with a condition of secrecy that the fisherman is unable to keep, succumbing to the nagging of his wife. Thereupon all the gifts are lost and the couple returns to their original desolate state. This scenario is repeated a second time with the same result, the wife's justification being that she would rather live in poverty than not know where their good fortune was coming from.

Nathalie Baratoff is a graduate of the C. G. Jung-Institute Zurich (1987) and training and supervising analyst at the International School of Analytical Psychology Zurich (ISAP), where she regularly teaches.

As the fish is caught for the third time, it bids the fisherman cut it up into six pieces and give two each to his wife and mare, and to plant two in the ground. The wife now bears golden twins, the mare golden colts, and two golden lilies spring from the ground.

As the twins come of age they decide to go out into the world. They comfort their sad father with the assurance that the lilies will indicate how they are doing: if the lilies are well, so are the twins; if they droop, the twins are in some trouble; if they drop, the twins are dead.

Coming to an inn, the twins are laughed at because both they and their horses are of gold. One twin is intimidated and returns home; the other does not allow their mocking to stop him and continues on his way.

This twin now comes to a forest full of robbers, but rides through unscathed by covering himself and his horse with a bearskin.

Arriving at a village, he meets a beautiful maiden, falls in love, proposes, and marries her. When the bride's father returns home and finds out about this he is very upset and wants to kill the groom (who is still wearing the bear-skin). Thanks to the bride's intercession the father refrains from harming the bridegroom, but his curiosity leads him to peek at the sleeping couple. How great is his surprise upon seeing his daughter in bed with a golden man!

During this night the golden twin dreams of pursuing a stag of great beauty through the forest. Awakening, he tells his bride that he means to go hunting, and will not be put off by her pleas.

He encounters just such a stag in the forest and rides tirelessly after it the whole day. When night falls, the stag disappears and the golden twin finds himself before a small house wherein sits a witch. This witch tries to entrap him by appearing in the guise of a little old woman, but her dog barks at him viciously. This annoys the golden twin, and he threatens to kill the dog. The witch now shows her true nature and turns the golden twin to stone.

Back home, the second twin sees one of the lilies drop and hastens to his brother's aid. Arriving at the witch's house, he is met in the same way, but he will not be fooled. He keeps his distance and threatens to kill the witch if she doesn't return his brother to life. This she does, though very unwillingly, and the two brothers are reunited. The fairy tale ends with one brother returning to his bride, the other going home to his father.

"The Golden Children" opens with the image of *a poor man and a poor woman who had nothing but a little hut and who sustained themselves by fishing and lived hand-to-mouth.*[1] The poverty of this initial condition indicates a drastic paucity of psychic energy. This is confirmed in the fisherman's reaction to what happens next: When he catches a golden fish, and a talking one at that, and the fish promises him a castle in return for its life, the fisherman's sole response is: "*What's the use of a castle if I have nothing to eat?*" Even after he has been promised a cupboard with an inexhaustible supply of food, he is unable to appreciate this miraculous gift of fate or to make any more use of it than to fill his stomach.

We might see this concretely as the state of a very common fellow without much imagination and focused on the basic necessities of life. We can, however, also see the fisherman's problem as a "common" one for man. In this sense "common" means "archetypal." This implies that it is an archetype that is responsible for this condition, and that it can be constellated in a fisherman as well as any other person with any other occupation or cultural niveau.

The soul geography of the fisherman in this tale shows him well positioned on the threshold between consciousness and the unconscious (land and sea). His occupation consists of bringing unconscious contents (fish) into consciousness (life), and the mention of a wife indicates wholeness and potential fertility (creativity). It is the fisherman's poverty, his total lack of vitality, that thwarts any development. It is the mother archetype in its negative manifestation that pulls all his energy away from life.

The libido of a man with a mother complex lies captive in the unconscious (with the mother). Very often he can only reach it in his fantasy, if at all. Unless he talks about his fantasies or gives them some kind of expression (writing, painting, modeling, dancing), no one ever knows of their existence, and indeed he himself soon forgets them. Since the unconscious usually reacts in a compensatory way to consciousness, we can safely suppose that our poor fisherman would fantasize or dream of success in fishing or about living in a beautiful house instead of a "little cottage." It comes as no surprise, therefore, to learn that he has caught a golden fish in his net and that he has, indeed, been offered a splendid castle. His inability to do anything with this gift is the tragedy of this fisherman, as well as of any other man with a mother complex: he is unable to integrate such a treasure into his conscious life.

The golden fish symbolizes an unconscious content of the highest value. Its appearance in the fisherman's life is pivotal. It breaks through his uneventful and frustrating existence and offers a possibility for change. The story tells us that the fisherman's astonishment was great upon finding the fish in his net, but there is no awe, no understanding of what has taken place. He might have built an altar and made offerings. Later on, when his wife tried to extract his secret from him, he might have told her to hold her tongue and be thankful for God's grace lest she try His patience and provoke His wrath. He does none of this, and he is willing to throw the fish back into the water in exchange for a cupboard full of food.

This attitude helps in understanding why the fish offers a castle as ransom for its life. As something that protects and shelters, the castle displays mother characteristics. It would hold the fisherman and satisfy his hunger. It might, however, also open him up to the world. Wanderers, knights, minstrels, merchants might come to the castle; such contacts would broaden his horizons and show him possibilities for bettering his situation in life. Although this castle is a gift of the fish, it is a prototype of a structure built by human hands and hence an example of consciousness and willpower. In order to build a castle, man needs skill and thought and knowledge and strength and, above all, effort. And so, the castle might have provided the fisherman with a base for making the transition to a more active attitude towards life. But none of this happens, because the fisherman lacks the energy and understanding of what has taken place.

At this point we might ask what role the fisherman's wife plays in this fairy tale. She is certainly very curious. She is unwilling to accept the gift without knowing who the giver is. This curiosity is a thirst for consciousness. If she had not been curious, the two would have continued to live in the new castle with its magic cupboard in a naïve, unconscious way. Although this may be likened to Adam and Eve before the fall, there are important differences: Adam and Eve did not get a second or third chance. They had to face the hardships of the world and find a way of surviving in a situation very different from the Garden of Eden. Furthermore, the fisherman and his wife did not start out with a castle and the magic cupboard. They were familiar with the difficulties of life and, as it seems, they were unable to make their way out of them as the first couple did.

If we see the wife as the fisherman's anima, we might say that he had the curiosity and the striving for consciousness within him but lacked the willpower to carry this through into life. This is demonstrated by the fisherman's returning to the sea both times after losing the castle without having learned anything from the experience. If he had really wanted to know, as his wife did, he might have started asking himself where this fish came from and what its miraculous appearance and gift meant. But none of this happened. The fisherman could not think symbolically; he was caught in the concrete, in the *materia*. This was the effect of the mother complex, pulling all energy away from life and paralyzing his spirit.

Had the golden fish not returned a third time, and had it not sacrificed itself, nothing would have changed in the fisherman's life.

After falling into the fisherman's net for a third time, the golden fish comes up with a new and rather surprising solution: it asks the fisherman to cut it up into six pieces, to give two pieces each to his wife and to his horse, and to plant the last two in the ground. If the sea symbolizes the unconscious and the golden fish an extremely valuable content of the unconscious, then this new development witnesses to the insistence of the Self in making a change in the fisherman's life. Through the symbol of the fish, the Self is now incarnating in the fisherman's life. This is a moment of Self-sacrifice and requires dismemberment because the ego would not be able to survive confrontion with the Self in its wholeness.

It is worthy of note that the fish instructs the fisherman to distribute the six pieces among three distinctly different realms: the human (the twins), the instinctive (the colts), and the vegetative (lilies). This shows that it is a thorough, all-embracing transformation that has now been set in motion.

We can say, in short, that the twins born to the fisherman's wife would stand for a new consciousness, and that the colts will serve as their master's instinctive carrying force.

I would like to consider the symbolism of the lily in more depth. The lily has always been seen as a royal flower. It appears on the coats of arms of many peoples, e.g., the French Fleur-des-Lis, the emblem of the French kings since the twelfth centrury, where it stood for majesty and power.

In the Sermon on the Mount, Jesus tells his disciples that the beauty of the lily surpasses Solomon in all his glory.[2] This is an important comparison, for Solomon was not only great and powerful and rich; he was especially venerated for his wisdom. The repeated mention of the lily in the Song of Songs, attributed to Solomon, puts the lily in the role of sponsa—as a mystical expression of Yahweh's love for Israel and, later, in the New Testament, of the love of Christ for the church. According to *The Oxford Annotated Bible*, the Song of Songs is a symbol of "the ultimate experience of divine love in the individual soul."[3]

In our fairy tale, the lily has a connecting function. As the twins ride out into the world, they assure their troubled father that he will know how they are faring by looking at the lilies: *If they are fresh, then we're in good health. If they droop, then we're sick. If they drop, then we are dead.* Later on in the tale, the twin who has remained at home realizes that misfortune has befallen his brother when one of the lilies drops. Thus the lily represents the Eros principle, the man's anima, his soul.

That the lily represents the soul in this fairy tale is supported by another amplification. In contrast to the human and to the instinctive realm, the vegetative realm has the potential for renewing itself after death: the plant dies, its seed falls into the earth, a new plant arises. In the case of the lily, it is not the seed but the bulb from which the new plant grows. Still, the visible part of the plant dies and a new one grows from the earth. Symbolically it refers to that part of us which continues to exist after death.

A central motif of this tale is the number two: the twins, two colts, two lilies. In fairy tales as well as in dreams, we sometimes encounter images that appear in twos without there being any apparent reason for this. Jung postulated that such double phenomena are caused by the approach of a hitherto unconscious content towards the threshold of consciousness.[4] Before such contents cross over into consciousness, they can only be perceived as two. There is no differentiation between them because only consciousness is capable of differentiation. This doubling of an image testifies to the ambivalent nature of all unconscious contents.

When such previously unconscious contents approach the threshold of consciousness, they can just as easily fall back into the unconscious as step over the threshold. Hence, the appearance of the twin motif bespeaks a very tentative stage in development: it can go one way or it can go the other. The initial situation shows how easily any development could have been nipped in the bud by the fisherman's lack of energy and willpower. When, however, such contents do make it over the threshold, when they are grasped by consciousness, then they show themselves for what they truly are—a pair of opposites.[5]

In the tale at hand, when the twins come of age they decide to leave home and venture out into the world. Coming to an inn, they are met with ridicule because of their golden color. An inn, being a collective place with people sitting together and drinking, inevitably leads to a sinking of the level of consciousness and to the dregs of mass psychology: whatever is not familiar is not appreciated, even if it is of high value. The people at the inn find the twins and their horses hilarious: *When they caught sight of the golden children they began to laugh and make fun of them.*

One of the twins hears the mocking and is shamed. The other twin pays no attention to what the people are saying. He seems to realize that this is the way people behave in groups and when they are drinking. He doesn't let them keep him from going on with his plans. The first twin is intimidated and returns home to his father.

This response of the twins suggests seeing them as personifications of the two psychological attitudes, extraversion and introversion. It is characteristic for the extravert to show good adaptation to the outer world. The extravert knows what to expect of the collective and is lenient towards its faults. In contrast, the introvert is poorly adapted to the outer world, intimidated by the collective, avoids confrontation, and seeks refuge in what is familiar…and so the introverted brother turns back and goes home.

But what does it mean that the twins reveal themselves to be attitudinal polarities? As the fisherman's children, the twin boys represent his future and his newly developing consciousness. They are a product of an impulse from the unconscious to come to grips with the initial state of poverty and passivity.

"The concept of energy implies that of polarity, since a current of energy necessarily presupposes two different states or poles, without which there can be no current. Every energetic phenomenon…consists of pairs of opposites: beginning and end, above and below, hot and cold, earlier and later, cause and effect, etc. The inseparability of the energy concept from that of polarity also applies to the concept of libido."[6] The implication of this statement is that if one goes through life one-sidedly, as either introvert or extravert, sooner or later one's libido will come to a standstill because it has nowhere to flow. Standstill or stagnation is precisely the condition of the fisherman's state at the beginning of the tale.

The scene at the inn shows that the unconscious impulse working for a change in the fisherman's psyche has crossed the threshold into consciousness. The two sons of the fisherman are no longer seen merely as twins; this image now breaks up into the one who goes out into the world (extravert) and the one who goes back home (introvert).

After this, our fairy tale follows the extravert. Leaving the inn, he first comes to a forest full of robbers, and we see him riding safely past them by concealing his and his horse's golden nature with a bearskin. Robbers are shadow figures, and represent an unconscious temptation to use the high value with which the hero is endowed (gold) for shadowy purposes. They might also represent envy attacks from others who see the hero's great value. The bearskin must therefore be seen as a sort of instinctive persona that guards the hero from his own shadow as well as from that of others. Let it be mentioned only in passing that the Germanic berserkers would be an important amplification to the bearskin.

Gold, the highest value, represents some talent or creative potential. Being endowed with such always carries the responsibility of protecting it from shadowy influences from within and without and, more generally, for doing "the right thing" with it.

This extraverted twin manages to get past the robbers without any loss to himself (the new consciousness) or to his horse (the instinctive energy that carries this new consciousness forward). Had he faced the robbers and tried to fight them, he would surely have been outnumbered.

The scene that follows is surprisingly short. The hero comes to a village and meets a beautiful maiden: they fall in love, get married, and a difficulty with the girl's father is quickly resolved. This could easily have been followed with: "and they lived happily ever after." The script of this tale runs differently, however, for, after marrying the maiden, the hero dreams of hunting a splendid stag. Waking up in the morning, he tells his wife that he must go hunting—the day after their wedding! When she begs him to stay, fearing something terrible might happen along the way, his only reply is: "*I must and will go forth.*" Here the hero appears very hard and unrelated. The unconscious has grabbed him with its impersonal, inhuman hand and has pointed him in a new direction. The dream of the stag introduces a very different experience into the fairy tale. Our hero knows nothing of what lies ahead; he doesn't know that the stag will lead him to the witch and that she will turn him to stone.

As with the typological functions, so too with the attitudes: the inferior one—because it has been less used—stores up a great deal of energy. When this energy of the inferior attitude breaks through into consciousness, it can be overwhelming. In the case at hand, the extravert, who is oriented towards the outer world, may experience the unconscious in a far more powerful way than the introvert, whose adaptation is towards this part of the psyche. For the introvert, it doesn't come as such a great surprise, and he has already had experience in dealing with it. For the extravert—it is a revelation! He is fascinated and swept along. This is what now happens to our hero. All his knowledge of the world, his perception of the situation and of what those around him experience and expect, all this extraverted adaptation is extinguished as he obeys the voice of his dream and sets out after the stag.

The stag is an image of powerful masculine energy. This is probably why, for ancient people, it was connected with the invincible sun. The stag sheds its antlers once a year and replaces them by the time of the rutting season, so that the "ladies" will be impressed and the "gentlemen" discouraged from encroaching upon his preserves and threatening his harem.

The stag's swiftness gave rise to another popular belief: legends speak of the stag leading into the depths of the forest; to an abyss; to the virgin, giant, magician, witch; to a magic land; to the beloved or to a dead mate.[7] Von Franz writes that "the deer symbolizes an unconscious factor which shows the way to a crucial event, either toward rejuvenation…or into the Beyond…or even to death."[8] Thus the stag can be seen as a *psychopomp*, a guide to the unconscious.

For alchemists, the stag's fleeting nature associated it with Mercurius. Mercury or quicksilver was for them an ever-changing, volatile, evasive, irritating, and fascinating element that they worked with in their operations. One of Mercurius's epithets was indeed *cervus fugitivus* (the fugitive stag).

To summarize, the tremendous strength of the stag, his fecundity and swiftness, have made him a symbol for dynamic spirit and a striving for consciousness (sun symbolism). The yearly shedding of its antlers has come to stand for transformation or renewal.

We watch our hero riding the whole day in pursuit of this marvelous creature—*over ditches and through bushes*—until night falls, when the stag suddenly vanishes. The hero has been blinded in broad daylight by a powerful instinct that he is powerless to resist. This is not a biological instinct but rather the instinct for individuation. It is a force that wants us to become all we are capable of becoming. This force, which had been working all along in the extraverted hero figure, went into high gear when his further development was threatened by the comfort and well-being of his new settled life. The stag, in the role of psychopomp, has fulfilled its mission very well indeed. It has maneuvered the hero onto the witch's doorstep, and there is now very little he can do but make her acquaintance.

We need to take a closer look at this meeting. When the stag suddenly disappears, the extraverted twin finds himself *before a small cottage, and inside sat a witch*. The text continues: *Then he knocked, and a little old woman came out.* The German original uses the word "Mütterchen," a diminutive of "Mutter" with the touch of endearment that most diminutives carry. Both statements come from the narrator and no explanation is given for the discrepancy between them. How are we to understand this? As an extravert, this twin can be expected to go by what he sees. But might the information about there being a witch inside the little house be seen as coming from the unconscious of the hero as an intuition or suspicion? In this case, he is confronted with two contradictory impressions. Being an extravert, he will surely put his trust in what comes from the outside.

This has fatal consequences, and ends with the witch turning the extraverted twin into stone, whereupon one of the lilies back home drops. The introverted twin now rushes to his brother's aid, and it is interesting to compare this twin's reaction to the witch. Here we read: *The old witch came out of her house and called out to him. She wanted to entrap him too.* The German word is "berücken," which means to charm or to enchant. The situation is, of course, different: the second brother comes prepared for trouble because one of the lilies has fallen over. Still, he knows that it is a witch that stands before him, because he trusts his inner voice and because he does not let outer appearances affect his perception: he does not let the witch entrap him.

Fairy tale heroes are usually able to see through a witch's tricks and to frustrate her evil intentions. This is especially apparent when the hero is preceded by his brothers. In one such Russian fairy tale, a witch welcomes her guests and offers them her beautiful daughter's bed. Not realizing that a witch is a witch, regardless of how sweetly she speaks or what a beautiful daughter she has, the first two brothers find themselves in the witch's cellar. The third brother knows better and responds to the witch's "hospitality" with the following words: "No, little aunt! A visitor must not do that without first making certain preparations."[9]

From this example we may be tempted to think that the second brother, the introverted twin, is the true hero because he knows how to cope with the witch, but this is too simple. The extraverted twin has accomplished a great deal up till now: he did not let himself get discouraged at the inn, and he didn't return home as his brother did; he knew how to get past the robbers in the forest, and he didn't give up his journey by succumbing to the troubled words of his new bride.

In part, the extraverted twin knows quite well how to respond to the witch. For example, he doesn't allow her to question his courage. The witch's first words, "*What are you doing so late at night in the middle of the great forest?*" imply that this is a dangerous place to be. Here we see one of the witch's favorite tricks. By asking such questions she tries to undermine the hero's self-confidence, to make a little boy of him; on the other hand, she could also be testing him. The extraverted twin chooses to ignore the witch's provocative question. He responds with: "*Have you seen a stag?*" It is difficult to judge whether he is consciously avoiding the issue. After all, why shouldn't a hero be in a great forest late at night? Or is he still so much under the influence of the daylong chase that he hasn't reoriented himself?

We must also see that he is a bit inflated. He has become unconsciously identified (*participation mystique*) with the beautiful stag; he is blinded by the powerful thrust of the stag's energy, with the result that he cannot realistically assess the danger before him. But recall the fisherman who had so little vitality and drive. If the twins represent the fisherman's future development, then we can also see how important such inflation can be.

The extraverted twin's naiveté towards the threat presented by the witch is further demonstrated by his response to her dog. Witches often appear in the company of dogs. The Greek goddess Hecate was not only accompanied by the howling of dogs, she herself sometimes appeared as a dog.[10] Both the Greek dog Cerberus and the Egyptian dog Anubis guided the souls of the dead into the underworld. Cerberus was portrayed as a fierce watchdog who could, however, be bribed, while Anubis was instrumental in resurrecting the dead. Both were closely connected with the threshold between the two worlds—psychologically, the threshold between the conscious and unconscious parts of the psyche.

A dog has an excellent sense of smell. Interestingly enough, witches usually don't see well but they can smell things out. As the witch in the Russian tale "Vasilisa the Beautiful" returns home—riding in a mortar, prodding it on with a pestle, and sweeping her traces with a broom—she approaches the gate to her yard, stops, sniffs the air around her, and cries out: "Fie, fie! I smell a Russian (human) smell! Who is here?"[11] and does not see Vasilisa standing close by. This acute sense of smell that the witch and dog share can be psychologically understood as intuition. It is what allows one to perceive the invisible. This is what our extraverted twin is sorely lacking or unable to trust. He only sees what is visible, and in the forest—i.e., in the realm of the unconscious—this can be a great handicap.

When the extraverted twin approached the little house, he did not register the fact that it was a witch who sat inside. Now, when the little dog runs out and starts barking at him, this lack of information, together with his inflation, keep him from realizing the perilousness of his situation. The little dog, making such a nuisance of itself, is really the witch's instinctive reaction to the hero. Unless perverted by humans, animals do not normally conceal or falsify their feelings. They are incapable of deceiving by playing a role, as the witch has done. They wag their tales when they like and trust you, and they bark and bite when they don't.

Cerberus could be bribed. Perhaps the witch's dog would have quieted down if the hero had thrown it a bone or a piece of meat. Perhaps the extraverted twin would have done so if he saw what he hadn't seen. Now it is too late. He has missed his chance. In an uprush of affect, he swears at the dog and threatens to shoot it. The witch is furious. She now shows her true nature and turns the hero to stone.

Petrification may be described as an inability to move by oneself, to initiate action. A stone will roll if pushed by some outside agent, but it cannot do so by itself. Symbolically, it implies that one cannot change or adapt to demands of life: one becomes rigid, inflexible. Petrification also means that one cannot feel, one cannot empathize with others. It is interesting to note that it is precisely an extravert who must now suffer petrification. His entire adaptation to outer reality is destroyed: he is paralyzed in his essential way of reacting to life. This is the consequence of living an attitude one-sidedly. A time comes when the repressed introversion gathers so much energy that it takes over and completely subdues the extraverted attitude. The witch who is responsible for this, the negative mother complex, now overwhelms the conscious ego and renders it helpless.

This is the extremely important message of typology, namely, that any one-sidedness is contrary to individuation. The psyche appears to insist on the ego's *opus contra naturam*—in other words, that one not only follow one's natural inclination (in this case to live in an extraverted way) but also strive towards wholeness by integrating the opposite attitude.

The introverted twin doesn't know what really happened to his brother, only that he has gotten into very serious trouble. Being an introvert, his adaptation is towards the inner world, and he will hence not be so easily fooled by what he encounters in the forest. As the extraverted twin demonstrated knowledge of the outer world (inn, robbers), so the introverted twin knows more about both the positive as well as negative aspects of the inner world. He is not naïve about the unconscious. We see that he does not come too close to the witch. This shows that he is aware of her power. He has, however, seen through the "Mütterchen," and he won't tolerate what she has done to his brother. He stands up to her and for this he is rewarded. The text reads: *She touched the stone with her finger, but ever so unwillingly, and the brother regained his human form at once.*

We have seen some of the ways in which a witch attempts to disarm and destroy a hero. She may entrap him with seductive proposals that inevitably lead to his peril, or she may try to undermine his courage by provocative questions. As we can see from another Grimm fairy tale, "Hansel and Gretel," she may also capture him and fatten him up in order to eat him herself. Here she brings about a regression to infancy with focus on food, something we have seen earlier in the fisherman. By all such means, the witch, if she is successful, keeps the man from growing up and interacting with the world. This makes him passive and severely damages his instinctive sphere. But what fairy tales repeatedly tell us is that if a man can see through the witch's tactics and can challenge her by standing up for himself, he will succeed in thwarting her intentions. More importantly, by doing this he can effect a change in her attitude, for she then often becomes helpful and supportive. Psychologically speaking, such a confrontation induces the archetype to show its other side: the negative mother turns into a positive one. The witch's meanness can also be seen as a challenge: if he is a true hero, he will know what he has to do and where he needs to go, and he will not be intimidated by her provocation.

At the start of our tale, we find a man who is lamed without knowing it. As the story unfolds, we become aware of his passivity and defeatist attitude. At the same time, we register an expectation on his part that everything will be provided for him. This basic attitude prevails even when he receives a very precious gift. He doesn't seem capable of using it to advantage because he has no energy and willpower to do so. This, as we said, is descriptive of a man in the grip of the negative mother complex. But the Self appears to mean well by him: it offers itself up for integration and brings him two sons, who end up defeating the witch—the very source of his trouble. This is a mutual effort; neither twin is capable of doing it alone. The extraverted attitude, personified by the twin who goes out into the world, appears at first to be the cure for this condition, but, as we see later, the problem cannot really be solved with extraversion alone. What is ultimately called for is direct confrontation with the witch. As the tale shows, this is impossible without being both anchored in life (extraversion) as well as being aware of unconscious processes (introversion).

Fairy tales often end with the marriage of a prince and princess. Sometimes only one of the two is of royal blood, the other a commoner or even a fool. Irrespective of these nuances, it is the union of a man and woman, of the masculine and feminine principles, which heals through wholeness and promises a creative solution to the problem at hand. The tale of "The Golden Children" does not follow this pattern. Here the healing occurs through the mutual effort of the twin brothers who also represent polarities, albeit not those of the masculine and feminine. The message of "The Golden Children" is that this is the wholeness without which the resolution of the mother complex is impossible.

NOTES

1. All texts of this fairy tale are given in italics and are my own translations from the German: "Die Goldkinder," *Kinder- und Hausmärchen gesammelt durch die Brüder Grimm* (München: Winkler Verlag, 1978).

2. Matt. 6:25-34; Luke 12:22-31.

3. *The Oxford Annotated Bible* (New York: Oxford University Press, 1962), p. 815.

4. C. G. Jung, *Children's Dreams: Notes From the Seminar Given in 1936-1940*, ed. M. Meyer Grass and L. Jung (Princeton: Princeton University Press, 2007), pp. 465 ff. See also Hedwig von Beit, *Gegensatz und Erneurerung im Märchen* (München: Franke, 1983), pp. 279, 282-283.

5. *Ibid.*

6. C. G. Jung, *Collected Works*, vol. 6 (Princeton: Princeton University Press, 1971), § 337.

7. Hans Bächtold-Stäubli, *Handwörterbuch des deutschen Aberglaubens* (Berlin: Walter de Gruyter, 1987), vol. 4.

8. Marie-Louise von Franz, *An Introduction to the Interpretation of Fairy Tales* (New York: Spring, 1970), p. 87.

9. A. N. Afanas'ev, "The Bold Knight, the Apples of Youth, and the Water of Life," in *Russian Fairy Tales*, trans. Norbert Guterman (New York: Random House, 1973), p. 315.

10. Karl Kerényi, *The Gods of the Greeks* (London: Thames and Hudson, 1951), p. 36.

11. Afanas'ev, *Russian Fairy Tales*, pp. 441-442.

"Observe Nature and You Will Find the Stone": Reflections on the Alchemical Treatise "Komarios to Cleopatra"

ANDREAS SCHWEIZER

The Text and Its Authors

In the following essay, I will focus upon a small extract from a longer alchemical treatise, "Komarios to Cleopatra," which consists of two parts.[1] Marie-Louise von Franz discussed some aspects of the second part, which is about the alchemical resurrection mystery, in her book *On Dreams and Death.*[2] In a not-yet-published manuscript that was kindly given to me by the Foundation for Jungian Psychology, she also deals with this text, which according to her is one of the oldest and most important alchemical treatises that we have. It is the text of Komarios, or rather of Cleopatra. Evidence clearly suggests that the text stems from the first century C.E., and that it was written in the cosmopolitan city of Alexan-

Andreas Schweizer studied theology in Zurich and Egyptology in Basel. He is a graduate of the C. G. Jung Institute of Zurich and works in a private practice in Zurich and as training analyst and supervisor at ISAPZurich. He is president of the Psychological Club Zurich. His book on the Egyptian netherworld and its profound influence on alchemy and Jungian psychology will be published by Cornell University Press in the spring of 2010.

dria. At any rate, it is pervaded by an Egyptian-Hellenistic spirit such as would be found in that metropolis.

But who is its author—Komarios or Cleopatra? In a novel by Rabbi Lawrence Kushner, *Kabbalah, a Love Story*,[3] we find a lovely scene taking place between the famous assumed author of the Zohar, Moses de Leon (ca. 1250–1305), and a Spanish noblewoman, his pupil. In a flashback to the thirteenth century, the narrator describes how Moses de Leon argues some basic questions of Jewish mysticism with the noblewoman. It is his task to teach this woman, for whom he obviously feels an increasing love. The longer their dialogue continues, the more the reader gets the impression that it is in fact her feminine intuition and wisdom that is teaching him thrillingly new and inspiring ideas. It is as if she were the real author of the Kabbalah. While he discusses her statement that the divine spark emerging from the Nothingness of the *Ayn Sof* must completely *give itself away* and relinquish its very identity (*Tsimtsum*) in order to start the whole process of emanation and creation,[4] she answers, to his amazement:

> "Don Moshe, you do not understand because you are talk-ing like a philosopher and not a Kabbalist," said the señora. "Of course *according to logic* something cannot dissolve itself and realize itself simultaneously. But, Don de Guadalajara, *according to life*, yes. I know this happens."
>
> Moshe looked at his pupil as if she had just told him the *raza d'razin*—the secret of existence (which in fact, of course, she just had). "That would mean creation is not a point in space and time, but potentially everywhere and all the time. And every dissolution is also a creation."[5]

Thus it might be also with the text of Komarios. Officially, it is ascribed to the great and well-known master of alchemy, Komarios. But in reality, the major part of the preserved text seems to be a dialogue between Cleo-patra and the philosophers, in which Cleopatra comments on the mysteri-ous words of Komarios at the beginning of the treatise. If this hypothesis were to prove correct, we would have here one of the very rare documents of alchemy that reflects the alchemical *opus* from a feminine viewpoint.

Psychologically, we can interpret Cleopatra as the anima of Komarios or of the philosophers. But we can also understand her explanations in terms of feminine psychology, so that Komarios or the philosophers would represent animus figures of a positive kind. Be that as it may, as the last queen of the Ptolemaic kingdom Cleopatra is more suitable to represent the anima of antiquity than any other historical figure. Thus, her name is not chosen by mere chance. It alludes, as Marie-Louise von Franz states in her manuscript, to the royal mystery of the *hierosgamos*, to which the text refers and which the historical Cleopatra had lived out with Caesar.

The treatise has a truly feminine spirit. It mirrors a wisdom that is not so much expressed through Logos—that is, in an abstract way of thinking—but rather through nature and images of nature. Cleopatra emphasizes the continuing transformation of everything that exists, as well as love for the totally personal and thus unique life of the individual. The philosophers with whom she debates some of the fundamental alchemical issues recognize the special value of this feminine wisdom, since they frankly confess to her: "In you is concealed the most awesome and strange [i.e., miraculous] mystery. Illuminate us...."[6] In terms of masculine psychology, this means that the anima contains the mystery of individuation, which indeed she does! Accordingly, the philosophers ask their teacher, a woman, to reveal the well-protected mystery of alchemy to them. Psychologically, this reflects the fact that the anima as a rule does not reveal her secret without an effort being made. Unless a man has true humility, he will only be deceived by his anima.

The first part of the text (chapters 1-6) is of a completely different nature from the second part (chapters 7-17). To better understand the specific quality of the second part, I will briefly address some of the main issues discussed in the first chapters.

At the beginning, Komarios speaks of the monad, the "all-monad" or cosmic oneness, which is composed of the four elements. The elaborate teaching of Cleopatra, on the other hand, is more an abstract ordering system with a clear mandala structure. This system is arranged in the form of an Ogdoad, that is, an eightfold structure. It comprises the four phases of the alchemical opus, or process of individuation, arranged in a circular way—the *nigredo, albedo, citrinitas,* and *rubedo*—and of the activities corresponding to these phases: (1) becoming aware of the shadow in the *nigredo,* (2) the acceptance of feeling in the *albedo,* (3) the increasing consciousness and awareness of transpersonal tasks in the *citrinitas,* and finally (4) a *transgression,* that is, a transition into another form of existence in the *rubedo,* which the alchemists describe as a realization of the relationship to the *unus mundus* (the one world), i.e., the egression from the alembic in order to create cosmic wholeness.

The Ogdoad of Cleopatra according to Marie-Louise von Franz

The four phases of the opus:	The specific actions in the four phases:	…and their psychological meaning:
I Nigredo or blackening	Mummification and washing of the substances	Shadow work: washing of the heart, purification of thoughts
II Albedo or whitening	Mingling of the substances with the yellow water: creation of a wax-form	Acceptance of feelings
III Citrinitas or yellowing	Liquefaction of the gold	Transpersonal tasks
IV Rubedo or reddening	Decomposing and extraction of the gold as union of the opposites	Egression from the alembic; awareness of the *unus mundus* or cosmic wholeness; unification through the *ekstrophe* (egression or *transgressio*)

It is striking that Komarios connects the self of a man with the image of a monad, whereas Cleopatra describes the self of a woman using the eightfold ordering system of an Ogdoad. Whereas the male concept of the all-monad places the emphasis on a Being, that is, the "mind of the whole, who rules all things," as the Gnostic Simon Magus states it,[7] the feminine image of the Ogdoad describes the realization and unfolding of primordial oneness as a creation process and materialization of the One in the material world. It is Sophia (the anima) who brings the dormant (male) creative potential into closer relation to the human world. Sometimes I have the impression that this is one of the biggest conflicts between men and women, or animus and anima: the longing for the oneness of all beings (Komarios) vs. the desire for a fulfilled life (Cleopatra).

After this rather abstract but nevertheless profound introduction, we encounter, beginning with chapter seven, a completely new and nearly merry spirit. It is this chapter that I will deal with in the following reflections. It is still Cleopatra speaking to the philosophers:

> Observe the nature of plants and from whence they come. Some come down from the mountains and grow up out of the earth; others rise up from gorges and from plains. But observe how one approaches them. One must gather them at the right

moment, on the appropriate days. Pick them from the islands in the sea and from the upper plains. And observe how the air serves them, how the wheat embraces them protectively so that they are not damaged or destroyed. Observe the divine water that nourishes them, and how the air rules over them after they have incorporated themselves into one substance.[8]

THE ROLE OF NATURE IN ALCHEMY

Even if many details in this passage may not say much to us, nevertheless we immediately feel that it is pervaded by a spirit of nature and full of feeling, just as the imagery of our dreams often is. It speaks of plants, mountains and gorges, of islands in the midst of the ocean and of the heights of the upper plains. It is obviously not a dry philosophical text as are, for instance, some of the Dialogues of Plato. Instead, life is described as it develops naturally and by itself, for She—i.e., Nature with her transformational processes—is the great teacher of alchemy.

In antiquity, plants were often seen as metaphors for the mystery of resurrection. Probably the most famous example of this is the Egyptian Grain-Osiris. Out of earth and grain is formed a figure of the mummified god, Osiris. Upon being watered, seeds begin to germinate on the figure. They soon start sprouting, which symbolizes the revival of the ruler of the netherworld and, with him, the revival of all the deceased. The Egyptian Horus rises as the reborn Sun-god from a lotus plant. The son–lovers of the mother goddesses in Asia Minor, who suffer an early death, resurrect as flowers: violets flourish from the blood drops of the castrated Attis, while Adonis, also castrating himself, resurrects in the shape of a blood-red anemone. So if Cleopatra calls the alchemical opus a work of plants, this is a clear signal that she understands it as a transpersonal, eternal work, which requires eros to arise from the unfathomable ground of the soul.

Alchemical nature symbolism is very old indeed. It can already be found in one of the oldest alchemical texts, that of

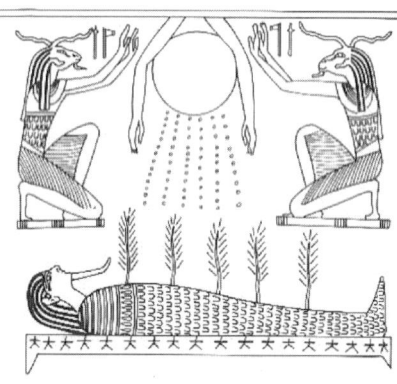

Figure 1: Grain-Osiris

Pseudo-Demokritos, to which our treatise alludes in several places. Especially one passage from Pseudo-Demokritos became a well-known alchemical axiom and was quoted again and again throughout the history of alchemy: "Nature delights in nature; nature conquers nature; and nature rules nature."

Figure 2: Uroboros

What does this mean?[9] The Latin alchemists occasionally changed the first clause slightly to say: "Nature *embraces* nature," or even "nature *devours* nature"— out of sheer *joie de vivre,* so to speak, out of pure love. According to Jung, this notion refers to the ancient (originally Egyptian) image of the Uroboros, the snake biting its own tale, which represents the union of the opposites par excellence. The oldest representation of the Uroboros that we know of stems from one of the shrines in the burial chamber of Tutankhamun (fourteenth century B.C.E.). In the context of death, this image contains a consoling message, namely, that all life is continuously renewed and regenerated within the eternal cycle of time. Psychologically, this means that the transformation of consciousness and of the collective *Zeitgeist* becomes possible whenever the opposites (head and tail of the snake) are united *Deo concedente*—"by the grace of God." In other words, unless we dare to do the impossible, nothing really new will come into existence!

The idea that nature delights in nature, embraces or even devours nature, soon became a central alchemical image or symbol of regeneration that, by definition, arises out of the union of the opposites. But now Demokritos continues: "Nature conquers or rules nature." This is obviously not a joyful embrace anymore, as in the first statement about nature. Here, in fact, a fiercely militant element is introduced, which brings up rather disturbing associations and fantasies. Nature is not static, since nothing in her remains the same forever, but rather she is full of opposites and contradictions that contend with each other without end. They destroy, repress, and dissolve each other. This is a difficult and quite dark, even painful, aspect of the individuation process. It speaks of the destruction of the old, namely, the dismemberment of the old king or the noxious dragon. In psychological terms, this means the destruction of values, convictions, and ideals that may have proven helpful for ages, in order to make space for new and mostly quite different ones.

Figure 3: The Double Nature of Mercurius

The alchemists did not promote the image of a safe world. Rather, they approach the world as it is, in its striking beauty but also in its wickedness and barbarian cruelty. Cleopatra does not embellish reality. At the end of her teaching, she even speaks of a murderous or deadly remedy pervading all bodies. Thus she is a true representative of the Great Goddess, like the Babylonian Ishtar, who is not only the goddess of love but also the mistress of war who lustfully rejoices in the blood of her victims. Such monstrosities pervade alchemical symbolism from earliest times, and are later consolidated in the image of *Mercurius duplex.* In his double nature, Mercurius proved to be the supportive spirit through whose help the gold could be produced, while with his incalculable and devilish moods he also drove the alchemists to despair, for "as quicksilver, he dissolves the gold and extinguishes its sun-like brilliance."[10] In brief, "he is their [the alchemists'] good luck and their ruin,"[11] as Jung says. We should not be misled by the charm of many alchemical images, for the *Dea naturae* and mistress of the alchemists indeed has two quite opposite sides!

THE ALCHEMICAL LAW OF ANALOGY

A further fundamental law of alchemy is implied by Cleopatra's reference to the *analogy* of the plants to the metals. In alchemical thought, organic as well as inorganic matter is something vivid and transformable, pervaded by a living (divine) spirit. Today's quantum mechanics shares this concept of matter insofar as it teaches the paradox posed by the mutual exclusivity of the description of light, which can be located adequately only through two contradictory, complementary conceptions: either as a movement of waves, or as particles. Waves and particles are two conceptions that exclude each other. What is true in the world of quantum mechanics is also valid in the cosmic world. Einstein affirmed that the universe is expanding, since a static universe would certainly collapse sooner or later.

According to the law of analogy, all things are interdependent. In interpreting alchemical texts, therefore, we meet the same difficulties as in dream analysis: to understand a specific dream symbol requires amplification of similar, that is, related, symbols. In order to interpret an alchemical text, one must know as many other texts as possible, for one text explains the other: *Librum libros explicat.* I will cite, in this perspective, a text of Zosimos that describes the analogy between plants and metals as assumed by Cleopatra, but in a much more explicit way. It runs like this:

> How does nature learn to give and to receive?…The metal gives, and the plant receives; the stars give, and the flowers receive; heaven gives, and earth receives….And everything is entwined and everything is dissolute; everything is mingled and everything is separated…everything remains and everything withers.[12]

Many analogies are mentioned in this text: metals – plants, stars – flowers, heaven – earth, etc. Whatever exists in the macrocosmic world has its reflection in the microcosm, and what grows, flourishes, and finally dies in the organic world is mirrored by the inorganic world of matter. All is pervaded by the same divine spirit, or as we would rather say in the terms of psychology, by one and the same creative spirit of the unconscious, which includes also matter and the body.

By treating the *prima materia*—let's say, for instance, the metals—with fire or by saturating it with the divine water, the alchemists intended to extract the divine creative power of the spirit from the darkness of matter and to transmit it into their lives. In matter the divine mystery is hidden. For the alchemist, material substance is the matrix one begins with, indeed the womb of the mother from which all new life proceeds. Psychologically, this is a projection of unconscious psychic totality, that is, of the collective unconscious, onto the darkness of matter. Cleopatra describes this psychic fact, as is usual in Hellenistic times, with quite drastic images: She speaks of bodies and spirits bound and oppressed in the gloominess and darkness of the depths of Hades, namely, the corpses lying in the retort. They are all yearning for redemption. Again, it is by analogy that Cleopatra illustrates their regeneration, for the imprisoned bodies and spirits or corpses, she says, "clothe themselves in splendid, bright colors, *like* [and herein lies the analogy] the flowers in spring."[13]

Our present text begins: "Observe the nature of plants and from whence they come." For the alchemist, this simple image evokes many fantasies and ideas that might be briefly summarized as: "Observe the metals, observe your body and the material world and its impotency. They are in front of you, bound and imprisoned like the dead in Hades. But keep in mind that one day they may awaken to new life and resurrect just like the flowers in the fields in springtime." Or, to put it into a more psychological language: "It may be that you feel half dead, a prisoner of your own dark and circling thoughts, but don't forget that nature is capable of regenerating and transforming even your inert psychic nature, for your distressed soul is like a plant yearning for spring. One day, for sure, she will flourish again—don't forget it!"

Despite all their freedom of imagination, the alchemists were well aware of the fact that they were dealing with a paradoxical mystery that is, as Cleopatra says, completely unknown—"that which cannot be recognized at all." Referring to this ineffable darkness of the mystery, Zosimos adds: "Silence teaches the art."[14] This is indeed what we also experience in analytical work: If after a painful experience in life some healing takes place; if one day, due perhaps to a dream, we step out from a state of depression or difficult period of stagnation to a new life—it is better to keep silent. After all, what could possibly be explained here?

ABOUT THE RIGHT PLACE

To approach the mystery of plants, namely, of body or matter, two things are decisive according to Cleopatra: first, *where* they are to be found, and second, *when* they are to be found—in other words, the right place and the right time.

First I will consider the question of the right place. Some plants come from the mountains, says Cleopatra, while others grow up out of the depths of the earth; still others come from the plains. One collects them on islands in the sea and on the upper plains. These images contain an idea that some centuries later was expressed in much clearer form in the *Tabula Smaragdina*. This problem, which is raised by the question of the philosophers to their teacher, Cleopatra, is stated as follows: "Tell us how the highest comes down to the lowest and the lowest up to the highest, and how the middle approaches the upper and the lower, and how they become one with the middle."[15]

This is, as far as I can see, the oldest formulation of an idea central to all of alchemy: the union of the opposites, above and below, in the center or middle. Here I will only briefly deal with this topic. People in general in Hellenistic times were deeply longing for redemption. Hardly any other question was more important to them than that of how to be redeemed from the curse of destiny (*Heimarmene*), that is, from a life that cannot be changed by any means since everything in it is predicted or set out in advance. This corresponds to the question often raised today: Does our life have any meaning at all? The hope reemerging throughout the whole history of alchemy was that the adept, like the initiand of the mysteries, could ascend to the highest celestial sphere by passing through the seven planetary spheres, in order to encounter the highest deity in that celestial region that is beyond every influence of *Heimarmene*—that is, of fate. Enriched by the encounter with the divine spirit, the adept then descends again to earth, now enabled to transform the world of matter and bodies with the assistance of the divine spirit. Psychologically, both the ascent to cosmic and spiritual dimensions and the descent to the material world represent an archetypal experience, that is, an experience of the self, which is indeed the only way enduringly to transform life.

Cleopatra describes this archetypal experience, not unlike our dreams do, with vivid images from nature, such as the islands of the sea and the highest regions of the mountains. They both seem to have the same meaning: On the shore of the infinite ocean, as in the magnificent world of the mountains, one can feel very alone and surrounded by a cosmic loneliness. But in both places one can also be filled with a deep feeling of oneness with the divine nature of the universe. In such moments, we become open and permeable to transpersonal life. A true alchemical experience, such as the individuation process, requires both: the experience of isolation (islands!) and loneliness on the one hand, as well as the awareness of being at one with everything that exists in the universe—or as the alchemists would rather say, with the *unus mundus*—on the other.

The alchemists' deep longing for redemption has to do with a cosmic—that is, with an archetypal—dimension. C. G. Jung and Marie-Louise von Franz often emphasized that only an archetypal experience can initiate a genuine healing process. In her book *The Cat*, Marie-Louise von Franz wrote: "As Jung pointed out, an archetypal experience is the only healing factor in therapy....If it doesn't happen, you can't do much. You might see some improvement with good counseling and so on, but there will be no real cure, no real help."[16] The alchemists were well aware of this. They clearly realized that the life of humans is based on creative forces that we nowadays associate with the collective unconscious. This bestows a great dignity on the individual, for most people suffer from the conviction that their life is more or less meaningless, even if in temporary periods of inflation they seem to believe themselves to be God knows how important and experienced. From a statistical point of view, the life of the individual among billions of people on earth today is indeed totally unimportant. Facing the always lurking danger of mass psychology, the alchemist knows of only one remedy—isolation and loneliness; or, as Cleopatra puts it, the reflection on the nature of plants in the midst of the sea and on the highest mountains. It is paradoxical: the very isolation in the alchemical laboratory or in the analytical vessel can teach us that we are not alone, but are instead intimately connected with a vivid spirit of the soul and of nature that secretly accompanies and supports life.

THE APPROPRIATE TIME

At the end of her speech in chapter seven, Cleopatra adds a further image of the union between the above and the below in the middle: "Observe how the air serves them [the plants]," she says, "and how the wheat embraces them protectively so that they are not damaged or destroyed." The air is an allusion to the presence of the divine *pneuma*, a vivid spirit essential for any success in the alchemical opus. Air clearly refers to the "spiritual" nature of the *coniunctio oppositorum*, the union of the opposites.

Wheat, on the other hand, in the context of Alexandrian Hellenism is a well-known symbol of the resurrection mystery, of the regeneration of life out of the darkness of the earth. Nourished by air, earth, water, and fire (sun), plants represent a living center. For the alchemists, this living center is the *one* substance that unites the opposites. The image of a plant or flower is quite appropriate. Through it, Cleopatra seems to express that the union in the middle can only be attained through feeling and eros. This reference to love is the decisive difference between the abstract idea of Komarios, i.e., that the oneness of the universe is seen in the all-monad, and the feminine conception of the realization and unfolding of the pri-meval oneness in the eightfold process of the Ogdoad. What Cleopatra has in mind is the individuation process as a *dynamic* process.

What about the right moment? "One must gather them at the settled instant, on the appropriate days," she states. It seems that humans do not

have much choice or freedom if everything in life is settled by divine powers or determined by the laws of nature. Here the alchemists recognized a
problem that brings synchronicity into our discussion. We meet the same
idea of *Kairos* in a Greek alchemical treatise with the title *The Prophetess
Isis to Her Son (Horus)*,[17] which originates, just as our text does, in the first
century of this era. Marie-Louise von Franz has broadly discussed this
treatise in her lectures on alchemy.[18] It says that after a certain passing of
the *Kairoi* and the necessary movement of the heavenly spheres, one of
the angels who dwelt in the first firmament saw Isis from above and
came toward her, desiring to unite with her sexually. But Isis refused him,
since she wished to learn more about the preparation of gold and silver,
that is, about the great mystery of alchemy. She finally succeeded in this
when another angel approached her and revealed the mystery to her. The
same idea that the whole of alchemy depends on the right timing (*Kairos*)
seems to be involved when Zosimos, in his treatise *On the Letter Omega*,
speaks of "the tinctures that can only succeed at the right moment."[19]

Psychologically, this means that each temporal moment has its specific value or feeling quality. The unconscious has its own time system.
We can call it a *synchronistic time structure*. Psychic contents come and go;
they emerge from the unfathomable stream of the collective unconscious;
they may reach the threshold of consciousness if only for a very brief
moment and then disappear again. If anyone wants to bring these contents into consciousness, that is, to understand them, they can only succeed if *Kairos* is given or, as myth would formulate it, if a messenger calls
on us as the Olympic gods Zeus and Hermes did in the beautiful story of
Philemon and Baucis.

These specific creative moments in life may give us the unique chance
to welcome a hitherto unknown divine visitor or, to put it into psychological language, to integrate a new psychic content of the collective
unconscious into consciousness. I think that such moments happen far
more often than we believe. If, however, the doubter is dominant in us at
such a decisive moment because we are too much involved with or preoc-
cupied by the linear time structure of ego-consciousness, then everything
may disappear again and flow back into the unconscious as if nothing had
happened. The *realization* of synchronistic time-quality, therefore, is of
greatest importance and has a lot to do with the creative principle in general. Besides the readiness to overcome one's own inertia, it requires above

all an attentive spirit, that is, the awareness of the specific quality of such a moment.

The alchemists had several symbolic images for this creative time-quality. I will here mention only the peacock, or phoenix. The play of colors of the *cauda pavonis* (the peacock's tail) emerges from the *nigredo*, that is, from those moments in life in which we are harassed by a noxious spirit, by anxieties, by sorrows. The many colors of its tail are able to kill the poisonous dragon, so that we are suddenly free of our dark fantasies. Indeed, the dragon's poison transforms into a remedy. As the alchemical stone, the peacock or phoenix produces all the colors. The *multi colores* initiate renewal and resurrection. From being completely depressed and overwhelmed by the misery and nonsense of our life, all of a sudden the colors of springtime break in because a divine visitor has shown up, in the shape of a dream figure or of a beloved man or woman who removes the dreary veil from our eyes.

But this does not happen as unexpectedly as it may seem, for even in chaos there is a secret order of creation. A true transformation will only take place if we are—I am tempted to say, only by chance—at the right place and if it happens in the right moment. It is not up to us to decide about the latter; it rather happens, as the alchemists repeatedly affirm, *Deo concedente*—by the grace of God. This, however, is not the whole truth, for every synchronicity requires human assistance, since only human consciousness is able to distinguish between the mere accidental coincidence of an outer fact with an inner-psychic experience and a true synchronicity. Pre-psychotic people, for instance, often experience countless so-called synchronistic events. But since they do not understand them, these events have no healing influence at all. In order to understand the specific and unique meaning of a synchronistic event, a strong ego-consciousness is required. It requires a human being to open the door for the unknown visitors, that is, for the gods. The key to this door is human understanding. I completely agree with Marie-Louise von Franz, who once said that C. G. Jung taught us with his psychology to keep our door open for the unknown visitor.[20] For the alchemists, the understanding of the secret order in chaos involves the participation of humans in the continuous work of creation. The alchemists even went so far as to proclaim that the human being who creates the stone is no less than a redeemer of the macrocosmic world!

I would like to summarize this range of ideas in a more imaginative than scientific way, as follows: "If you want to be alive psychically," according to our author, Cleopatra, "then more than anything else you need one thing: a true and clear spirit. Therefore overcome your inertia, that devilish antagonist of every development, and go up to the heights of the mountains and down to the depths of the sea. Bear your loneliness and confusion, and keep an attentive and vivid spirit despite your dark and endlessly circling fantasies. Then you will not miss that divine moment and unique place, and there you will find the remedy for the revival of your distressed soul!"

THE WATER OF LIFE

The work is not completed with the discovery of the plants alone. Cleopatra continues: "Observe the divine water that nourishes them and how the air rules over them." To begin, this can be understood in a biological sense, for water and air are exactly what plants need to grow and thrive. The water mentioned here, however, is not common water, but rather divine water. Similarly, the air is no common air but rather that divine *pneuma*, or spirit, that hovered over the primeval waters while darkness was still reigning over the world like the beloved of the creator, who even today pervades everything in nature with her divine spirit and light.

The philosophers express it even more precisely. They speak of the blessed waters flowing down to the dead like a remedy of life that awakens them so that they can revive.[21] This idea about the divine water, which can be found throughout the whole history of alchemy, probably originated in the natural phenomenon of the inundation of the Nile, which bestowed the blessing of a new period of fertility on the whole land of Egypt year after year. As the floodwaters began to subside, plants started to sprout again all over the now fertile land.

For many Greek alchemists, water was the primeval principle or source of life. Only much later did they develop the idea of the *aqua permanens*, that is, the arcane substance. Again it was Zosimos who described this conception in the most pregnant way. In his treatise *On the Divine Water*, we read:

> This is the divine and great mystery that we sought, for it is
> the whole [can also mean the All or the universe]. And from it
> is the whole and through the same is the whole. Two natures,
> but one substance; for one attracts the other, and one rules
> over the other.

> This is the silver water, the hermaphroditic [the male–female], which forever flees, yearning for one's own [nature]…
>
> For it [i.e., the divine water] contains life and spirit; and it is deadly. Whoever understands this possesses silver and gold.[22]

The divine water is the "spirit of life, not only indwelling in all living things, but immanent in everything that exists, as the world-soul."[23] Its effect reaches up to the highest regions of the sky and down to the lowest depths of earth and the netherworld. It unites the greatest opposites imaginable: "Two natures, but one substance," as Zosimos says, alluding to the axiom of Demokritos. The divine water is male–female, i.e., androgynous, like the alchemical Mercurius. Due to its ability to unite things that are totally alien to one another, the divine water is equated with eros. In her commentary on Ibn Umail, Marie-Louise von Franz says that in the context of Arabic alchemy and mysticism the divine water signifies "the creative loving emanation of Allah, the primary impulse of love in God towards man."[24] It is the intention of the alchemical opus to make this love conscious and to complete it.

Zosimos's statement about the divine water alludes to this eros: "It is the silver water, the hermaphroditic, which forever flees, yearning for one's own [nature]." The volatility of life, its mortality and futility, forces human beings to become what they are according to their own true and unique natures. Just because the secret of life gets lost or fails again and again, we are forced to search for the stone anew, or as Zosimos puts it, to search for the water that pushes us toward our own true nature, toward the uniqueness of an individually lived and fulfilled life. This exactly is what the words of Cleopatra aim at: an eros full of life, a life full of eros.

The divine water contains life (zoé) as well as spirit (pneuma), but it is also deadly (probably because of the toxicity of quicksilver, which Zosimos identifies with the divine water). As Karl Kerényi has shown in his book on Dionysus,[25] zoé refers to the indestructibility of life, that is, to the divine power of Dionysus that in its insatiable thirst and lust for life can increase even to the degree of madness. Such untamed life energy can indeed be deadly if the instinctual urge for life is not balanced or compensated by intellectual understanding. On the other hand, it is the stimulator of every true transformation in life. C. G. Jung once said that love by itself is useless if it does not also have understanding.[26] It is true that the divine water embodies liveliness in every form; however, what Zosimos really and most precisely meant is a vitality that accompanies an increase of understanding. This is also true for its shadow aspects. People who are confronted with difficult experiences, or who feel remorse for something they have done and are wrestling with their conscience, can be healed from their often compulsive and even demonic restlessness if they can, even in a fragmentary sense, understand what happened to them. From time immemorial, it was the major purpose of the religions, myths, fairy tales, and legends to comprehend in images, stories, and thoughts that which in the end is inexplicable, and thus to diminish the sinister power of the unknown.

Whoever is provided with this liveliness and gift of comprehension, says Zosimos at the end of his brief treatise, possesses silver and gold. Now the male and the female are reconciled with each other. The anima has attained a loving and healing effect on the psychic world, and the animus become a spiritual guide who no longer destroys feelings and eros but rather supports the individuation process in any form of understanding. In order to be successful, the opus requires both perspectives, that of Komarios and that of Cleopatra.

Returning once more to the speech of Cleopatra: "Observe the divine water that nourishes them, and how the air rules over them after they have incorporated themselves into *one* substance." The divine water and air are now united in *one* substance. At the end of her discourse, Cleopatra elaborates broadly on this union. After her excursus into the resurrection of the dead awakening from the darkness of Hades, she continues by saying that the mystery will be fulfilled only if body, soul, and spirit embrace each other: "For he (the body) clothed himself in the light of divinity, and the darkness departed from him, and all were united in love—body, soul and spirit—and all became one; in this the mystery is hidden."[27] The visible sign for this completion is the erection of a "statue filled with light and divinity." According to Jung,[28] this statue incorporates the concealed precious substance that the alchemists made so many efforts to produce. It symbolizes the final product of the alchemical process, namely, the *one substance* or the *lapis philosophorum*, the stone of the sages, which describes the divine, incorruptible, and eternal nature of humankind.

What Cleopatra has in mind, and what indeed is a precondition for the uniqueness of the individual, is a harmonic liaison and union of the divine water and air with the body, namely, the loving union between soul and spirit *in the body*! This is the spirit of the anima, the feminine self, who does not accept any form of transformation of the psychic-spiritual into a bodiless spirituality. And this is, as far as I can see, the spirit of early Greek alchemy, which is pervaded by a deep eros for concrete life.

The alchemical redeemer ascends to heaven, but only in returning to earth can his work be completed. For here is his home—in the body, on earth, and in the stone. Alchemists reach the most precious of all goods only if they accept their ordinary, common, daily life as completely as possible in order to understand it. They do this without continuously wanting to correct their life, as if they could know what serves them best. A rose will always be but a rose, a thistle but a thistle, and thus each of us can only become what we are. This unique reality of the individual, however, is precisely the stone that pervades everything with its colors and with its love.

Therefore let us slightly change the title given to these alchemical reflections: "Observe *your unique* nature and you will find the stone." This is, I believe, the core of Greek alchemy and of analytical psychology as it was taught to us by C. G. Jung and Marie-Louise von Franz. For this I am grateful to both of them. Each of us, according to his or her nature, will understand what we can understand of it. But if the alchemists were right, then the *one stone*, which becomes the cornerstone, stands behind this variety.

******

TEXT SAMPLES (Berthelot, *Collection des anciens alchimistes grecs*, pp. 292–297. Translation from Greek by the author.)

7 Observe the nature of plants and from whence they come. Some come down from the mountains and grow up out of the earth; others rise up from caves and from plains. But observe how one approaches them. One must gather them at the right moment, on the appropriate days. Pick them from the islands in the sea and from the upper plains. And observe how the air serves them, how the wheat embraces them protectively so that they are not damaged or destroyed. Observe the divine water that nourishes them, and how the air rules over them after they have incorporated themselves into one substance.

8 Ostanes and those who were with him responded and said to Cleopatra: "In you is concealed the most awesome and strange [also: miraculous] mystery. Illuminate us by casting your light from afar onto the elements. Tell us how the highest comes down to the lowest and the lowest up to the highest, and how the middle approaches the upper and

the lower, and how they become one with the middle…; and how the blessed waters flow down to the dead who are lying there, bound and oppressed in the gloominess and darkness of the depths of Hades; and how the remedy of life enters and awakens them, so that they revive for their creators….A cloud carries them upward. And the cloud that carries the waters rises up from the sea." When the adepts considered what they saw, they rejoiced.

9 Then Cleopatra spoke to them: The penetrating waters revive the bodies and the bound, weakened spirits [*pneumata*]. For they have suffered renewed affliction and have been hidden again in Hades. After a short time they begin to grow and to come forth and clothe themselves in splendid, bright colours, like the flowers in spring. And spring rejoices and indulges herself in the beauty that clothes them.

15 …And the soul united with the body, since the body had become divine through his relation to the soul, and dwells in the soul. For he [the body] clothed himself in the light of divinity, and the darkness departed from him, and all were united in love, body, soul and spirit, and all became one; in this the mystery is hidden. In this coming together the mystery was fulfilled, and the house was sealed. A statue was erected, filled with light and divinity. For the fire had made and transformed them into one, and it [the one] has come forth out of its womb.

17 …See how I tell you what the goal [of the one] is: when it is completed, it becomes a deadly remedy[29] that circulates quickly in the body. In the same way that it enters its own body, so does it also penetrate the [other] bodies. In putrefaction and warmth there is created a remedy which pervades every body without hindrance.

NOTES

1. Marcellin Berthelot, *Collection des anciens alchimistes grecs* (Texte grec, Reimpression de l'édition 1888; Osnabrück: Otto Zeller, 1967), pp. 289-299 (all translations from Greek by the author).

2. Marie-Louise von Franz, *On Dreams and Death: A Jungian Interpretation* (new edition with a foreword by Emmanuel Kennedy-Xipolitas and Vernon Brooks; Peru, IL: Carus, 1998).

3. Lawrence Kushner, *Kabbalah: A Love Story* (New York: Morgan Road Books, 2006).

4. Daniel C. Matt, *The Essential Kabbalah, The Heart of Jewish Mysticism* (New York: HarperCollins, 1996), pp. 93-99.

5. Kushner, *Kabbalah*, pp. 158-159.

6. Berthelot, *Collection des anciens alchimistes grecs*, p. 292.

7. C. G. Jung, *Mysterium Coniunctionis,* vol. 14 (1970) of *The Collected Works of C. G. Jung*, trans. R. F. C. Hull, ed. H. Read, M. Fordham, G. Adler, Wm. McGuire, 20 vols. (Princeton, NJ: Princeton University Press, 1953-1979)(hereafter *CW*) , § 160.

8. Berthelot, *Collection des anciens alchimistes grecs*, p. 292.

9. Jung, *Mysterium Coniunctionis*, *CW* 14, § 718; see also Jung, *Alchemy*, Vol. 1, ETH Lectures, November 1940–February 1941 (Zurich: Karl Schippert & Co., 1960), pp. 42-44.

10. Jung, *Psychology and Alchemy*, *CW* 12 (1968), § 84.

11. *Ibid.*

12. Michèle Mertens, *Les alchimistes grecs: Zosime de Panopolis,* Mémoires authentiques, Tome IV, 1re partie, texte établie et traduit par Michèle Mertens (Paris: Les belles lettres, 2002), p. 38.

13. Berthelot, *Collection des anciens alchimistes grecs*, p. 293.

14. Mertens, *Les alchimistes grecs*, p. 41.

15. Berthelot, *Collection des anciens alchimistes grecs*, pp. 292-293.

16. Marie-Louise von Franz, *The Cat: A Tale of Feminine Redemption* (Toronto: Inner City Books, 1998), p. 9.

17. Berthelot, *Collection des anciens alchimistes grecs*, pp. 28-30.

18. Marie-Louise von Franz, *Alchemy: An Introduction to the Symbolism and the Psychology* (Toronto: Inner City Books, 1980), pp. 43-63.

19. Mertens, *Les alchimistes grecs*, p. 1.

20. Marie-Louise von Franz, *Archetypal Dimensions of the Psyche* (Boston & London: Shambhala, 1999), p. 73.

21. Berthelot, *Collection des anciens alchimistes grecs*, pp. 292–293.

22. Mertens, *Les alchimistes grecs*, p. 21; Berthelot, *Collection des anciens alchimistes grecs*, pp. 143-144.

23. Jung, *Psychology and Alchemy*, *CW* 12, § 528.

24. Marie-Louise von Franz, *Muhammad ibn Umail's Hall ar-Rumuz ('Clearing of Enigmas')* (Egg, Switzerland: Fotorotar, 1999), p. 94.

25. Karl Kerényi, *Dionysos: Archetypal Image of Indestructible Life* (Princeton: Princeton University Press, 1976).

26. Jung, *Alchemical Studies*, *CW* 13 (1967), § 391.

27. Berthelot, *Collection des anciens alchimistes grecs*, p. 297.

28. Jung, *Mysterium Coniunctionis*, *CW* 14, § 559-569.

29. An all-permeating poison: see von Franz, *Hall ar-Rumuz*, p. 86.

Illustrations:

Fig. 1: Grain-Osiris. Erik Hornung, *Tal der Könige* (Darmstadt: Wissenschaftliche Buchgesellschaft, 1983), p. 181.

Fig. 2: Ouroboros. Logo of Eranos Tagungen, Ascona. Created by Andreas Brodbeck, Zumikon, Switzerland.

Fig. 3: Mercurius. *Mutus Liber, Die Alchemie und ihr Stummes Buch*, Vollständige Wiedergabe der Original-Ausgabe von La Rochelle 1677, Einleitung und Kommentare von Eugène Canseliet F.C.H. (Amsterdam: Weber, 1991), detail of plate 11.

LADY SOUL

DIANE COUSINEAU BRUTSCHE

Soul is a most familiar word, and yet such a mysterious reality.

A few decades ago, a semantic phenomenon started to happen around the word "soul." Previously reserved for religious or philosophical writings, while in the field of psychology "psyche" was the more or less synonymous term, "soul" progressively began to lose this strict semantic boundary and to appear more and more frequently in psychological contexts. It was as if it needed to be set free from its previous confinement.

Jung was indisputably one of the pioneers of this semantic emancipation. In the *General Index* of the *Collected Works*, for instance, there are more than three pages of references to the word "soul." This trend has been followed later by prominent Jungian authors of sometimes very different perspectives, such as Evangelos Christou, James Hillman, Thomas Moore, Murray Stein, and Wolfgang Giegerich, to mention only a few major contributors. The word has increasingly become familiar in psy-

Diane Cousineau Brutsche, PhD, was born in Montreal, Canada, and earned a doctorate in French literature from the University of Paris and a Diploma in Analytical Psychology from the C. G. Jung Institute of Zurich. She works as an analyst in private practice in Zurich and is a training analyst, supervisor, and lecturer at the International School of Analytical Psychology in Zurich (ISAP).

chology, alternating with "psyche" in mainly—although not exclusively —Jungian publications.

This semantic phenomenon may seem perfectly normal since "psyche" and "soul" are originally synonyms, distinct only because of their linguistic origins. However normal it may appear, yet it is still somewhat puzzling. One may wonder indeed why both terms would continue to be used in a psychological context if they were absolutely equivalent. In spite of its close kinship with "psyche," "soul" conveys something that the former does not convey as well.

We owe to Jung an important early attempt to differentiate both terms for psychology. "I have been compelled, in my investigations into the structure of the unconscious," he writes in 1921, "to make a conceptual distinction between *soul* and *psyche*. By psyche I understand the totality of all psychic processes, conscious as well as unconscious. By soul, on the other hand, I understand a clearly demarcated functional complex that can be best described as a 'personality.'"[1] For Jung, therefore, "psyche" refers to a global system (in close analogy to the self as system), while "soul" refers to a specific entity *within* this system. In Jung's writings "soul" often appears in too close an association, however, with the concept of anima, depriving it thereby of its universal meaning, which is independent of gender identity. At other times, "psyche" and "soul" are used interchangeably, depriving "soul" this time of its specificity. Apart from a few exceptions, the latter is also true for most works by contemporary Jungian authors, where both terms tend to alternate without acknowledgment of their differences.

Words are not mere abstract phonetic conventions. Each one of them has its own vibrations, which evoke in us a certain set of emotions or images. Words are therefore endowed with dynamic qualities, like living symbols or "powers," as Hillman would say. Like angels, words are emissaries carrying messages from a reality that is behind them.[2] The aim of this article is to bring a contribution to our understanding of "soul" as a specific psychological notion and to shed some light on the essential relevance of its being included as a term for psychology.

THE EVOCATIVE POWER OF THE WORD "SOUL"

Unless one's philosophical viewpoint radically excludes any spiritual or symbolic dimension, any one of us can have hints of what soul is about simply by letting the word assert its evocative power. Giving close attention, for instance, to the way soul is uttered in the analytical setting or in an intimate conversation with a friend, one can already perceive several features commonly associated with the word.

For most of us, the word psyche evokes, as it did for Jung, something global, impersonal, something like an inner "system," whereas soul is felt like a *more specific energy within this system.* In talking about one's soul, however, one would rarely, if ever, mean to say that it is merely a "functional complex" among others, like the anima is in its classical Jungian definition, for instance. On the contrary, one normally intends this word to mean one's own deepest identity, the *very core of one's psyche,* and something totally independent from one's gender identity. This sense of what the word soul means, which has been bequeathed to us by classical Greek philosophers such as Socrates, Plato, and Aristotle, definitely seems to have given expression to a universal intuition that has crossed centuries without alteration.

Such centrality brings "soul" close to the Jungian notion of "self" as the center of the psyche. Although both notions refer to a transcendent, numinous reality, the emotions evoked by them differ considerably. Like what Jung says about the biblical Yahweh in his book *Answer to Job*, the self is a "phenomenon"[3] that belongs to a dimension where none of our human values has meaning, among others our moral notions of good and evil. It rules over human life and triggers the process of individuation, but it can also crush human beings, leading them to their destruction, as witnessed dramatically in psychosis. Because of its amoral energy, which is so completely foreign to human desires and preoccupations, the self inspires awe. As for the soul, even when it forces the ego to tread on unknown and often disquieting territories, it nevertheless remains perceived as a *more benevolent entity, closer to the human reality*, evoking because of this more trustful respect than fearful awe.

On the other hand, invaluable hints about the soul are found in religious traditions, or more generally in initiatic traditions from very diverse cultures. Most of them, while acknowledging the spiritual nature of the soul, emphasize its essential link with body and matter. Religious and esoteric traditions often adhere to a tripartite view of human reality in which soul finds itself situated in a middle realm between the "higher" realm of the spirit and the "lower" one of matter. The medieval theologian Augustine, for instance, described the soul as a "*substantial*" entity. Being at the same time spiritual and material, holding both opposite dimensions within itself, soul appears to be a most *paradoxical reality*.

Whether it be through mythology, poetry, or iconography, soul, like her sister psyche, is universally represented with a *feminine symbolic quality*. This is reflected also in language. Soul is declined in the feminine, at least in European languages in which genders also apply to notions and concepts and not only to living beings. Christian theologians and mystics, moreover, often name the soul the "bride of God." In other words, in the mystical union of one's soul with God, individual human beings—male as well as female—experience themselves in the feminine role.

As a symbolic reality, on the other hand, soul could in no way be exhaustively described in rational terms. It has to be encountered in its own realm, in the symbolic realm and its manifestation through archetypal images. Individual and collective intuitions such as those mentioned above point in the direction of a feminine archetypal image as the foundation of our human notion of soul. Just as Jung sees the self as the *Imago Dei* within the human psyche, I propose to see the soul as the *Imago Deae* within the psyche, in other words as the "feminine" aspect of the self, intrinsically belonging, like the self, to the human psyche, independently from gender identity.[4] Consequently, in the rest of this article I will refer to soul in the feminine form, i.e., not as an "it" but as a "she."

THE ARCHETYPAL MOTHER OF THE SOUL

Archetypal images are innumerable. Embedded in cultures and historical periods, they can be compared in their relationship to the archetypal realm to the facets of a prism, each one of them reflecting a specific quality of the archetype, each one being a very precious manifestation of the transcendent reality at the center of the prism.

A most powerful feminine archetypal image to be found in the Judeo-Christian tradition is undoubtedly that of the Divine Sophia as she appears, for instance, in Gnosticism, in alchemy, and even more powerfully in the part of the Old Testament known as "Wisdom Literature."

It is no secret that the feminine part of God has been progressively eliminated from the predominant Western religious traditions, or at least her full meaning and divine quality mutilated through many centuries of one-sided masculine monotheism. The God image in these traditions is that of a lonesome Father, having forgotten about the existence of his female partner, who *"was beside Him, like a master worker"* when He created the universe.[5] Even if important texts about Sophia have remained included in Christian Bibles as "Divine Wisdom," she is not perceived by official theology as a divine entity *per se*, but rather as an attribute of the masculine God. Because of this, symbolic manifestations of the Divine Sophia, God's essential feminine partner in the process of creation, practically can only be found in esoteric or more generally initiatic traditions on the fringe of official churches in which she was (and in some cases still is) venerated in spite of the general repression.

One of the richest symbolic representations of Sophia can be found in the series of tapestries entitled "The Lady and the Unicorn," found in Paris at the Museum of Cluny. This stunning work of art comes from the French fifteenth century and stems from an initiatic tradition known as "Courtly Love." Intimately linked to alchemy since its Sufi Islamic origins, and to the Grail movement,[6] "Courtly Love" was, like alchemy, an initiation process under the spiritual leadership of the feminine divine principle, mostly known in alchemy under the name of Sapientia, Sophia's Latin name.[7] It was, on the other hand, a very unique religious phenomenon in Western cultural history in that it was essentially centered on the experience of love as path to initiation, but love not only in its agapaic quality, as we usually find it in Christianity, but in its erotic, sexual dimension.[8] The very center of the cult was the Eternal (Divine) Feminine perceived by the lover as being embodied by the beloved Lady.[9] Sophia was meant to be encountered on the earthly plane through a human, incarnated love. Because of these characteristics, Courtly Love can be considered as a genuine "soul religious path," as compared to the "religions of the spirit" that aim more at transcending the incarnated condition.

There are six individual panels in the tapestry series. Each of them shows the Lady, surrounded on either side by a lion and a unicorn, in a more or less similar setting each time, and in most of them she is accompanied by another female figure of smaller size. The latter is usually referred to, in the literary tradition around the Lady and the Unicorn, as being the "Maid" or the "Servant," because of the role of assistance she seems to play for the Lady. On each panel the Lady is involved in a different activity. Five of them have to do with a sensory activity: touching, smelling, tasting, hearing, and seeing. The sixth panel is different from the others in that it does not refer to any sensory activity in particular, and it also contains an important visual element that is absent from the other panels: a pavilion decorated on its outside with tongues of fire symbolizing its spiritual quality, and completely empty inside. The canopy of the

Tenture de la Dame à la Licorne: A mon seul désir (entre 1484 et 1500; 4e quart du 15e siècle/1er quart du 16e siècle; Carton: Paris, tissage: Pays-Bas du Sud; Cl. 10834; Paris, musée national du Moyen Âge_Thermes de Cluny; © RMN/Frank Raux.

pavilion bears a highly enigmatic inscription that for centuries and still nowadays has given rise to unending interpretations: "A Mon Seul Désir" ("To My Only Desire" or "To My Unique Desire"). This particular panel is usually referred to as the main panel and is considered to be the spiritual center of the whole series, its core.

The following comments will focus on this central image and attempt to convey some of the intuitions it triggers.

LADY SOPHIA/LADY SOUL

Many symbolic elements in the series of tapestries point toward the identity of the Lady as the Divine Sophia, as she finds residence in our earthly world. Approaching the core panel from a Jungian point of view, on the other hand, we find that it presents itself as a mandala, a representation of psychic totality. By allowing it to speak to us, we can progressively identify the different symbolic levels and elements that are part and parcel of the psychic wholeness it presents.

The empty pavilion decorated with tongues of fire seems apt to evoke the domain of the *Deus absconditus*, the completely transcendent, invisible Godhead or, in psychological terms, the archetypal realm as such: the realm of pure potentiality from which all that exists emerges, the realm of the self.

"*I came forth from the mouth of the Most High*," says Sophia, "*and covered the earth like mist.*"[10] Following her movement, the Lady comes out of the pavilion. She sets foot on an "island," a circular piece of land, the earthly dimension—or, more expansively stated, the created, visible universe as a whole in which her creative energy is to unfold. Purely spiritual in origin, Sophia's vocation is fulfilled within the realm of visible, material reality. Like her archetypal Mother, one could say that the individual soul originates from the self but comes "out" of it to merge with nature and matter. As *anima mundi*, the Lady Sophia enlivens each aspect of the created universe, and as the individual human soul she brings life to each aspect of a person's existence.

Because of its circular shape, the island on which the Lady stands could be seen as another symbol of the self, the circle being the geometric figure typically associated with the self. But here it is also a limited space, compared with the background of the tapestry where no frame can be seen, as if it could extend indefinitely. The Lady's island therefore evokes the idea of boundaries: the boundaries of the created universe, Sophia's domain, and the limitations generated by incarnation, the realm of Lady Soul.

All around the Lady one sees a rich variety of plant and animal shapes, as well as a human figure. Similar elements, however without any human representation, are also seen beyond the boundaries of the "island," like still uncreated potentialities that belong to the archetypal dimension. They evoke the potentialities of the collective unconscious, still out of reach to human consciousness or meant to remain so. Compared with this unlimited background, one could associate the Lady's island to what Jung calls "psychic reality."

"*I was…rejoicing in his inhabited world and delighting in the human race*," says Sophia in another classical passage from the Wisdom literature of the Bible.[11] A few steps away from the Lady stands the other feminine figure, the "Maid." Because of her smaller stature and her role as assistant, she could represent the human being in its relation to the divine, or in psychological terms, the ego in its relationship with the soul. Serving Lady Soul in fact expresses what should be the normal role of the ego.

The Maid is presenting a jewel box to the Lady out of which the Lady takes a necklace. A necklace symbolizes a link between the person who gives it and the one who accepts it. It also evokes a yoke, which means an attitude of submission. By taking the necklace offered to her by the young woman, the Lady accepts forming a bond with her, sharing her reality and even sharing with her the yoke of the incarnated condition. In each of the five other panels she is shown involved in a specific sensory activity, expressing her bond with bodily reality. Through the activities of the senses, Soul experiences herself and acquires her "substantiality." She becomes a "substantial spirit."

In each panel, the Lady occupies the center of the image. In such a central position she is associated with the self in its quality as central subject of the psyche. She appears, however, as a specific aspect of the self: a symbolically feminine aspect of the self, immersed in material reality, closer to the human ego and its humble, daily life.

All these aspects of the Lady represented in the tapestry correspond very closely to the intuitions about the reality of the soul enumerated earlier. They bear witness to the intimate symbolic link between the archetypal image of Sophia and our notion of the individual human soul. For this reason, while interpreting the different elements present in this work of art, I felt it was important not to separate the mythological level from the psychological one.

THE CREATIVE DYNAMICS OF SOUL

Observing now how the different elements presented in the picture are related, one gets an insight into the specific role of Sophia in the creation and the specific role of soul in our individual lives. Analyzing all the elements of the tapestry would bring us far beyond the limitations of this article, so I will discuss only the most relevant ones.

Standing between a lion on her right and a unicorn on her left, the Lady is shown at the center of what I would call a "horizontal" pair of opposites, which are an integral feature of the constitution of the psyche. I suggest seeing the lion, the king of animals, as representing here the pole of the instincts, the "infra-red" pole of Jung's metaphoric psychic spectrum,[12] and the unicorn on the other side as a mythical representation of the spirit, the "ultra-violet" pole that Jung designated as the "spiritual" or "archetypal" pole. Compared to the Lady, the Maid's position is always off-center. She is in a humble position and thus leaves the central place to the one to whom it properly belongs. Off-center also expresses the challenge that the psychic polarities represent for the ego, which is caught within their dynamics, being attracted by either one or the other pole, or alternating between the two.

Standing in the very middle between the two opposite principles, the Lady appears as the one who differentiates them, keeping them separated while at the same time mediating their relationship and affirming thereby their equally essential roles. Doing this, she supports the ego in its necessary task of differentiation, without which no consciousness can arise. On the other hand, she appears to offer an invitation addressed to the ego to come closer to the center and to endure the excruciating tension generated by the psychic opposites, thereby preventing the ego from remaining stuck in neurotic one-sidedness.

Allowing the image to speak some more, one can perceive another pair of opposites, something that I would call a "vertical" one. This is the opposition between the pavilion—the upper, spiritual realm—and the lower realm of animals, plants, and the Maid—the natural realm. Here again, Lady Soul appears as a mediator between the transcendent realm of the self and the mundane world of the ego. Mediating their relationship, she protects the ego from a neurotic imprisonment in daily, horizontal reality by providing a relationship with the beyond. Standing in front of the pavilion, on the other hand, she keeps them apart, differentiated but at the same time related. This position also shows her as a guardian of the threshold, protecting the ego from a potential identification with the self, in other words from an inflation that could crush it, as happens in psychosis.

With this paradoxical position Lady Soul permits the coming together of opposites without loss of their differentiation. In other words, she fulfills the role of the transcendent function. I therefore propose to see the soul as the active *subject of the transcendent function* while being, like the alchemical stone, at the same time its means and its goal.[13]

A LONG EXILE

Following the path towards the soul, one can in no way avoid being confronted with a problem that pertains to our very psychic constitution. Whether we like it or not, there is and always will be a distance between the realm in which the activity of the ego takes place and the one in which the reality of the soul is meant to unfold. Their mutual encounter requires from the ego a radical change of its center of focus. Accessing the soul is, like alchemy, an *opus contra naturam*, therefore always the fruit of an initiation, whatever the culture may be in which an individual is embedded. The challenge is, however, particularly demanding for an individual molded by modern Western culture. Millenniums of one-sided masculine monotheism have resulted in a drastic exclusion of a feminine divine mythical representation. Like the apocalyptic "woman clothed with the sun,"[14] Sophia has been sent into exile, leaving us orphaned. Severed from her archetypal foundation, soul progressively vanished from the culture's collective consciousness, leaving its denizens psychologically alienated from their very center as human beings. As a result, "loss of soul" has become "the great malady of the twentieth century,"[15] a phenomenon so often noticed in analysis.

In many of its aspects, the major Western philosophical developments throughout the last centuries appear as a direct outcome of an exclusively masculine monotheism, and this trend has contributed to eradicating even more severely an awareness of soul that had survived in earlier periods. The predominant philosophical and scientific collective path has been marked by a progressively strong emphasis on a rational-objective approach to reality, which found its culmination in the nineteenth-century "positivistic" movement. In spite of all the wonderful achievements we owe to this development, it also bears baleful consequences for our inner life. As soon as rationality, the activity of the so-called "masculine" brain, ceases to be but one legitimate and essential approach to reality and becomes the only legitimate one—the one that sets the very standards of reality (as was the case in the positivistic movement)—it automatically rules out anything that escapes its purview. Rationality being a function of differentiation, it operates on the principle of "either/or." Soul, as well as the whole symbolic dimension, because they belong to a paradoxical realm that is not either/or but both/and, suffer the same fate as the once revered philosophical notion of "paradox": they end up being rejected as non-realities, mere fantasies, and even as non-sense and absurdities. While quantum physics nowadays is increasingly adopting a paradoxical perspective on reality and discovering that mind and matter form what can be called a "uni-duality"[16] (the very definition of a paradox), most of our contemporaries keep adhering to a positivistic approach, blocked in a rational dead end and cut off from the symbolic realm.

The overwhelming predominance of rationality goes hand in hand with the predominance of the ego in our culture. As center of consciousness, the ego is, like rationality, a function of differentiation inevitably leading to a dualistic perspective. Such a perspective, essential for our orientation in the world and for our sense of identity and our values, automatically results also in creating hierarchies between the different orders of reality or value that are differentiated: spiritual or material, noble or vulgar, sacred or profane, Christian or pagan, monotheistic or polytheistic, etc. A one-sided ego-consciousness naturally tends to identify with the polarity that appears to be superior, rejecting the opposite pole as inferior or even undesirable.

Lady Soul, on her part, invites us on the contrary to marry these opposite principles, to bring them into a relationship of uni-duality. Needless to say, this challenges drastically the ego's mode of thinking and perceiving. It may be felt as an affront to its most precious spiritual ideals, its very best moral, heroic aspirations. It may even appear as threatening consciousness itself.

One of the most powerful symbols of the mutual creative energies of the divine archetype is to be found in the Hebrew Star of David. This image is formed of two intertwined triangles, one pointing upwards, called the "masculine" triangle, the other one pointing downwards, the "feminine" one. As for the path indicated by soul, it follows the direction of the "feminine" triangle, bringing spirit into matter. Instead of seeing it as the essential complement of the masculine one, in a dualistic perspective it is mostly perceived as its antagonist. It has disappeared, for instance, from the God symbol in Christianity, which has retained only the "masculine" one.

The aim however is to create, in harmony with the energy represented by the "masculine" triangle, a third realm of reality at the point of encounter of both worlds that were earlier separated and differentiated by the masculine creative act: visible/invisible, manifest/potential, spiritual/material, profane/sacred, lower/upper, temporal/eternal. This would be a realm of reality where all opposites embrace each other, drawn by a single, mutual movement, which is Lady Soul's "Seul Désir." This is what I would call the "second act of creation": a feminine creative act, responding to and fulfilling the creative process initiated by the masculine energy.

The growing integration of the notion of "soul" in our contemporary psychological language seems to herald a potential shift in psychology. Our civilization has performed wonderful creative accomplishments following the path of the "masculine" brain. However, the development of that kind of consciousness, which was absolutely essential in the past, has progressively tended towards one-sidedness, leading us now ever deeper into a dead end. Our collective consciousness is in dire need of a new paradigm, a new understanding of ourselves and of our relationship with our neighbors (individual and collective) and with nature. The path to the Soul leads us towards what we are not yet but urgently need to become: human.

NOTES

1. C. G. Jung, *Psychological Types*, vol. 6 (1971) of *The Collected Works of C. G. Jung*, trans. R. F. C. Hull, ed. H. Read, M. Fordham, G. Adler, Wm. McGuire, 20 vols. (Princeton, NJ: Princeton University Press, 1953-1979)(hereafter *CW*), § 797.

2. James Hillman, *A Blue Fire: Selected Writings by James Hillman*, ed. Thomas Moore (New York: Harper, 1991), p. 28.

3. Jung, "Answer to Job," in *CW* 11 (1969), § 600.

4. Diane Cousineau Brutsche, *Le Paradoxe de l'Âme* (Genève: Georg Editeur, 1993), pp. 36 and 94.

5. Book of Proverbs 8:30, *The Holy Bible: New Revised Standard Version with Apocrypha* (Nashville: Thomas Nelson, 1989), p. 591.

6. T. P. Cross and W. A. Nitze, *Lancelot and Guinevere: A Study on the Origins of Courtly Love* (Chicago: University of Chicago Press, 1930); Emma Jung and Marie-Louise von Franz, *The Grail Legend* (Boston: Sigo, 1986), p. 21; Denis de Rougemont, *L'Amour et l'Occident* (Paris: Plon, 1939), p. 208.

7. Marie-Louise von Franz, *Aurora Consurgens* (New York: Pantheon, 1966), p. 143; C. G. Jung, *Psychology and Alchemy*, *CW* 12 (1968), § 464-479; Matthew Caitlin, *Sophia Goddess of Wisdom: The Divine Feminine from Black Goddess to World-Soul* (London: Aquarian, 1992), pp. 255-265.

8. James A. Schultz, *Courtly Love, the Love of Courtliness and the History of Sexuality* (Chicago: University of Chicago Press, 2006), pp.

150-156; Jean Markale, *Courtly Love: The Path of Sexual Initiation* (Rochester, VT: Inner Traditions International, 2000), pp. 40-41, 60, 212.

9. Markale, *Courtly Love*, pp. 145, 146-148, 155-157.

10. Ecclesiasticus 24:3, *The Holy Bible*, p. 87.

11. Proverbs 8:31, *The Holy Bible*, p. 591.

12. Jung, *CW* 8 (1969), § 414.

13. Cousineau Brutsche, *Le Paradoxe de l'Âme*, p. 93.

14. Book of Revelation 12:1-6, *The Holy Bible,* p. 252.

15. Thomas Moore, *Care of the Soul* (New York: Harper Perennial, 1992), p. xi.

16. David Bohm: *Wholeness and the Implicate Order* (London: ARK Paperbacks, 1983), p. 197.

THE WILD FEMININE: RECONNECTING TO A POWERFUL ARCHETYPAL IMAGE

KATHARINA CASANOVA

To begin, I would like to reflect on the meaning of "wild" and "wilderness," which evoke visions of uncharted landscapes and untamed animals. We think further of the primordial, primitive, strange, unknown, dark, and fear-inspiring. For ages, humankind has sought to penetrate and control such territories. Following the biblical command, "thou shalt subjugate the earth," humans have conquered continents and subjugated their inhabitants.

Everyone knows by now that this rapacious attitude threatens Mother Earth and humanity, for it stands to destroy our remaining and precious life resources. These considerations about the outer world apply as well to the inner world: if we lose connection with the wild, primordial, primitive parts of our souls, then we lose a vital source of energy for psychological life, and we can become sick.

ANIMALS IN DREAMS

Taking this point of view, I have come to pay special attention to the

Katharina Casanova received her diploma from the C. G. Jung-Institute Zurich in 2001. She was among the founders of ISAPZURICH and was Director of Studies from 2004 to 2008. Her main interests are psychology of dreams, picture interpretation, feminist history of religion, and theory of complexes.

appearance of animals in dreams—of my own and of my clients. Animals in dreams usually represent instinctive, sometimes very neglected or oppressed, sides of our souls. If we succeed in understanding their messages, we may obtain precious hints for our daily lives. An example is given in the following dream of a woman of twenty-eight years. She dreamt that there was something strange in her bathroom, and when she went there to look she found an enormous male bear. He was very angry because he had been in the washing machine, and now he wanted to attack her. She managed to close the door and thereupon awoke fear-stricken and with a wildly beating heart. This young woman suffered from recurring depressive periods in her life. She had a tendency to adapt herself too much to her surroundings, to become overly dependent on her partner, to do everything in order to be nice and well accepted. She had difficulty accepting that the bear in her dream was part of herself, and that he was angry about her treatment of him. In therapy she discovered that she felt much better when more centered upon herself, when listening to her inner voice and permitting herself to take some freedom in space and time. When she tried to repress or "clean up" these deep instinctual needs, like trying to wash the bear in the machine, she felt sad and empty.

I choose this example because in Switzerland bears are actually a very current topic. Some years ago, bears were released into nature again, but they do not always behave as expected. In the last few years, two wild bears had to be killed because they had lost their natural fear of humans. The newspapers are full of debate as to whether bears deserve space in the mountains or are too dangerous and should be exterminated. Should we give these wild animals a chance to live in our country, or should we eliminate them? The same discussion rages concerning wolves, some of which have been killed illegally by farmers because of the threat to their sheep. Biologists and gamekeepers defend the keeping of sheep in the mountains, provided they are well tended by shepherds and herd dogs. If we do not look upon the land as strictly a food resource for our domesticated animals, but rather expand our respect and knowledge of the natural habitat, we find that there is room enough for humans and their domestic animals *and* for wild animals. For the life of soul, this translates as: a well-developed consciousness need not repress the wild, primitive layers of the psyche, provided they are treated with respect and knowledge.

I would like to cite another dream. This client was a student with many fears and phobias. He could hardly stay seated through an hour's lecture and had to make sure of a ready way of escape by sitting near a door. After being in therapy for many years, he dreamed that he found himself working in a house near some woods. Suddenly a big silver wolf came out of the woods and stood in front of the house. My client knew instinctively that this wolf was waiting for him. He saw its wonderful wild eyes and had no fear—on the contrary, for the first time he felt safe and protected. He then walked away from this place with the silver wolf at his side. He felt deeply moved by this dream. After this dream, my client had the impression that the silver wolf, unseen by others, was accompanying and protecting him everywhere he went. How can we explain this dramatic change from a psychological perspective?

The dream, we can easily see, images the outcome of a process whereby my client found a positive connection to a deep, instinctual area of his soul, as symbolized by the wolf. With the protective image at his side, he was able to start a new kind of life that was much freer of anxiety. The suddenness of the wolf's appearance is quite typical of the emergence of transformational energy: it comes up unexpectedly and with the impact of powerful emotion, such that changes and new directions in life become possible. We can also surmise that the young man was ready for this change, since he was working in a house near the wood, an image for the long previous analytical work with and near the unconscious.

As he came near the end of therapy, the client dreamed that he had to go to an old industrial area with ugly grey buildings to take some measurements. There he was very astonished to find that nature had taken back her territory: he found a lush green meadow with all kinds of wild plants and flowers, which had overgrown the old industrial buildings. He himself expressed his understanding of the dream in a few brief words: "If this can happen in nature outside, it can also happen in nature inside, in my soul." The dream shows an impressive image of what can happen when we find a connection to our deeper roots: life can grow and develop again.

THE WILD FEMININE AND THE DRAGON

In reading about nature and wild animals, one may well ask where the *wild feminine* can be found. The answer is that it is present in all these images. Let me explain why I am connecting all things wild to the feminine. Going back to the roots, to the beginning of the world, to the beginning of life, directly into the wilderness, we discover that in many creation myths the snake plays a central role. The ancestral wild dragon-snake stands not only for the beginning, but also for the end of the world, when it opens its voracious mouth to devour everything.

Taking a closer look at the dragon-snake, we notice it is a symbol that appears universally across cultures and throughout the history of man-kind. Huge in its appearance and spitting fire, it is terrifying and presents us with an image of concentrated, primordial power and energy. In the East, dragons have retained a positive meaning. Here the heavenly dragon is held to be a divine, good-natured, and luck-bringing creature; it is the essence of wisdom, of creative power, and of the capacity for transforma-tion. It is responsible for the harmony between heaven and earth, for fer-tility, and therefore for the prosperity of the whole country. As a spiritual authority, it is associated with Yang-energy.[1]

At the roots of our Western culture we find tales of an *original female* dragon, who lives in the water and represents primordial chaos. The Babylonian creation myth, *Enuma Elish*, describes the sun god and divine hero, Marduk, battling the primordial sea-snake, Tiamat, the ancestral mother of the world.[2] "Tiamat" means salt water, the ocean, and the first original waters. Tiamat's male companion is Apsu, whose name means the original moisture, fresh sweet water. According to the myth, the Cos-mos begins to unfold when Tiamat and Apsu allow their waters to flow together. As a fruit of their union, the first gods are born and the first sandbars form, which in turn give rise to the first mainland. The myth thus far can be understood to provide a symbol for the creation of a con-sciousness with boundaries.

In the first ancestral family that follows, some very human-like con-flicts take shape, and finally the young god Ea slays his father. On this father's grave Marduk is born, the glorious son of the Sun. Intending to tame her querulous descendants, Tiamat gives birth to all kinds of mon-sters: snakes, dragons (the red dragon and the sphinx), the mighty lion, and other creatures. However, this proves to be of little help, as Marduk slays Tiamat herself. Out of her body arise heaven and earth, ocean and land, light and darkness, above and below, life and death.

Joseph Campbell notes that Tiamat, although slain and cut into pieces, still remains indestructible—and moreover that Marduk and all his gods were created from Tiamat's substance.[3] On this basis, Campbell suggests that one could understand the battle from another standpoint and find that the impetuous chaos burst into pieces all by itself and placed these pieces into the world order.

Marduk is a sun god. With Marduk, the power of light manifests to oppose Tiamat's realm of darkness and primordial depths. From this time onward, these two are understood to be hostile, oppositional forces. The mythical story says further that Marduk created men from the blood of Tiamat's divine monsters. Humans therefore stand between Chaos and Cosmos, inheriting the difficult task of resolving this tension. The mythological tale has its origins in the development of nature. Eventually, however, it takes sides with the "upper" principle.

In Western culture, the ancestral snake belongs to the "lower" principle—that is, to the female, to wild and uncontrollable nature, to darkness, and to evil. The original female snake stands for beginnings, for the primordial sea out of which life was born. To contact the snake is to reach symbolically to the deepest archetypal level of the collective unconscious. The limbic system represents the biological equivalent.

THE DRAGON IN PSYCHOLOGY

Jung recognized the life power of the dragon. In *Symbols of Transformation*, he says: "The hero who fights against the dragon has many things

Figure 1: St. George and the Dragon

in common with it, respectively he takes over some peculiar characteristics of the dragon, i.e., its invulnerability, the snake eyes, etc."[4] In Jungian psychology, the heroic dragon slayer becomes a symbol for the individual who struggles to separate consciousness from the unconscious. Jung tended to interpret the dragon as an aspect of the terrible mother, who wants to devour her son.[5] In the dragon fight, the hero kills this terrible side of the feminine and liberates the fertile and blessed part, which is represented by the figure of the virgin. Psychologically, this virgin would be the image of the anima, which has been separated from the mother archetype.[6] And yet, a number of paintings of the dragon myth continue to intrigue me in their portrayal of a perhaps unexpected relationship between the dragon and the virgin. A good example is Paulo Uccello's renowned *St. George and the Dragon*, completed in 1456 and housed in the National Gallery in London.

In this and other paintings, I discovered that the dragon and virgin are often depicted as having a strong bond, whether or not this was consciously intended by the artists. Thus I began to wonder to what extent—if at all—the conventional Jungian understanding of dragon-slaying is of value for the female psyche. How feasibly can we maintain that feminine consciousness positively identifies with the hero who kills the dragon? Or is it rather identified with the virgin—who, as in Uccello's painting, holds the dragon on a loose cord? Could the motif "woman and dragon" even be a very old, nearly forgotten archetype, which has undergone reinterpretation in the course of time?

SAINT MARTHA AND TARASQUE

Following this question has led me to the holy women Martha and Margaret,[7] each of whom is known for her taming of a dragon. They may be seen in paintings and sculptures with dragons sometimes lying at their feet or in their arms, or even featured as riding-animals. I shall concentrate on Martha and her personification of a particular kind of "female relatedness" with the wild dragon.

In the Bible, Martha is known as the sister of Mary and of Lazarus. Jesus is said to have visited them and to have enjoyed Martha's cooking.[8] In the Bible we see Martha's energy. It was she who persuaded Jesus to go to Lazarus's grave, whereupon Jesus awakened him after he had been deceased for four days.[9] According to *The Golden Legend*, an imaginative medieval hagiography, unbelievers put Martha out in a rudderless boat to drift in the ocean—together with her sister Mary, her brother Lazarus, and Saint Maximinus—after Christ's ascension.[10] By the providence of God, the boat arrived at the South of France. According to legend, Les Saintes Maries de la Mer in Provence was their landing point. Elsewhere it is said that Mary and Martha were accompanied by a black servant named Sara. Sara is venerated by gypsies all over the world as their patron saint. On Whitsuntide they assemble at Les Saintes Maries de la Mer to commemorate the saint in an ecstatic procession. This story points to the positive valuation of a "primitive," wild, and numinous side of the feminine. Martha's taming of the dragon in the dense woods in the South of France is described in *The Golden Legend* as well as in some fairy tales of that region.[11] Here is my summary of the story, based on several sources:

A long time ago, when the Rhone River flowed wild and impetuous and was bordered by tremendous woods, a huge beast emerged one day from the sea and took it over as her very own kingdom. It was a female dragon, half-beast, half-fish, taller and stronger than twelve elephants, with teeth as sharp as swords and skin as strong as iron. She was an offspring of Leviathan, the cruel and dreadful sea-dragon, and Onachus, the terrible monster snake. Her name was Tarasque.

When she drank water and spat it out, she caused ships to burst and the ferrymen to drown. With a single stroke of her huge paws, Tarasque was able to destroy houses, and with her breath she made an infernal fire of whatever was around her. The men of Provence were brave and bold and risked battling her, but none of them succeeded and they all lost their lives. For seven years Tarasque spread her reign of terror and brought poverty, death, and misfortune to the people.

One day a shepherd saw Tarasque's skin glittering in the sunlight and thought that Tarasque was dead. Little did he know that what he had seen was nothing but the dragon's shed skin, left lying on the ground. Akin to the ordinary snake, Tarasque had to slough off her skin every seven years.

So another seven years passed, and the people suffered more than ever under the cruelty of Tarasque. She tore down all the bridges and killed everyone who tried to cross the river. The people on both sides were forced to get along without each other and their lamenting and wailing never stopped.

Finally the people decided to defeat the beast by a ruse. Not far from the city of Avignon there was a deep marsh, and whoever entered it was lost forever. Into that marsh they planned to lure Tarasque. To do this, they tied horses along the path to the marsh, and they tied sheep and goats to the trees. And indeed, Tarasque followed that trail of easy bait. However, when she arrived at the marsh, something strange happened. Instead of gobbling up the last bait, she roared three times like peals of thunder, and the earth quaked. Then she turned around and went back to the Rhone. All the disappointed and astonished people could do was to escape. The marsh was a place of the devil, and Tarasque herself was a satanic creature. Therefore, that evil place could not bring her to harm.

One day, Holy Martha came to the area where Tarasque dwelled. When Martha arrived at the gates of Jarnegues, the people fell to their knees in front of her. They had heard a lot about Martha's miracles, and they implored her to liberate them from the beast.

So Martha set out for the woods down by the river. She went alone, barefoot, dressed all in white and without any weapons to defend herself, only a little jug of holy water. Eventually, she found Tarasque. When the beast saw Martha, she roared loud in delight at the new offering and moved towards her. But when Martha raised her hands and made the sign of the cross, Tarasque's power broke like wild waves break on cliffs. Then Martha raised her hands and sprinkled holy water on the beast's head, whereupon Tarasque grew as gentle as a lamb.

Martha tied her blue belt around Tarasque's neck and guided her like a willing horse to the city of Jarnegues. The gates were wide open. The people were jubilant. But they also raged over Tarasque and the suffering and misfortune she had brought upon them. So with lances and stones they killed the dragon. Although Martha cried bitterly about Tarasque's death, she forgave the inhabitants of Jarnegues, who built a church to honor her and renamed their city Tarascon.

This tale refers to an ancient time when the River Rhone was wild and humans did not dominate nature to the extent they do today. The emphasis on three times seven years points to a cyclical non-patriarchal time. With her molting every seven years, Tarasque herself seems to have constituted the cyclic order of that time. Her sloughed-off skin glitters in the sunlight—it seems to be golden, very precious.

Tarasque is a part of wild and frightful nature. She is familiar with the deep marsh, which will not harm her. She roars three times, and the earth shakes. Such attributes express her power, a force not easy to remove. After three times seven years, the time has come for Martha's appearance.

She arrives alone and barefoot, dressed all in white and bearing no weapons, in marked contrast to the well-armed St. George. Martha's epiphany echoes, among other things, the medieval belief in a supernatural wild folk who inhabit the forests.[12] Going barefoot and with long unkempt hair, they sometimes helped humans. Martha also recalls the Greek goddess Artemis striding through the woods. The white dress is a sign of her virginity, in the original meaning of female independence as described by Esther Harding.[13]

Martha does not kill the dragon. Instead, she tames her with the sign of the cross and holy water. These are well-known Christian signs of protection against evil. However, I would like to go a bit further. The cross is a very ancient universal symbol. Rooted in matriarchal culture, it represents a first arrangement of order and a sign of the Great Mother.[14] When Martha makes the sign of the cross, this could also be taken as a sign of reverence for the Great Mother. Her sprinkling of holy water over the head of Tarasque can be interpreted similarly, because water is the original element of snakes.

I suggest that Tarasque becomes gentle because Martha approaches her with respect and does not see her as a monster to be broken and destroyed. Nicole Lazzarini's collection of fairy tales based on our legend supports this interpretation.[15] There it is said that Martha speaks with Tarasque and explains where she comes from. She says that Tarasque cannot harm her and that she is not afraid. Upon hearing these words, Tarasque becomes gentle because she finally feels loved ("parce qu'enfin aimée")![16]

Martha ties her blue belt around Tarasque's neck and guides her with it. Is this not a sign of a deep union? It seems that spiritual energy flows from one to the other. Perhaps this is Martha's way of asking the people for understanding for the wild dragon—but in vain, as we know, because the people kill the dragon. Martha cries bitterly about Tarasque's death. Did Martha realize that she could not change the course of time? She forgave the people of Tarascon, who recognized her as a holy one, but they were unable to value her way of taming the dragon above the heroic mode of slaying it.

In the legends and fairy tales about Martha, we find pagan and Christian elements coming together. The former point to an archaic feminine goddess possessed of great healing powers. Beyond this, it is said that Martha could awaken the dead. Here the legend links her to the story of

Jesus resurrecting Lazarus, but also to the ancient life-giving Great Mother. Even the grass in Martha's garden was held to be miraculous,[17] and many healings were said to have occurred at her grave. Her sarcophagus lies in the crypt of her church in Tarascon. According to legend, the French king Clovis visited this church every year, after his conversion to Christianity, to receive Martha's healing.[18]

We can imagine that the old religion did not disappear from one day to the next. It was rather a gradual process. Old divinities were still venerated after the conversion of the people to Christianity, and in the course of time they merged with the Christian saints. Martha leading the dragon by her belt is a perfect image for this process: pagan religion is not violently eliminated and overcome, but rather is integrated, as if gently led on a blue ribbon. This is a very wise feminine attitude.

Saint Martha is perfectly suited for the integration of an old goddess into the Christian religion. She is noble, self-confident, independent, and caring in the mode of the sheltering Great Mother. In the preface of the book *La Tarasque*, Maurice Pezet suggests this view when he states: "*La draperie chrétienne enveloppant sainte Marthe*," implying that "the Goddess is wrapped in the veil of a Christian Saint."[19]

The figure of Martha seems to have been subsumed to a patriarchal world in which the principles of masculine consciousness rule: the now tamed dragon is overwhelmed and killed. Wild nature is conquered and depleted for human purposes. Yet aspects of the Great Goddess shimmer through in the legend—the dragon is tamed and, who knows? may live on unbeknownst to us. The wild characteristics of the old goddesses are specifically the ones that were eliminated in the features of many female Christian saints. The dragon fight can destroy such features and split them off, but one can also esteem the dragon and tame and integrate her values.

Martha is called a "virgin." Psychologically speaking, this has little to do with sexual chastity but more with an independent spirit, as mentioned before. The epithet of virginity is here used in order to conceal Martha's original wild power. In many aspects, she reminds one of Artemis, the daughter of Zeus and Leto, a goddess of nature who stands for a fruitful relation between "above" and "below." Artemis is the goddess who strides through the woods accompanied by her companions, nymphs and hunting dogs. She is called the "mistress of animals," especially of young ones. Artemis is the huntress who never misses her aim, which also represents her dark side.[20]

In the figure of Artemis one finds a manifestation of woman living independently, capable of caring for herself and focused on important aims. Like Martha, who connects to the dragon with her blue ribbon, Artemis has a deep connection to her own wild side and the realm of the Great Mother. This points to a type of consciousness that is deeply rooted in instinct.

The Great Goddess and Her Animals

Turning to ancient myth, we know that at the Babylonian New Year's festival the verses of the *Enuma Elish* were performed, and that the king, Marduk's representative, was confirmed as the ruler for another year. The ritual procession passed through the Gate of Ishtar in honor of the Great Goddess. The ritual path has been reconstructed in the National Museum of Berlin with the bricks that were dug out of the site in Babylon.[21] The beauty of this work is moving, especially the frieze with lions that borders the path to the Gate. The Gate itself is decorated with alternating bulls and dragons. This is an image that refers to the old mother goddess Tiamat, in honor of Ishtar. The presence of lions and bulls in this work points to the ancient meaning of the Great Mother as the Mistress of wild animals.

One of the most touching representations of the Babylonian Goddess is from around 4000 B.C. It is a sculpture showing her as an archetypal mother, holding her child in her arms. Remarkably, both mother and child are portrayed with snake heads. The German researcher Vera Zingsem has shown a clear development from Inanna to Ishtar.[22] I mention this because Inanna is often depicted as the Mistress of ani-

Figure 2: Babylonian Goddess

Figure 3: Cylinder Seal of the Great Goddess

mals and vegetation. Sometimes she is portrayed as seated upon or riding a lion. Of special relevance here is a relief that shows the Great Goddess with a wild lion on a leash. The goddess holding a tamed wild animal seems to be the first of an iconographic series leading later to Martha with the dragon.

In a written prayer in cuneiform script to Inanna of Ur, one can read that the goddess herself was compared to a dragon: "You have filled the country with snake poison, like a dragon."[23] Another song says, "Goddess of Ningal, you were born for joy, like a dragon you have the power to destroy."[24] She is also called "Queen, riding on wild animals,"[25] and a "wild cow without reins."[26] In another prayer she is called "splendid lioness among the Gods,"[27] or "bull burning with anger."[28]

It is significant that the Goddess was recognized and venerated both in her light *and* dark aspects. "When you thunder like Ischkur, vegetation will grow, you Goddess, who brings the big flood down from the mountains."[29] "Inanna of heaven and earth, high Goddess, who spreads flaming fire-rains all over the world...."[30] Here we recognize her as the mighty dragon. In other passages, we see her as a merciful "magna mater," that is, the Great Mother: "Great Queen of all Queens,...wise Queen of all countries, full of understanding,...merciful woman who gives us life, your heart shines strongly."[31]

Inanna is a courageous fighter. Like a lioness, she will defend her people. The fact that she is always ready to fight seems to be as well an expression of her ability to love. Aggression and love do not exclude each other, but rather they exist naturally together and are characteristic features of the wild feminine. This archetypal image may be difficult to comprehend, because today these two aspects seem to be so contradictory.

In the original versions of many fairy tales, the light and the dark sides are still contained in the figure of the mother, whereas in later versions the destructive side is attributed to an evil stepmother. She chases her children away when time has come for them to become independent, just as wild animals do. The frightful dragon contains these opposites. I do not deny that the wild dragon contains very dangerous shadow aspects, but it is not a solution to project the frightful, or to repress it or split it off. The violent killing of the dragon is a pseudo-solution. The shadow parts need to be looked at and integrated.

RECONNECTING TO TODAY

Here I would like to tell about a 60-year-old client. Because of severe family problems, she worked with me for many years in analysis. Due to many disappointments in the course of her life, she had lost her previously sustaining religious faith. Her disillusionment with the church was accompanied by many negative emotions and feelings, and she formed the conviction that she was a "bad woman." Towards the end of our work she began to imagine what she described as a sister, and later a goddess, whom she called "Sibylla Veronica." Sibylla Veronica was said to be big, strong, and red-haired. My client had talks with her every day, experiencing her "friend's" caring and sharing of energy. As a steady invisible companion and protectress, Sibylla Veronica helped my client to accept her own shadow and to develop understanding and love for herself. With Sibylla's support, my client rediscovered a "religious attitude" in the broad sense of reconnecting with nature and something larger than herself. Sibylla Veronica arising spontaneously from the unconscious recalls the earlier-mentioned dream in which a silver wolf suddenly appeared out of the woods and accompanied the dreamer thereafter as his assistant.

It is useless to split off the wild dragon side. The untamed and unnourished animal will take revenge. In banishment, it will do all the evil that one wanted to avoid. Situated in the deepest region of our soul, in its archaic instinctual ground, it will overtake the whole personality from behind and paralyze it with fears, phobias, and depressions. This is why it is so important to go back to the roots again and again in therapies with women *and* men. There we can move toward taking up respectful contact with the dragon within, with the long-banned, archaic, wild and dark feminine. This deserves to be acknowledged and nourished, since it belongs to the deepest energy-giving part of our soul and finally to our Self.

NOTES

1. Catalogue to the exhibition *"Der Drache: Himmelssohn oder Ausgeburt der Hölle?"* Text, Urs Ramseier and M. L. Nabholz, Museum für Völkerkunde und Schweizerisches Museum für Volkskunde (Basel: Museum für Völkerkunde, l996), pp. 1-4.

2. B. Stamer and V. Zingsem, *Schlangenfrau und Chaosdrache in Märchen, Mythos und Kunst: Schlangen- und Drachensymbolik im Kulturvergleich* (Stuttgart: Kreuz, 2001), pp. 133-139.

3. Joseph Campbell, *The Hero with a Thousand Faces*, Bollingen Series Vol. XVII (New York: Bollingen Foundation Inc., 1949), p. 246.

4. C. G. Jung, "The Dual Mother," in *Symbols of Transformation*, vol. 5 of *The Collected Works of C. G. Jung*, trans. R. F. C. Hull (Princeton, NJ: Princeton University Press, 1990), § 575.

5. *Ibid.*, "Symbols of the Mother and of Rebirth," § 374.

6. Uwe Steffen, *Drachenkampf: Der Mythos vom Bösen* (Stuttgart: Kreuz, 1984), p. 29.

7. Rosa Giorgi, "Margareta von Antiochien" and "Marta," in *Die Heiligen: Geschichte und Legende* (Berlin: Parthas, 2003), pp. 231-233; 252-256.

8. Luke 10:38-42, *The Holy Bible*, Authorized King James Version (Wheaton, IL: Tyndale House Publishers, 1987).

9. John 11:1-44.

10. "Martha," in *The Golden Legend* or *Lives of the Saints*, vol. IV, compiled by Jacobus de Voragine, Archbishop of Genoa, 1275; English by William Caxton, 1483; from the Temple Classics, F. S. Ellis, ed., 1900/1931, *Internet Medieval Source Book: Saints Lives*, Paul Halsall, ORB Sources ed.: http://www.fordham.edu/halsall/sbook3.html (accessed 18 February 2009), pp. 64-67.

11. "Das Ungeheuer Tarasque," in *Märchen von Drachen*, ed. Sigrid Früh (Frankfurt: Fischer, 1988), pp. 61-63.

12. A. Rapp Buri and M. Stucki-Schürer, *Zahm und Wild: Basler und Strassburger Bildteppiche des 15. Jahrhunderts* (Mainz: Ph. von Zabern, 1990), p. 52.

13. Esther Harding, *Women's Mysteries: Ancient and Modern* (Boston: Shambhala, 1971), see, e.g., p. 102, and chapter 9, pp. 117-127.

14. Carola Meier-Seethaler, "Die matrizentrischen Wurzeln universeller Symbole" (lecture at the C. G. Jung-Institute, WS 91/92; personal notes); see also Marija Gimbutas, *The Civilization of the Goddess* (San Francisco: HarperSanFrancisco, 1991), e.g., p. 316, and fig. 13, p. 317.

15. Nicole Lazzarini, *Contes et Légendes de Provence, Sainte Marthe et la Tarasque* (Rennes: Editions Ouest-France, 2002), pp. 181-187.

16. *Ibid.*, p. 187.

17. "Martha," *The Golden Legend*, p. 65.

18. *Ibid.*, p. 67.

19. Louis Renard, *La Tarasque: Le Temps Retrouvé* (Marguerittes, France: Equinoxe, 1991), preface by Maurice Pezet, p. 3.

20. Jean Shinoda Bolen, *Goddesses in Everywoman* (San Francisco: Harper & Row, 1984), see chapters 3 and 4, pp. 35-75.

21. J. Marzahn, *Das Ishtar-Tor von Babylon. Die Prozessionsstrasse. Das babylonische Neujahrsfest*, Staatliche Museen zu Berlin, Vorderasiatisches Museum (Mainz: Ph. von Zabern, 1995), pp. 17-30.

22. Vera Zingsem, *Göttinnen grosser Kulturen* (München: DTV, 1999), p. 100.

23. *Ibid.*, p. 80.

24. *Ibid.*, p. 85.

25. *Ibid.*, p. 80.

26. *Ibid.*, p. 81.

27. *Ibid.*, p. 95.

28. *Ibid.*, p. 96.

29. *Ibid.*, p. 80.

30. *Ibid.*

31. *Ibid.*, p. 81.

Illustrations:

Fig. 1: Paulo Uccello, *St. George and the Dragon*, 1456, National Gallery, London: http://www.nationalgallery.org.uk/cgi-bin/WebObjects.dll/

CollectionPublisher.woa/wa/work?workNumber=ng6294 (accessed 15 June 2009).

Fig. 2: Babylonian Goddess. Adele Getty, *Goddess: Mother of Living Nature (Art and Imagination Series), the Babylonian Goddess* (Ur, around 4000-3500 b.Ch., terracotta, height 15 cm) (London: Thames and Hudson, 1990), p. 33.

Fig. 3: Cylinder Seal of the Great Goddess. Othmar Keel, *L'Eternel féminin. Une face cachée du Dieu biblique. "Sceau-cylindre montrant Ishtar maîtrisant un lion"* (Mésopotamie, Elam, env. 2340-2190 av. J.-C., pierre noire, hauteur 4,2 cm.) Musée Bible + Orient (Genève: Editions Labor et Fides, 2007), p. 94.

AND THE RIVER SWELLED
WITH HORSES

ELEONÓRA BABEJOVÁ

As a small girl I was captivated by an image of Cinderella riding her horse through the forest.[1] In retrospect, this image represented beauty, freedom, and also a connection to the body, to one's nature, instincts, and desires. After all, Cinderella rode on her horse to the ball at the castle, where she danced with the prince. Although aided by three magic hazelnuts hiding beautiful clothes, she got to the castle on her own horse and did not have to be spirited there by any exterior magic. She was connected to the love in her heart and was able to ride her desire and instinct to win the prince.

Apart from my fascination with this image I have never paid much thought to the horse's symbolic or literal power, despite growing up in a small town in Slovakia well known for its annual horse races, and taking some riding classes ten years ago. Yet the horse galloped out at me through a recent dream. I used the *I Ching* to amplify one of the images in the dream, and the mare arrived in hexagram 2, Space: "Trial belongs to the female horse."[2] The horse here is a "symbol of spirited strength in the natural world, earthly counterpart of the dragon."[3] The horse in the Chi-

Eleonóra Babejová is training as a Jungian analyst at ISAP Zurich. She has been a research scholar, translator, instructor in adult education, and a tutor for teenagers with learning disabilities, as well as a facilitator of spiritual retreats.

nese cosmology also stands for courage and energy. So I started to reflect on the meaning of this symbol and its relevance to my individuation journey.

Symbol dictionaries provide an overwhelming wealth of meanings for horse images throughout different cultures, mythologies, and historical periods. Rather than offer interpretations of the symbol, in this paper I would like to "animate the image," so that its power and symbolic content can step forward by giving soul life to the animal itself rather than draining its life through attempts to pin down its meaning.[4]

Although the horse lends itself to heroic imagery with its immense physical power and vitality, important aspects in themselves, I want to move closer to the horse's sensitivity and the kind of knowing that has been associated with the feminine, going along with the image of the "female horse." Similar to the female figure in the Tarot card *Force*, effortlessly holding open the jaws of a lion, the horse stands for the poise of a person able to contain their vitality, to identify and process their emotions, and to be powerful without losing their connection to the earth. It is the meeting of two ways of being: the active mode of the forward rush of a hero, and of *wu-wei*, not doing. I want to show the symbolic power of the horse to carry for us humans a knowing that comes through our bodies, our senses, proprioceptive imagery, and imagination. Human knowing and horse knowing are strung together by a resonance more akin to the vibration of a sensitive instrument than the sound of a whip. As Jung says: "The symbols of the self arise in the depths of the body and they express its materiality every bit as much as the structure of the perceiving consciousness."[5]

In this essay I will move with the horse image through following several links. First I return to the image of my distant ancestors, who a long time ago roamed the steppes of Eurasia on horseback before they migrated to Europe, where they finally settled. This will open the way to bring the horse and the human into a relationship. Then I will consider the human–horse relationship as a place of overlap of two different kinds of consciousnesses, human and equine. This will initiate a process of metamorphosis, moving between the horse and the human and vice versa, in which the horse acts as a psychopomp. The horse is seen as a creature that can move between different worlds in different ways: between the world of humans and the world of gods, between the realm of the living and the realm of the dead, between the conscious self and "lost soul parts" in the unconscious. The horse will not only be a traveler between worlds but also between shapes, so that the boundary between the human/horse grows transparent. Finally I will enter the wilderness of the horse/human body, ending up in the horse's belly, the source of power and the place of alchemical transformation.

NOMADS OR CENTAURS?

The horse played an important role among the numerous nomadic tribes of Eurasia, in the Celtic world, in Norse and Teutonic mythology, and in the Islamic world as well as in Christianity.[6] Evidence of contact between humans and horses goes back as far as 15,000 years ago.[7]

Horses are "natural nomads." I would agree with Kohanov that "domestication" worked both ways: horses and humans came together for the benefit mutual cooperation offered.[8] This view takes humans away from the center of the world and opens space for seeing and experiencing the horse as a being on its own rather than as an appendage to humans. For nomadic people, the horse was an invaluable means of transport and movement, the basis of their army, and a companion. But the horse was also seen as carrying magic qualities, the most notable the ability to move between the world of the living and the world of the dead.

Much of the literary record of the nomadic people comes from the writers of the sedentary civilizations. Inevitably, nomads were seen as "barbarians" (in its original Greek meaning denoting those who speak an incomprehensible tongue, but later acquiring a definite derogatory meaning as those opposed to the sedentary, "civilized" peoples) when they came into contact with settled peoples in Europe, who projected the monsters of the human psyche onto them. With their rapid attacks and what seemed like magical riding skills they evoked the terror of the settled population, who saw them as brutal killing beasts.

Among these nomadic "scourges" were also Huns, the ancestral link on the Hungarian side of my family that I am following in this paper, as the old Magyars might have been one of the Hunic tribes. Maenchen-Helfen notes that Huns were demonized very early on. Both Greek and Latin writers considered the invaders "bandits and deserters."[9]

When the Hunic tribes (at this point more seminomadic than nomadic) invaded Europe in the fourth century, they absolutely terrified the local population, largely because of their riding skills, extreme mobility, and the ability to shoot from their bows with great accuracy while galloping at full speed.[10] The strength of the nomadic way of waging war rested on high maneuverability, a speedy attack and quick dispersal to all sides, which broke the enemy's ranks, swiftly followed by other forces waiting on the wings, at first hidden from sight.[11] The nomadic riders were described by observers as almost glued to their horses, so as to leave the impression of mythical creatures, half human, half horse:

> You would think that the limbs of the man and horse were born together, so firmly does the rider always stick to the horse. Other people are carried on the horseback; these people live there.[12]

The horses of the nomadic Huns were different from the finely bred Roman horses: smaller and sturdier, able to endure cold and heat, patient, and—in the eyes of Roman observers—ugly as well as less intelligent and noble than the Roman fine breeds.[13] The very look of the horse must have amplified the impression of a mythical and a rather stupid beast. One can say that the aesthetics of nomads' horses would have been closer to the element of earth than the element of fire or wind exemplified by the long-limbed, fine stallions preferred by Romans. As Huns also had different, Asian features (which were also described as ugly by Roman historians) and clothing, they must have seemed like a materialization of certain mythical creatures, perhaps even centaurs, at this time being pushed more and more into the dark rooms of the unconscious psyche as Christianity was consolidating as an ideology and ancient gods were dying or retreating underground.

WHEN CENTAURS ROAMED THE WIDE PLAINS OF ARGOS

As the nomadic rider metamorphoses into a mythical centaur, the play *Equus* follows the similar metamorphosis of an adolescent boy into a nomadic rider/centaur, and its dire consequences. In the play, the psychiatrist Martin Dysart, in his fantasy, longingly goes back to those mythic times when centaurs still trampled the wide plains of Argos.[14] This fantasy conjures up a time when passion and ecstasy were still alive for him, something he does not experience in his work with disturbed children and adolescents where, as he notes with bitterness, he serves the "God of Normal."

Dysart is challenged when he is given the case of a seventeen-year-old boy, Alan Strang, who blinded six horses. As the boy's story unfolds, the psychiatrist starts to question the very ground of his work. He feels that if he heals the boy of his pain and makes him a normal and well-adjusted member of human society, he will also remove this boy's passion, "his self-chosen pain," the intense connection between the religious and the sexual that makes him alive.

Alan has created a sacred ritual: once every three weeks he takes a horse out at night, undresses, and then rides the horse naked, enjoying its power and the sensual contact with the horse's sweaty body, participating in worship of the great god Equus in which the dogmatic Christianity of his mother commingles with pagan sensuality and his own sexuality. As Dysart notes, the boy is the modern centaur in the fields of Hampshire trying to ignite "the flame of original ecstasy in the spiritual waste around him."

Dysart feels jealous as he realizes that he has never experienced such passion in his life, even though Alan is destroyed by his passion. And so he remains with the image of being inside a horse's head, tortured now by the realization of the split between his intellectual enjoyment of ancient Greek myths, gotten through leafing through illustrated books or even regular visits to Greece, and the visceral, somatic experience of passion that is not mediated but experienced in the now. That passion comes alive for Alan in the contact with the sensual reality of the horse, which mediates for him a connection with his own instinctual drives and enables him to experience the power of embodiment.

The centaur is a mythological creature combining the lower body of a horse and the upper body of a human. The first centaur was an offspring of Ixion and Nephele (the cloud made in the image of Hera). Centaurs inhabited the mountains of Thessaly and they were fierce, benevolent, and sensuous. In their sensuous aspect, they were associated with the Sirens in the orgies and processions of Dionysos. The best-known centaur was Chiron, personifying wisdom and knowledge of healing arts and archery, a tutor to famous heroes such as Achilles and Jason. As the symbol dictionary states, the centaur represented the "lower" animal nature conjoined with the "higher" nature of judgment and virtue.[15] Such division reflects the ancient split between the animal/human, body/mind, wild/tame, and a clear value placement with the tame and civilized. I will return to this split when I talk later about the space "in-between."

According to another symbolic dictionary, centaurs were actually divided into two families: the children of Ixion represented blind, brute force and lust while the children of Philyra and Cronos represented strength and nobility, as in Chiron.[16] So here the division runs between the raw power of instinct and the instinct that has been tempered and contained, yet not repressed, as in the above mentioned Tarot card *Force*.

TÁLTOS, OR THE ONE WHO TRAVELS ACROSS BORDERS

In ancient Hungarian mythology, we encounter the *táltos*, both as a human being and a magic horse. The word was used by the ancient nomadic Magyar tribes for their shamanic figures, who were born miraculously with full human teeth or six fingers. Their special destiny was determined during the prenatal phase; therefore they already came into this world with special gifts. They could predict the outcome of battles but also cure illness. They used the horse as the means of travel between the world of humans and the world of spirits.[17] But as the word *táltos* refers to both the shaman and the horse, there is a certain merging of the two into one on this magical journey, a centaur-like being traveling through the liminal space of in-between. A *táltos* horse also has prophetic gifts and psychic powers, just as the shaman. This belief is not limited to old Magyars but is universal, as the horse is seen as being able to bear messages between different worlds, to see the spirits of the dead, and to have foreknowledge.[18]

We encounter this magical *táltos* in Hungarian and Slovak fairy tales (here as *tátoš*), but similar horses are also part of the Slavic and Germanic mythology.[19] First we see this horse as an ugly, thin, neglected animal, seeming more dead than alive as it lies on a garbage pile or heap of dung. Not unlike as in alchemy, the gold is found in the dung or dross, but only by the wise who know where to look. So the real nature of the horse can only be recognized by a *táltos* or by the hero in the fairy tale. The miraculous power of the horse comes to life only when purchased or acquired by the right person. Then the horse changes to a golden, silver, or diamond horse with golden hooves that flies through the air or moves through the water, connecting different realms and accomplishing miraculous acts.[20] The horse advises the hero, teaches him about hidden things, and helps him with its supernatural abilities. Without the horse's advice the hero would be lost or dead. The heroic ego narrowly focused on its goal cannot accomplish much without the use of horse wisdom that is grounded in the body and knows from the body.

The Jungian analyst Jerome Bernstein came up with the term "Bor-

derland Personality" (different from borderline personality), which refers
to individuals who are a kind of contemporary *táltos*. He noticed that
many of his clients had frequent nonrational experiences that were impossible to explain within the framework of cause-and-effect logic and did
not fit the Western mainstream paradigm at all. As a result, they feel
abnormal and alienated, and they are often pathologized when they seek
out help. These people display an extreme sensitivity to nature, animals,
and the environment. Bernstein sees the growing number of such people
as an emergence of a new kind of consciousness that bridges the mind-
body split. He sees the Borderland Personality as a kind of person who
inhabits the "psychic space where the hyper-developed and overly rational
western ego is in the process of reconnecting with its split-off roots in
nature."[21]

The symbolic power of the horse lies in its capacity to carry out this
borderland travel. By "symbolic power," I don't mean its many symbolic
meanings, but rather its mediating capacity that rests on a felt sense of a
consciousness deeply connected to the messages of the body and its environment, consciousness that "in-dwells," in Winnicott's term. It does not
need to separate. And any such separation is merely conceptual or ideological. If we talk in our culture about the Cartesian split between the
body/mind, it means that an awareness of their inseparability has fallen
into the unconscious, yet this split does not reflect a real division. As Jung
wrote:

> Since psyche and matter are contained in one and the same
> world, and moreover are in continuous contact with one an-
> other and ultimately rest on irrepresentable, transcendental
> factors, it is not only possible but fairly probable, even, that
> psyche and matter are two different aspects of one and the
> same thing.[22]

THE SPACE IN-BETWEEN

According to Morris Berman, the domestication of animals laid
down the fundamental distinction between two categories: wild and
tame. This split has formed the basis for later forms of thought in terms
of exclusive oppositions. Plants became edible or inedible; animals were
good/domesticated/tamed or bad/those that attacked human crops. The
ability to inhabit the space in between decreased, and many subtle differ-
entiations and intricacies of an interconnected whole—where there is no

either/or polarity but rather a both/and relation—have been lost. The larger part of the animal world became Other, there only to be subjugated, controlled, tamed, and overcome. Anything that fell into the category of the Other shared the same fate, including the body. As Berman observes, "For many centuries now, and I suspect millennia, 'we' (i.e., our minds) have regarded our bodies as somehow untamed, unruly—animalistic....Like animals, they don't 'listen to reason.'"[23]

A vital connection gets lost in the long civilizing process as animals are juxtaposed to humans and what is "animal" in the human has to be controlled and suppressed because it is unworthy of the "higher" spiritual part or reason. I do not want to suggest that the civilizing process can or should be reversed or to propose a return to nature. I would just like to point to the genesis of the split entailed in the civilizing process, and also to highlight that this process of splitting has been taking place at many interwoven levels, including that of the body.

In his classic description of the civilizing process, Norbert Elias points out that the creation of table manners and etiquette was a somatic experience, a disciplining of the body. It created a form of social distancing, as one modified behavior based on how one was seen by others, creating an observer within who was now controlling the body in order to comply with a set of outside rules. The educated classes of Western Europe learned detachment and emotional restraint in their bodies before the scientific revolution laid down the principles of scientific objectivity in Western science. The methodology of the emerging science reflected this distancing from one's sensory experience and spontaneity. The immediacy of the somatic experience of being in the world was lost. Being reasonable and objective entailed psychic distance and somatic disengagement.[24]

Yet as Winnicott also points out, psyche and soma are integrally connected: "The basis of psyche is soma, and in evolution the soma came first. The psyche begins as an imaginative elaboration of physical functioning."[25] In contrast to the ideal of disembodied rationality, there is a different kind of body-based reason, that of a horse, which one might describe as the psyche speaking through the body. The horse as a symbol can mediate this split as it has been universally seen as a magic creature moving through the in-between space, between life and death, the Lower and the Upper World, back and forth. And through an act of shape-shifting, through recovering "horse wisdom," a person can recover access to vitality, emotions, and also develop a different kind of awareness that does not focus like a laser beam but is softly alert and takes in its sensuous environment.

Relating to the soul of the world and ultimately also to one's own soul is possible only if such immediacy of experience is maintained. This kind of relating does not need a "return to nature," but rather feeling one's way into what could well be called an animistic conception of the world, where everything is alive and everything has a soul. Including the horse. That soul-fullness and aliveness can be perceived only in an immediate engagement with the world and an awareness of that engagement in one's body. Van Löben Sels talks about the "capacity for primary experience" as one's firsthand experience of being alive. It is a place where there is no defense, as body awareness cannot be argued against because it just is.[26] Or as Reich wrote: "Truth is immediate, full contact between life that perceives and that is being perceived."[27] Of course this kind of knowing can be rationalized away, which is the most common defense of a laser-like focused ego. I suggest that one way of accessing this awareness is by imagining that one is a horse or imagining a horse moving between the intellect or reason and the "sensation-al" radar that humans have embedded within their bodies as their "animal" part.

Let us move now with the horse to the waters of the unconscious and the unwanted fire hiding in their depths.

AND THE RIVER SWELLED WITH FIRE HORSES

The nine-year-old heroine Eve of the film *Eve & the Fire Horse* comes from a Chinese family that emigrated to Vancouver in Canada and is trying its best to adjust to the life there.[28] Eve is born in 1966, the year of the Fire Horse, which occurs every sixty years. She tells the story of how, long ago in China, nobody wanted children, especially not girls, born in this year because of their strong will. Parents were so afraid they even drowned babies born in this year in the river. And the river would swell with the spirits of the unwanted fire horses. The movie shows Eve's imagining of fire horses floating in the river's depths, not dead, but moving with their powerful bodies through the water.

Fire horses are drowned because they are too potent, carrying too much vitality, energy, and independence, and are not likely to fit in with the collective norms demanding obedience and conformity. In Japan, women born in the year of the Fire Horse were called *hinoeuma*. They were considered too dangerous, headstrong, and deadly for men, so a whole generation of women born in 1906 were unable to marry and faced poverty and deprivation in their old age. While the 1966 generation had an easier time, they still faced a lot of prejudice, as women were expected to be quiet and subservient, definitely not qualities associated with the fire horse.[29] The image of the fire horse stands here as a symbol for all that is unwanted by the conscious self—whether individual, parental, or societal—and is consequently drowned in the river.

I would like to return to the symbolic potency of a body of water filled with fire horses moving around—all the vitality, both physical and mental, drowning in the deep waters of the unconscious, suppressed and sent there to be kept out of sight as its expression is not allowed. In a similar way, this vital aliveness can get imprisoned in childhood while a false self is developed that shows no signs of the immense potency hidden in the depths.[30] In addition to the common association of water with the unconscious, Jung also wrote that water is the "valley spirit" and psychologically means spirit that has become unconscious.[31] The fire horses don't die, but continue moving around, stirring in the waters of the unconscious. They erupt in sudden blazes of anger or manifest as depression, addictions masking emotional pain that has no voice, or continuous sadness and emptiness as the connection to vital parts of self is lost.

The horse as a *táltos* can create a connection to the lost parts of the human soul, just as in a soul retrieval the shaman *táltos* brings back soul parts that have left. The soul is considered to be the person's vital essence, and if parts of this essence separate from the person, the consequence is a disease. While in the past the main reasons for soul loss were seen as fear or theft, at present it is often the result of trauma. The person does not feel fully present, is depressed, or has a sense of missing vitality.[32] Jung comments on the universal belief in a plurality of souls in an individual when he talks about the fragmentation of the personality.[33] He considers psyche not an indivisible unity but a whole consisting of different parts that are connected to each other but also relatively independent. Jung called these parts autonomous complexes.[34] He wrote:

> [A] traumatic complex brings about dissociation of the psyche. The complex is not under the control of the will and for this reason it possesses the quality of psychic autonomy.[35]

Lost soul parts can then be seen from the psychological perspective as the disassociated parts of one's psyche. The notion of a plurality of soul parts points to a plurality of relatively autonomous complexes. Jung distinguishes between soul and spirit complexes, the first connected with the personal and the other with the collective unconscious. In the case of soul loss we are dealing with the soul-complexes. They belong to the ego, and when they get dissociated from the ego, it seems that certain portions of the psyche have disappeared.[36] In shamanic cultures this loss is seen as a soul loss. The lost soul part needs to be brought back in order to restore the vitality and health of the individual.

When something traumatic happens to a horse, for example when it is attacked, it freezes. A biological mechanism is set into action so that the horse (like other animals) does not feel pain when being dismembered by a predator. But in this moment the mind separates from the body (and yes, I do presume the existence of a horse mind here). Similarly, soul parts of a human leave when the person is faced with an unbearable situation. Yet those dissociated parts do not just simply return once the unbearable situation is over. Dissociation allows the external life to continue but, as Kalsched remarks, at an enormous internal cost. The unbearable experience gets distributed into different parts of the body and mind, especially into their unconscious aspects.[37]

In fairy tales, the magical horses, often associated with the fire element, can not only fly through the air but move through the water. Just as the *táltos* connects the realms of humans and spirits, so does the horse-*táltos* connect the different elements and realms, moving down under the surface of water, in the unconscious of locked-away emotions, memories, and parts of oneself that escaped in order to survive. This is the non-ordinary reality accessed by the shaman.[38] In some cultures (for example the Yakut and the Buryat of Asia), the drum shamans use to travel to non-ordinary reality is made of horsehide, so, metaphorically speaking, it is the horse that takes the shaman into a different realm, inaccessible to average mortals. This drum is called the shaman's horse.[39] The Buryat also use a horse-headed stick, and the state of ecstasy that takes them into a different reality is induced by dancing astride this horse.[40]

During the soul retrieval ceremony of the Buryat, someone holds a horse outside the yurt near a tree, as it is believed that the horse would be the first one to perceive the return of the soul and would show this by quivering.[41] It is the horse, our animal body, our sympathetic system, that picks up resonances and false notes that move like waves from an underwater volcano that is still alive. Yet one needs a very sensitive seismograph to register these waves. This is where the equine and human consciousness overlap, as their sympathetic nervous systems (and their related enteric and parasympathetic systems) resonate like the strings of a viola d'amore.[42] This seventeenth-century instrument had two sets of strings: one attached to the fingerboard that could be plucked or played with a bow, and another set underneath the stringboard that could not be accessed directly, but vibrated each time the player would play a tone that resonated with one of the strings below. In a similar way, the sympathetic system can be seen as a system that "resonates with" rather than just reacts to stimuli.[43]

Jung also talks about the sympathetic system as a system that enables us to resonate with others' inner states, as he stresses also the earthy quality of water (besides its spiritual aspect) and of the unconscious, their connection to physicality. So water is:

> …earthy and tangible, it is also the fluid of the instinct-driven body, blood and the flowing of blood, the odor of the beast, carnality heavy with passion. The unconscious is the psyche that reaches down from the daylight of mentally and morally lucid consciousness into the nervous system that for ages has been known as the "sympathetic." This does not govern perception and muscular activity like the cerebrospinal system, and thus control the environment; but though functioning without sense-organs, it maintains the balance of life and, through the mysterious paths of sympathetic excitation, not only gives us knowledge of the innermost life of other beings but also has an inner effect upon them. In this sense it is an extremely collective system, the operative basis of all *participation mystique*.[44]

The civilizing process affected the value placed on the responses of the autonomic nervous system, which originates in an earlier stage of human evolution that connects us with animal nature, from which "civilized" humans have been trying to free themselves. The autonomic nervous system is not as much under the control of conscious intention as parts of the central nervous system. With the overvaluing of conscious control, together with a cerebral and rational approach to life, the manifestations of the autonomic nervous system are often written off in the same way we like to dispose of those strange inklings, moods, and longings that rise up from the unconscious. Or, within the mechanistic framework of modern medicine, these autonomous manifestations are medicated, disciplined, and considered as dumb as the body itself. Escaping rational explanation, they are often considered sinister and strange, requiring elimination through suppression or by simply ignoring them for as long as possible.

Yet all humans use their "gut sense" in making decisions. Perhaps intuition does not need to be pursued as some miraculous psychic or spiritual ability, as in fact it is wired into the human body, its roots connecting us to our animal ancestors. This is the place of our "horse wisdom," of body intelligence that is underestimated as the rational control of life is overvalued and all that is in the way of efficient functioning is discarded. The sympathetic is a part of the unconscious and is invaluable in signaling when we are emotionally incongruent, when we dissociate, when we do not want to or are not able to face certain emotions. As children, we might have learned to shut off our disagreeable emotions and find it hard to connect to them. Or the interpretation of these subtle cues becomes confused as the system keeps overreacting after trauma. It becomes unreliable and produces false alarms or gives false information.[45]

Those who spend a lot of time with horses notice how the one thing that confuses horses most is incongruity between the rider/caretaker's actions and their emotional state. This could be related to the "wisdom of the prey" that horses possess.[46] Because they were often preyed upon, they learned to read their environment for warning signals. Theirs is a more diffuse awareness that notices discrepancies as potentially dangerous, as if a red flag went up communicating threat and warning other members of the group of imminent danger. That is why horses also notice if humans who approach them are just putting on a nice face when they are really angry, frustrated, or terrified. Horses pick up those false tones like the silent breathing of underwater volcanoes of which humans remain unaware, as we have been taught to tune out such subtle messages.

Yet our internal horse reacts to such incongruity just as an external horse would, kicking its feet like the fire horses in the river. It can hear the imprisoned fire horses moving underneath. This sensitivity and intelligence of horses is at the basis of equine psychotherapy: humans are led to recognize their emotions, to connect and understand the messages of their sympathetic system and the gut, to touch the difficult places within themselves through contact with horses. So we encounter the horse again as a *táltos*, the creature that connects the conscious and unconscious realms for humans, taking them to encounters with terrifying gods and demons hiding in the depths. Now that we don't believe in horse magic anymore, we experience it differently as therapy. Yet the horse is present in the function of a psychopomp, of the creature able to move in-between.

The human psyche includes both predator and prey. According to Kohanov, it was the prey aspect that forged the cooperation between nomads and horses. It is this prey wisdom of the horse that returns us and mediates the way to our "animal" sensitivity, to a sensuous perception of the world. But as humans have come to identify with the predator, either through control by reason or in the dominant hero myth embedded in popular culture, the wisdom of the prey has been ignored. Maybe it is not necessary to choose either the prey or predator perspective, but rather to choose fluidity and movement. Imagine the flowing movements of a galloping horse or a fairy-tale *táltos* flying through the clouds.

Thus the centaur might not be a joining of the "higher" and "lower" nature, but rather a paradox: a way of being that moves fluidly in-between the two and finds them equally valuable without any hidden agenda to tame and control. The centaur probably stands at the juncture between two different modes of awareness: the more diffuse "horizontal" awareness of hunter-gatherer societies, and the focused "vertical" concentration of the first civilizations that has stayed with us and become more pronounced with increased specialization. Diffuse, "horizontal" awareness can also be characterized as attentive alertness and receptive readiness to act as needed, without anxious waiting. It includes the ability to scan the whole field and yet be attentive to details at the same time, rather than only being able to move between the two extremes.[47]

Moving with the internal horse then means being connected to the sensitive inner system that scans for incongruity and being able to read its messages. The horse is a psychopomp for recovering a crucial awareness that allows one to be aware of and to relate to one's emotions and to participate in the world with all senses. It involves recovering trust in one's somatic perception rather than relying on a stream of secondhand information and expert knowledge.

Perhaps here lies the origin of the symbolic power of the horse, coming from ancient times when everything had a soul and the horse was perceived with his/her magic qualities as they were right there, not yet abstracted in dictionaries of symbols. Imagination was part of the everyday reality rather than an impractical fancy of those few elected, crazy, or impractical enough to indulge it. "The mysterious paths of sympathetic excitation" are the paths of the horse as the carrier to the realms of our emotions and gut feelings and our unconscious, which is the contemporary residence of gods.

Becoming a horse is a magic transformation and an act of shape-shifting. The horse takes us magically to our own body or body-mind and our "sympathetic intelligence." It helps us to locate which of the strings under the stringboard of the viola d'amore start to vibrate when we are with others. This shape-shifting back and forth could also be expressed in the questions: What kind of a rider am I to my horse? And what/who is riding me as a horse? What possessed me? Which spirit, or in other words, archetype or complex? Connection to my internal horse might bring me closer to a way of living where, paraphrasing Rilke, I might be able to live the questions and eventually live into the answers—rather than wanting final answers, interpretations, and meaning—wrung out of both conscious and unconscious manifestations of my life.

SITTING IN THE HORSE'S GUT

> When man concentrates on the kettle down in his belly, he discovers that something happens. He pushes his libido down into the original primordial instinctive centers. It is just as if all the incompatibles in his consciousness, the raw materials, were gathered together and thrown down into the dark abyss of his sympathetic system, into the warmth of the body, well protected, and there begin to cook, to be transformed.[48]

Horses are creatures of immense physical power and vitality. As such they stand for sexuality and fertility, as shown, for example, by the Gallic goddess Epona, the Divine Horse, introduced into Britain and later adopted by the Romans.[49] Yet horses also have extremely sensitive enteric nervous systems. The small intestine automatically becomes inflamed as a protective response when the body feels threatened. Yet the horse's digestive system is so delicate that it cannot withstand this inflammation for long, and horses that are under prolonged stress conditions are more likely to get colic, which is the leading killer of domesticated horses. Horses that are around stressed humans who, however, lie to themselves and others about their emotional state, are more likely to develop colic.[50]

So here we enter the gut again, the origin of the "gut instinct" and part of the horse wisdom. While the sympathetic nervous system works through resonance, the gut responds with a strong reaction, as we often refer to "being hit in the gut" by something or someone. While the human gut can withstand inflammation longer than the horse gut can, it does not benefit from long-term unacknowledged stress either.[51] Anatomically, a network of fibers of the autonomic nervous system runs from the brain down to the gut. There the nerves wrap around the intestines and cause them to contract. So when we feel that something is "gut-wrenching," it is literally so. There are also rich connections between the amygdala in the temporal lobe of the brain and the stomach, which allow intense emotions like fear, anxiety, anger, rage, and threat to be felt in the stomach and the abdomen. As the amygdala also plays a part in memory, it is connected to the way in which traumatic experiences create changes in the gastrointestinal tract.[52] So when "something is sitting in our gut," it means that we are unable to digest it, whether it is physical food or emotional experience.

In Taoist alchemy, the stomach and spleen are the place of the earthy *yi* spirit that is at the center of the alchemical opus. It is located between the upper alchemical cauldron (chest) and the lower alchemical cauldron (the pelvic bowl). The *yi* spirit allows the yang energy of the mind to mix with the yin energies of the body. The *yi* holds the center and is the place of communication between above and below, between Heaven and Earth, without which Tao is lost. It is a middle ground between Spirit and Matter. It is in *yi* that vision and imagination find their way into a concrete form.[53]

So what then does sitting in the horse's gut mean? Or sitting in the human gut? As Hillman notes, there are different ways of dealing with our horse, horse here referring to our desires, strong emotions, and all those impulses that would fall under the heading "instinct."[54] After Buddha achieved enlightenment, he abandoned his horse and the horse died of grief. We can also try to slay the horse or let go of it. Yet there is another way: getting inside the horse to sit in the fire of its belly. To get into the horse's belly is to endure the fire of our emotions and desires. Sitting in the horse's belly we digest events, and brood on them. It is a place of incubation. The fire is contained. Now the fire horse sits within its fire rather than being buried in the river. This is an alchemical process. Within a sealed container we transform that which seems difficult, unbearable, or so ugly we want to bury it or drown it in water. The "raw materials," as

Jung calls them, are the alchemist's *prima materia*. Within the warmth of the belly they begin to cook. And the transformation process has begun.

CONCLUSION

In this essay I have focused on the horse as a symbol that can mediate between different worlds: the conscious and the unconscious, humans and the gods, body and mind, the soul and its lost parts, the ego and the gods and demons buried in the waters of the unconscious. In order to bring together the equine and human consciousness, I revisited my imaginal nomadic ancestors. This primeval connection of horse and human opened the way to a closer look at shape-shifting, whether as nomadic riders, centaurs, or the shamanic *táltos*, in both human and horse shape. I looked at the ability of horse as psychopomp to connect consciousness with the dissociated parts of the self, as has been done by shamanic practitioners from many different cultures. In this way, the horse with its symbolic potency can become aware of the drowned fire horses in the water of the unconscious.

I emphasized the ability of the horse to connect us with our "animal" wisdom, with the sympathetic nervous system that allows "resonating with" others and our sensory environment like a sensitive musical instrument. The horse is the being that can connect us to our gut instincts and teach emotional congruity, whether through imaginal shape-shifting or a more direct contact with the real horse as in equine therapy. The horse is the connection to our "wisdom of the prey" where emotional truth resides, and helps us bridge to a different kind of awareness: alert and attentive, embedded in its sensuous environment where it "in-dwells."

Finally, I entered the belly of the horse where the alchemical transformation from raw materials into the alchemical gold can happen. I believe that the symbol of the horse can connect us with the wilderness within, a wilderness that has retreated within while the outside has become increasingly civilized and tamed. To conclude this essay, I would like to quote Robin van Löben Sels:

> [T]he body is a landscape of truth-telling. It is as if an ancient, undivided world lies curled inside us with an ancestral memory of wilderness….Our true experience of the wild is inside us, beyond our ego or mental control, with rules and laws that do not obey our human will.[55]

NOTES

1. This image is from the fairy tale *Tři oříšky pro Popelku* [Three nuts for Cinderella] coproduced by DEFA - Studio für Spielfilm (East Germany)/Filmové Studio Barrandov (Czechoslovakia), directed by Václav Vorlícek, 1973. This is a different version from that of the Grimm brothers, as the feminine is more active. The union with the masculine comes from Cinderella's initiative.

2. Rudolf Ritsema, Shentana Augusto Sabbadini, *The Original I Ching Oracle* (London: Watkins, 2007), p. 84.

3. *Ibid.*, 85.

4. See James Hillman and Margot McLean, *Dream Animals* (San Francisco: Chronicle Books, 1997), p. 28.

5. C. G. Jung, quoted in Robin van Löben Sels, "When a body meets a body," in *Body and Soul, Spring* 72 (2005): 232.

6. J. C. Cooper, *Dictionary of Symbolical & Mythological Animals* (London: Thorsons, 1992), pp. 131-133.

7. The remains of the earliest domestic horses from Ukraine and some scattered sites as far west as Central Germany date back 6,000 years, although the earliest evidence of human-horse contact comes from the Magdalenian phase of the Upper Paleolithic in France and Spain, about 15,000 years ago. Ancient burial grounds reflect the sacrificial role of the horses who accompanied their owners to the otherworld, as was found in the tombs of Scythian nomads. The most famous horse sacrifices were Vedic, and also the ancient Roman October Horse festival. Juliet Clutton-Brock, *Horse Power: A History of the Horse and the Donkey in Human Societies* (Cambridge, MA: Harvard University Press, 1992), p. 11.

8. Linda Kohanov, *The Tao of the Equus* (Novato, CA: New World Library, 2001), p. 54. A similar argument is made by Michael Pollan in *The Botany of Desire: A Plant's-Eye View of the World* (New York: Random House, 2001), according to which humans did not domesticate plants (exert control over them), but plants intelligently used human desire to propagate themselves, seducing humans into believing they were the active agents—the masters in this process.

9. Otto J. Maenchen-Helfen, *The World of the Huns: Studies in Their History and Culture* (Berkeley, CA: University of California Press, 1973), pp. 2, 6.

10. Here I follow back in history the Hungarian part of my ancestry. The ancestral connection between the Huns and the Old Magyars has not been proved by research. Although some Hungarian historians like to claim continuity between the two, there is no evidence of such continuity, although Old Magyars might have been one of the tribes that comprised Huns, who were not a homogeneous ethnic group.

11. István Kiszely, *A magyarság őstörténete (Mit adot a magyarság a világnak)* [The ancient history of Magyars (What was the Magyars' contribution to the world)], vol. 1 (Budapest: Püski, 1996), p. 155.

12. Quoted in Hugh Kennedy, *Mongols, Huns & Vikings: Nomads at War* (London: Cassell, 2002), p. 29.

13. Maenchen-Helfen, *The World of the Huns*, pp. 205-206.

14. *Equus*, by Peter Shaffer; film version directed by Sidney Lumet, United Artists, 1977.

15. Cooper, *Dictionary of Symbolical & Mythological Animals*, p. 44.

16. Jean Chevalier and Alain Gheerbrant, *The Penguin Dictionary of Symbols*, trans. John Buchanan-Brown (New York: Penguin Books, 1996), p. 173.

17. Arnold Ipolyi, "Magyar mitológia" [Magyar mythology], in Vilmos Diószegi, ed., *Az ősi Magyar hitvilág* [The world of beliefs of the ancient Magyars], (Debrecen: Gondolat, 1978), pp. 211-212.

18. Cooper, *Dictionary of Symbolical & Mythological Animals*, p. 133.

19. The examples of such fairy tales would be the Magyar fairy tales "The tale of a prince, a king, and a horse" and "The tree that reached up to the sky"; the Slovak fairy tale "Popolvár, the greatest in the world"; the Russian fairy tale "The golden-bristled pig, the golden-feathered duck and the golden-maned mare"; and the Tartar fairy tale "Golden feather."

20. Ipolyi, "Magyar mitológia," pp. 211-212; Linda Dégh, *Folktales of Hungary* (Chicago: University of Chicago Press, 1969), pp. 311-313.

21. Jerome S. Bernstein, *Living in the Borderland: The Evolution of Consciousness and Challenge of Healing Trauma* (London: Routledge, 2005), p. 8.

22. C. G. Jung, quoted in Judith Harris, *Jung and Yoga: The Psyche-Body Connection* (Toronto: Inner City Books, 2001), p. 22.

23. Morris Berman, *Coming to Our Senses: Body and Spirit in the Hidden History of the West* (London: Unwin, 1990), pp. 63-72, quotation p. 64.

24. *Ibid.*, pp. 131-135.

25. Quoted in John P. Conger, *Jung & Reich: The Body as Shadow* (Berkeley, CA: Northatlantic Books, 2005), xiv.

26. Van Löben Sels, "When a body," p. 233.

27. Wilhelm Reich quoted in Will Johnson, *The Spiritual Practices of Rumi: Radical Techniques for Beholding the Divine* (Rochester, VT: Inner Traditions, 2007), p. 141.

28. *Eve & the Fire Horse*, directed by Julia Kwan, Red Star Productions, 2005.

29. For information on *hinoeuma* see Janis Cortese, "Onna no hinoeuma: What it means to be a fire horse woman," http://www.io.com/~cortese/hinoeuma/index.html (accessed 4 Jan 2009).

30. Mario Jacoby, *Individuation and Narcissism: The Psychology of the Self in Jung and Kohut* (London: Routledge, 1990); Alice Miller, *Drama of the Gifted Child*, rev. ed. (New York: Basic Books, 1997).

31. C. G. Jung, *The Collected Works of C. G. Jung*, trans. R. F. C. Hull, ed. H. Read, M. Fordham, G. Adler, Wm. McGuire, 20 vols. (Princeton, NJ: Princeton University Press, 1953-1979)(hereafter *CW*), vol. 9/1, § 40.

32. Sandra Ingerman, *Soul Retrieval: Mending the Fragmented Self* (San Francisco: HarperSanFrancisco, 1991).

33. Jung, "On the Nature of the Psyche," *CW* 8, § 365.

34. Jung, *CW* 8, § 582.

35. Jung, quoted in Donald Kalsched, *The Inner World of Trauma: Archetypal Defenses of the Personal Spirit* (New York: Brunner-Routledge, 1996), p. 13.

36. Jung, *CW* 8, § 586-594.

37. Kalsched, *The Inner World of Trauma*, p. 13. In this paper I will not go into a deeper discussion of trauma, as it is not its focus.

38. My knowledge about soul retrieval is based on the way it is taught by Sandra Ingerman and Michael Harner's Foundation for Shamanic Studies. Harner's research was focused on the Upper Amazon forest of South America, western North America, and Mexico. See Michael Harner, *The Way of the Shaman* (New York: Bantam, 1982).

39. Mircea Eliade, *Shamanism: Archaic Techniques of Ecstasy* (New York: Pantheon, 1964), pp. 168-176.

40. *Ibid.*, p. 408.

41. *Ibid.*, p. 217.

42. Kohanov, *The Tao of the Equus*, p. 86.

43. *Ibid.*, p. 88.

44. Jung, *CW* 9/1, § 45.

45. Miller, *Drama of the Gifted Child*; Jacoby, *Individuation and Narcissism*; Kalsched, *The Inner World of Trauma.*

46. Kohanov, *The Tao of the Equus*, pp. 101-132.

47. Morris Berman, *Wandering God: A Study in Nomadic Spirituality* (Albany, NY: State University of New York Press, 2000), pp. 19-47.

48. Jung, quoted in Conger, *Jung & Reich*, xxiv.

49. Cooper, *Dictionary of Symbolical & Mythological Animals*, p. 132.

50. Kohanov, *The Tao of the Equus*, pp. 142-148.

51. See, for example, Gabor Maté, *When the Body Says No: The Cost of Hidden Stress* (Toronto: Vintage Canada, 2004).

52. Mona Lisa Schulz, *Awakening Intuition: Using Your Mind-Body Network for Insight and Healing* (New York: Three Rivers Press, 1998), pp. 203-205.

53. Lorie Eve Dechar, *Five Spirits: Alchemical Acupuncture for Psychological and Spiritual Healing* (New York: Chiron Publications/Lantern Books, 2006), pp. 229-234.

54. Hillman and McLean, *Dream Animals*, p. 51.

55. Van Löben Sels, "When a body," p. 228.

THE FOUNTAIN OF MEMORIES— BURIED AND UNCOVERED

MARIA ANNA BERNASCONI
Translated by Heidemarie Fehlhaber

In this paper I will speak about the tradition of legends in the Valais, a mountain canton in southwestern Switzerland, and describe how this tradition had almost disappeared and then was revived. The attitude towards these legends has always been influenced by whether the *Zeitgeist* was open to this kind of tradition or adverse to it. I want to depict certain aspects of this development, showing which are important for the Valaisan tradition of legends. Furthermore, I want to show how these traditions have been revived and how this revival appears today. Finally, I will try to understand the processes from a Jungian point of view. I also refer to Jung's concept of symbolic life as presented in his work "The Symbolic Life."[1]

THE TERM "LEGEND"

First of all, I offer a short definition of the term I will be using throughout this essay. Legends tell about the strange—the totally different and monstrous—that breaks into a well-regulated and usually quite

Maria Anna Bernasconi is a graduate of the C. G. Jung Institute of Zurich and is a lecturer and participant at ISAPZurich. She wrote her diploma thesis about the Valaisan legends of the dead. Her interest is in ethnology and folklore, and she works as a Jungian analyst with expressive arts. She is also an artist.

comprehensible reality. Folk legends happen at a particular place and on a given site. Often the earthly protagonists acquire names, and sometimes there is a time specification. The figures in the legend are quite ordinary people, but in the legend they face something superhuman, ulterior, and numinous.[2] For this reason, the Jungian analyst and folklorist Gotthilf Isler believes that the alpine legends have religious meaning.[3]

THE *ZEITGEIST* OF THE REFORMATION AND ENLIGHTENMENT

What about folk traditions in Europe today? They were favored or rejected in varying degrees during particular historical eras. Christianity, which the nobility had adopted around 700 A.D. in the Alemannic territories of Central Europe, had to compromise a great deal in order to establish itself. Therefore it tolerated many of the pre-Christian traditions and allowed them to live on. It was Luther who brought a totally different spirit into Christianity. He and his fellow Protestants wanted to fight the old superstitions and to free Christianity from the tangle of a pagan underground. Calvin and Zwingli, in particular, questioned the value of images because they thought these distorted the message of the Holy Scriptures. So in various regions of Europe a fiery iconoclasm broke out, in which pictures and sculptures of saints and Christ were destroyed and defiled. At the same time, other folk traditions in all areas of life were looked upon with deep suspicion and were abolished if they were found to be pagan. Especially the charnel houses prevalent all over the country were terminated in the Reformed areas, and of course there were no relics in the Reformed churches any more. In the twentieth century, both charnel houses and relics have increasingly been abandoned in Roman Catholic areas as well.

The old folk traditions were challenged to an even greater extent by the spirit of the Enlightenment, which actually endeavored to wipe them out totally. Only the rational, provable, and explainable was considered valid. Even the senses were seen as unreliable because they could easily be misled. While one can appreciate this great cultural turn, it also had a shadow side. From this time on, anything emotional and irrational was fought against and suppressed. With the Enlightenment, the local legends of people along with other traditions were dismissed as superstition.

CULTURAL DEVELOPMENT IN THE VALAIS

At this point, I want to elucidate the specific circumstances in the

Valais in more detail. It seems to me that the mentality of the people in this mountain canton was strongly influenced by geography. The Valais lies in the southwestern part of Switzerland and essentially consists of a deep valley amidst high mountains. The valley runs from east to west with a slightly southern inclination, until in the lower Valais near Martigny it makes a short bend to the northwest and opens out to Lake Geneva. Aside from Mont Blanc, the highest mountains of the Alps are located in the Valais, among them the world-famous Matterhorn. Originally the Valais, which is the valley of the Rhone river, could only be reached through the narrow bend near Martigny. All the mountain passes into it are at a high level and hardly accessible. Until the beginning of the nineteenth century, the Valais could keep up quite well with the other mountain cantons, but beginning in the age of railway traffic it fell more and more behind. While Kaspar Stockalper, the famous merchant from Brig, located in the center of the Valais, definitely played his part in the best European circles during the Baroque era, circumstances changed enormously later on. In the nineteenth and twentieth centuries, traffic accelerated more and more, and the Valais could not keep up with this development because its high mountains functioned as massive barriers in almost all directions. As the main valley does not intersect the Alps from north to south, the expansion of the transportation routes for European traffic was not relevant either. This was reserved for the region of the Gotthard. It was only around 1900 that the important tunnels at Simplon and Lötschberg were constructed.

The Valais virtually got stuck in the seventeenth century, and so Biffiger writes:

> Everything is just old, very old in this region which during the superficial Christianization—like that of all Germanic peoples—has never adopted a transvaluation of the old values, it refrained from the Reformation and closed its doors against the Enlightenment, and only today it has entered a new era of thinking and acting.[4]

The Valais remained Roman Catholic, which also contributed to the fact that the old traditions were maintained to a great extent. Also in its dialects it preserved a strongly archaic quality, both in the German-speaking and the francophone areas. Besides Middle High German, the German dialect has preserved many Old High German elements, and therefore is sometimes hard to understand for the other German-speaking Swiss. But even the Valaisans from different villages sometimes did not

understand each other in former times, because—at least during the wintertime—they lived very isolated from each other and therefore developed
dialects of their own.

The Valaisans in the old times were mountain farmers. They lived on
livestock farming, some crops, and viticulture. By means of an elaborate
irrigation system, the land was kept very fertile, but since it is spread out
over the mountainsides and up to great altitudes, the farmers were forced
into a seminomadic way of life. From springtime on into summertime,
they moved higher and higher with their cattle, but at the same time they
had to return to work in the fertile fields and vineyards further down in
the valley, which meant a constant movement to and fro. Regarding their
daily bread, they were self-supporting. Most of them were poor because
the ground only yielded fruit if a lot of work was invested. Extraordinary
work like the construction of houses out of larch wood and the annual
cleaning of the vitally important aqueducts was done cooperatively.
Social cohesion was very important. The scarce free time, too, was spent
together. However, this closeness implied a very high degree of social control. Just as the mountains limited the horizon, the perspective of individuals, and particularly of women, had narrow limits. Men could at least
become priests, while for women there was just a terrible amount of work,
childbirth, and child-raising.

THE EVENING SEAT

So what to do during free time? As there was no radio or television at
that time, people had to entertain one another. And so they sat together
and talked to each other, sometimes working a bit together, the women
knitting or spinning, the men giving them a little assistance. Sometimes
they also sang or even prayed together. And of course they told stories. As
all of this took place in the evening when there was time for it, it was
called *Abendsitz*, "evening seat or sitting." These kinds of communal
gatherings were common all over Europe. Sometimes they were called
Abendsitz, sometimes *Spinnstubeten* ("spinning parlors") or *Lichtstubeten*
("light parlors").[5]

TELLING LEGENDS

At such evening sittings the people told stories and legends. While
this tradition was also common in other places, nowhere in Europe was it
kept up as intensively as it was in the Valais. Here this custom remained

intact until the 1950s. Forty- to fifty-year-old residents of the Valais can still report that they experienced such meetings. The last of these meetings took place in the alps, where most families had their cattle grazing during the summertime. All reports describe what a memorable experience it was to listen to such legend-telling at the evening seat. Old and young alike shuddered when they were told about an eerie ghost encounter.

In what follows, I will primarily be speaking about the Upper Valais, which was settled from the north in the eighth and ninth centuries by Alemannians. I do this because my paternal ancestors were Upper Valaisans, and therefore I am more at home in this part of the canton. Unfortunately it is the case that the two parts of the canton hardly ever deal with each other, which is so for historical reasons; to specify these reasons would not be useful here. Also in cultural matters the two parts of the canton have little influence on each other. Yet much of what I say about the German Upper Valais also applies to the French Lower Valais.

THE POOR SOULS

In the Valais many archaic customs have been maintained, but principally it was known among folklorists for its legends because there was such great abundance of them. The legends about the Poor Souls, in particular, are numerous among them. The Poor Souls are the spirits of the deceased who have to wander on earth for some time, with or without a reason. Partly this wandering is a specific version of the Christian purgatory, partly the idea of this procession of the dead has developed from the Germanic idea of the army of the dead moving through the air at night with Wotan. The Valaisans in particular knew about these spirits of the dead, and in former times all children knew what to do if they met such a spirit or even a procession of dead. Many of these characteristic religious beliefs are hardly to be found at any other place, e.g., the idea that the dead must expiate their purgatory time in the glaciers. Even in the 1970s I met people who were absolutely convinced that the dead appear to the living.

During my study of the legends of the dead among the Alemannic peoples of the Valais, I found out that nearly all the popular beliefs were packed into these legends. A central motif is the idea that the dead appear to the living, who are supposed to help them reach salvation. Sometimes the dead also help the living, but this help is not always evident. Since the living often fall into danger when meeting the dead, the legends of the dead include behavioral instructions. Thus the belief in spirits of the dead generates many rituals that should be followed. Doubtless this belief in spirits of the dead includes a remainder of age-old ancestor worship. I possess a tape-recorded broadcast of Radio Rotten Oberwallis, where several old people tell about the Poor Souls and that they actually had always prayed to them[6]—*to* them, not only *for* them, as is mostly said.

It is certainly not by accident that the spirits of the dead and anything connected with death are so prevalent in the Valaisan legends, since life was often extremely precarious in this hard and rough landscape, and dealing with death and dying was almost routine.

The first to record these legends were two priests, Moritz Tscheinen and Peter Joseph Ruppen, who published them in 1872.[7] Like many other educated people in Europe, they had been inspired by the Brothers Grimm not only to collect fairy tales but also old folk legends. From 1960 to 1963, the folklorist Josef Guntern visited all the villages in the Upper Valais and systematically compiled—before they were likely to vanish—all the folk tales and evaluated them scientifically. He also set up a list with details on particular narrator personalities.[8]

The Valais in the Twentieth Century:
Decline of the Old Traditions

The old economic and cultural life in the Valais came to an end with the construction of new roads, cable cars, and the emergence of mass tourism after the war and during the time of postwar prosperity. The Valaisans were abruptly torn out of their tranquillity, but also out of the austerity of their mountain farming life.[9] What lightly developed industry and the Enlightenment had not managed to achieve now happened: the Valaisans wanted and needed to catch up with the times if they did not want to face the young folks' emigration and an increasing depopulation of the villages. The Valaisans wanted to belong to modern times now, and they did not want to be laughed at as hicks and excluded in the lowlands because of their peculiar language and their strange customs. Their legends did not fit into the present time. So the Valaisans began to disdain and feel ashamed of their own traditions. When in 1997 I started to question old Valaisans about the legends, they made it very clear to me that they were not so stupid as to believe in those old stories! Interestingly, people who had moved out of the Valais had a more positive attitude towards the old traditions.

Revival

At about the same time, I discovered a kind of local revival of these old traditions. Some tourist offices began to offer "evening seats" during the summer high season. My research showed that this revival had started some fifteen years before. The initial impression that these events made on tourists has not been reported. Whenever I attend them, I see that most of the participants by far are locals.

New CDs with Valaisan legends have been produced, partly told in dialect, but also in High German.[10] The theme "legends" was mentioned in most of the prospectuses meant for tourists, e.g., in the prospectus of the Matterhorn-Gotthard railway.[11] Not only the legends, but also the motif of the spirits of the dead has been mentioned again and again in books on the Valais and in folklorist literature. Thus it is said about the Natischerberg near the Massa Canyon, for instance, that according to legend the Poor Souls are allowed to roam here at night, between the witching hour and dawn, from All Saints Day until the fourteenth of January.[12] A publication from 2003 on living in the Upper Valais refers to the house as a controversial place of the spirits: "And as we are speaking about the paranormal dimensions of residing here, we also want to point out the controversial function of the house and the residence as a place of *bozen* spirits."[13] Another publication tells about the shrinking of the glaciers and the increasing tourism and raises the question of how the Poor Souls may fare as a result.[14] Also, in the nature study publication of Laudo Albrecht on the Aletsch region, it is reported that in the crevasses innumerable Poor Souls still await salvation.[15] In a reference to the Chapel of the Poor Souls in the Trämel, it is explicitly mentioned that this chapel is above the Massa Canyon and close to the Aletsch Glacier, where according to popular belief the Poor Souls do penance and the procession of the dead passes through. The Valaisan mountain village Eischoll gave a path the name Gratzugweg,[16] Procession Path, presuming that the procession of the dead will always take particular paths that are precisely known. The legends about the dead are strongly prevalent in the new preoccupation with legends.

The theme of the spirits of the dead is also being treated in all kinds of artistic productions. A play from the beginning of the last century, "D'alt Schmittja," with a prominent Valaisan figure of legend, has been put on stage again.[17] Particular people specialize in legend telling. Andreas Weissen, a well-known legend teller from Brig, told me that he can live, though modestly, on legend telling. The hotel keeper Bernhard Schmid offers an evening seat for his guests every Wednesday night in the Hotel Glocke in Reckingen, where he tells Valaisan legends. A small group of women, the Boozu-Team,[18] annually organizes a legend evening where they tell legends on a stage in a performance-like way together with other inhabitants of the Agarn village. New plays that are written for these very active amateur theater groups often deal with legend themes. The group "Szenographie," for example, creates plays where the performances are embedded in the landscape of Visperterminen. The old cots and barns serve as sites for particular scenes. The performance even includes an aerial cableway ride that leads over the small chapels of a Way of the Cross.[19] Frequently the performances are designed with the local legends of a specific village or little town. For several years the well-known holiday village, Fiesch, in the Goms, has organized night hikes at the full moon during the summertime, where the telling of legends takes center stage, the so-called "Gratzugnacht,"[20] procession-of-the-dead night. The hike leads from Fiesch Village through the Fiesch Valley to Lake Märjelen on the brink of the Aletsch Glacier, which again is a place that is linked with many legends.

There is a piece by the alternative folk music group, "Oberwalliser Spillit," called "Armeseelenjodler," Poor Souls Yodel.[21] The two Valaisan singers Erika Stucky and Sina together sing a song about their mothers, where they lament that now the mothers are dead they have to go all alone to the land of the Poor Souls.[22] Artists illustrate a legend book with the appropriate drawings.[23] Paintings with legend motifs are created.[24] One of the figure groups of Katrin Riesterer is taken as a motif on a label for a red wine from a well-known Valaisan wine village.[25]

When I spoke with Katrin Riesterer, she told me that in preparing her figures she got into contact with old people who told her about their own experience and beliefs regarding the Poor Souls. I mentioned above that meeting with the Poor Souls required specific behaviors from the living. In former times, they always took care that they cleaned the paths that the spirits of the dead would tread of all obstacles. If you did not do that, it might turn out badly for you. Katrin Riesterer said to me that an old man from Saas Fee admitted that he still sees to it that the paths of the dead are clean.

In many different ways, it can be seen that local traditions are being revived in Central Europe. It seems that the time has come to rediscover one's own "Indians," after decades of spotting them only on foreign continents. Being occupied with the non-native obviously led to discovering parallels in one's own traditional culture.

Only fifty years ago the Valaisans epitomized a backwoods character; today Valaisan people and their dialect are seen as original and interesting, yet somewhat different and special.

What Has Disappeared?

The old belief in the spirits of the dead certainly does not exist anymore. While in my father's generation nobody doubted the existence of these spirits, this is no longer true for people today. Also, the many rituals linked with the belief that the Poor Souls have to wander are gone now. People do not devote milk spilled by mistake to them anymore, nor do they leave a window open a slit during wintertime to give them a chance to warm themselves. There are no water vessels deposited for them anymore to let them satisfy their thirst. The alp pastures are not left vacant during the wintertime anymore; instead a major flood of tourists comes there for winter sports. In former times, the alps belonged to the spirits from October 16, St. Gallus Day, on. And even less does it occur to modern people to remove an alp hut because otherwise the procession of the dead will go right through it. Scarcely anybody will clear the streets, like that old man, in order to let the procession have its way. For many years, no one has heard that a Reverend had to ban a spirit because it was raising too much trouble.[26] Nor do I ever hear of the "Quatember children"[27] now, persons who because of the time of their birth have second sight and therefore, unlike other people, can see the spirits.

Other things have vanished that certainly no one regrets. Even in the Valais the rigid sexual morals of yore do not prevail anymore, and the position of women has crucially changed for the better—surely a state of affairs that nobody wants to reverse.

What Has Remained?

Yet some rituals and symbols have lasted. People still deposit candles for the deceased at the few remaining charnel houses. And in the Upper Valais there are still two Poor Souls chapels—one in the outer Aletschji, the other in the Trämel, both of them in the communal region of Naters. Following the old tradition, people hang up little memorial pictures that appeal for prayers for the dear deceased. There, too, we see candles burning and little pictures added all over again.

WHAT HAS BEEN REDISCOVERED?

There has been a great revival of the tradition of legend telling and of putting legend themes onstage. It seems worth mentioning that the legend themes are presented in such a way that they can be experienced. Often they are transferred into a contemporary artistic form. The treatment is, at least as regards the contents of the legends, mostly based on written traditional texts. But often these are slightly altered, humorous elements are added, and certain motifs are adapted to modern thinking. What remains evident is the love and respect for the tradition, even though sometimes there are also ironic and critical tones, particularly towards ecclesiastical traditions. Surprisingly, the sometimes really eerie and horrible motifs are not at all moderated or eliminated. An example follows.

DANSE MACABRE ON THE EGGA

Once, in late autumn, a young man had been lumbering in a hamlet high up the Natischerberg, and in the evening on his way home he passed an old building from whence he suddenly heard the sound of music. He wanted to see what was going on there, and so he peeped through the door. He saw people in old-fashioned clothes dancing in circles, and their clothes were decorated all over with icicles jingling at each step. He realized at once that these were deceased people, and when he thought he recognized his girlfriend, who had recently died, he panicked and ran away helter-skelter.

At home, he went to bed immediately and hid under the blanket. But it did not help him. The front door opened and so did the door to his room, and he heard the jingling of the little icicles. An ice-cold shadow bent over him and something slipped into his bed. Out of fear he shouted: "Jesus, Mary and Joseph, who are you?" At that moment he lost his fear, and the ghost, upon being addressed by a living person, could answer: "I am Emma, your recently deceased sweetheart. I come from the Aletsch Glacier, and I must dance here with the others on the holy days because I did that again and again during my lifetime, so this is my penance. Now I ask you whether you want to help me and the others, but it is going to be hard." The young man agreed, and they went on talking for a long time.

Afterwards he never said a word about what she had told him and what he had promised her. From that time on, he was a different person. He did not get married, and remained a steady friend of the Poor Souls just as if he had entered into a spiritual marriage with Emma. The one thought for his lifetime was Emma. As he came to die and he heard the name "Emma," he smiled as if he remembered a good deed.[28]

So far the wording of the traditional legend. Today the idea of the good deed obviously is no longer up to date, so this part of the story has been replaced. It now says that after their encounter that night, Emma and the young man lived in marriage, and when it came time for him to die they blessedly stayed together in the other world. For modern people, it is obviously not enough that they meet in the other world only. Perhaps the archetype of the *coniunctio* needs to be visible at a more concrete level today. Yet the relationship still lasts beyond death!

Certainly one cannot say that the belief in spirits of the dead who have to wander after death has come back. Today people rather think that we do not know all of what exists between heaven and earth, and that there actually may be more than science can explain. Around 1960, Josef Guntern's interviewees often said that they did not know what to believe, but that the father, the grandmother, or the uncle who had told them about a legend were no liars.[29]

It seems to me that with the revival of the old legends a piece of the old community life has returned. The local people go to these performances because they are also about the legends of their ancestors. The performances offer an opportunity for identification; people have the same cultural roots just as they have the same ancestors. Not all of the motifs of the Valaisan legends may be unique, yet this world of legends has a unique coloring that cannot be found anywhere else. This world of legends has a special character.

The feeling quality of the evening seat is something that has also been revived. As far as I can see, the eerie features, characteristic of so many legends, have not been removed in these performances, and the audience may definitely shudder in the face of the drastic images.

WHAT CAN BE SAID FROM A JUNGIAN POINT OF VIEW?

This new interest in local, idiosyncratic things appears like a counterpoint to globalization, and here I would see Jung's idea of enantiodromia at work.[30] In other words, the revival of the tradition of legends, particularly in the forms it actually took, seems to confirm the creative ability of the unconscious psyche, all by itself as it were, to hit upon the proper remedy to prevent the impending split in the psyche between a superficial adaptation to modernity with its corresponding loss of meaning, on the one hand, and the archaic heritage, on the other. This archaic heritage carries a tremendous power, as we are gradually coming to understand now. To tell one's own legends actually has a lot to do with rootedness, which is, in my view, something people really need today. The legends are always connected with a particular place in a particular landscape and with particular people, and when the legends are told again they reestablish this connection. In his writings, Jung never ceased to underline the paramount importance of maintaining a connection with the ancestors up to the furthermost distances in time.[31] I cannot easily imagine anything more effective in bringing about a sense of rootedness than dealing with the ancestors' traditions.

We know from his autobiography, *Memories, Dreams, Reflections*, that Jung himself had seen spirits of the dead, namely, in the tower at Bollingen.[32] Furthermore, there are passages in his correspondence where he refers to Wotan's procession of the dead in a dream interpretation.[33]

SYMBOLIC LIFE

As we know, it was in 1939 when Jung gave his lecture titled "The Symbolic Life" to the Guild of Pastoral Psychology in London. There he said that during forty years of psychotherapeutic practice he treated only very few actively practicing Roman Catholics. He thought that there was something in the cult, in the religious practices themselves, that led to the fact that believing Catholics suffered less from neurotic symptoms.[34] According to Jung, the holy Mass of the Roman Catholic Church includes a living mystery: the transformation of bread and wine into the body and blood of Christ, which then is shared with the believers in a mystic communion. There are many other holy rites and rituals of the church as well: holy water dispensed on special occasions, the preparation of the baptismal water, etc.[35] If all these things are seen as really alive and effective, they are not merely physically or metaphorically suggestive actions, and therefore they have a profound psychological impact on the believers. Jung's note on the age of these ritual actions is very important: without exception, they all have ancient pre-Christian origins and go back into prehistoric times. Symbolic life always seems to be nurtured by rituals, i.e., by actions that are done with the body and are available to the senses (for example, the censing during a high Mass).

Jung mentions rites in India where he had seen that people had a corner in the house, separated by a curtain, where they could execute their private rituals for their gods.[36] Of course, the "Herrgottswinkel," the Lord's nooks, occurred to me right away. These were an inherent feature in the parlors of the Valaisan farmhouses and were similarly present in other Catholic regions in Central Europe as well. There would be a cross, a statue of the Virgin Mary, or a picture of a saint. There was also somewhere a little niche in the wall for a statue. Especially in the Valais, Catholic rituals influenced the whole of everyday life, and these routines were maintained for a very long time and to a high degree. The archaic was preserved much longer in the Valais because of its isolation.

The folk traditions, too, with their great abundance of sometimes age-old rituals, belong to the symbolic life of the common folk.[37] In former times, the priests also joined in the folk belief in the spirits of the dead. Often they functioned as exorcists; certain saintly priests were in close contact with the deceased, and their advice was sought when someone had encountered a spirit. Those priests obviously knew how to adjust the Catholic dogma to the spiritual needs of the parishioners entrusted to them, and thus really care for their souls. In turn, the people willingly accepted the idea that the deceased had to wander, as a kind of purgatory in penance for their sins. The idea of penance is rejected by most of today's legend tellers.

The custom of the evening seat is itself a ritual and a form of rootedness with the people present, and the mystery of the *numinosum* ("*fascinosum et tremendum*") is experienced with all the senses. I think this is also one of the factors that is involved in this revival: The contents are transferred through the senses, playfully and artistically. The psyche obviously needs the eerie motifs beyond all reason, and that is why they are passed down. Mirjam Britsch said in 1994 that the Valaisans had lost a piece of their soul in giving up the evening seat.[38] With the revival of the legends and the evening seat, the Valaisans may have regained a bit of their soul.

Jung says that doubt kills the mystery.[39] For the Valaisans, too, the old belief in the spirits of the dead has perished in its traditional form. But the legends and their contents live on, and they are actually celebrated. It is as if the archetypical energy enclosed in these legends cannot be annihilated and breaks through into life in a new form. Maybe it is important for them to be artistically framed, to be shaped quite consciously, or this energy might otherwise have a destructive impact.

Can Jungians contribute to the continuing success of such pleasurable revivals? Jung himself has shown us that we should take traditions seriously if somebody brings them along to us in analysis, and if necessary we should trace them back as far as possible. He indicates exactly when it is necessary or, more precisely, the dreams indicate it.[40] Individuals who need to reconnect themselves with their traditions are advised through dreams, fantasies, or symptoms. So we as therapists must not oppose it, but we should rather find a positive attitude towards the traditions and see them as something precious. We should not dismiss them as superstitious nonsense or as obsolete and uptight Christian morality, but rather look for the positive in the cultural shadow. In my view, it is one of our most important tasks to help our clients reassess particular factors of their psychic life, and this often involves their cultural identity. This can be crucial in individual work with people from foreign cultures, who actually often have an ambivalent attitude towards their own culture. Many foreign cultures are strongly discriminated against in our West-oriented countries.

Another possible contribution of Jungians is being made by colleagues in many areas of the world who are highly interested in registering cultural phenomena including traditions in all their details, describing them and gaining deeper understanding. Many Jungians have written papers dealing with religious and folk-religious symbolism. Jung says the symbol always exceeds our conscious knowledge of a matter. As long as it is alive, a genuine symbol can never be totally interpreted. As Jungians we always approach symbolic material with respect for its being as such, and for its liveliness.[41] It is fatal for a symbol if we think: "It is nothing but…"[42] We should rather maintain a beginner's spirit, as Jung recommends for dreams. He says that when listening to a dream he made it a rule to tell himself: "I have no idea what this dream means."[43] Only then would he be able to start exploring the dream. Sometimes an appropriate interpretation can deepen the experience; sometimes we have to let the energy work as we are used to doing with the material of active imagination. Always helpful is enriching with other archetypal material by amplification —and interest, curiosity, suspense, surprise, and playful handling are absolutely essential when dealing with symbolic material. Sometimes ruminant circling around is much better than the endeavor to understand too much too quickly.

NOTES

1. C. G. Jung, "The Symbolic Life," in vol. 18 (1976) of *The Collected Works of C. G. Jung*, trans. R. F. C. Hull, ed. H. Read, M. Fordham, G. Adler, Wm. McGuire, 20 vols. (Princeton, NJ: Princeton University Press, 1953-1979)(hereafter *CW*), § 608-696.

2. Max Lüthi, *Volksmärchen und Volkssage: Zwei Grundformen erzählender Dichtung* (Bern/München: Francke Verlag, 1961).

3. Gotthilf Isler, *Lumen Naturae: Zum religiösen Sinn von Alpensagen, Vorträge und Aufsätze*, Jungiana, Beiträge zur Psychologie von C. G. Jung, series B, vol. 5 (Küsnacht: Verlag Stiftung für Jungsche Psychologie, 2000).

4. Karl Biffiger and Oswald Ruppen, *Wallis, Erbe und Zukunft* (Bern: Verlag Paul Haupt, 1975), p. 126. For cultural-historical development in the Valais, see also Mirjam Britsch, *Wallis im Wandel* (Gümlingen/Bonn/Wien: Zytglogge Verlag, 1994). Mirjam Britsch is a psychologist and ethnologist and thus well suited to report on this cultural change.

5. Hanns Bächtold-Stäubli, ed., *Handwörterbuch des deutschen Aberglaubens* (Berlin: Walter de Gruyter, 1987), s.vv. Lichtabend: vol. VII, p. 754; Lichtstuben: vol. VII, p. 674. Also see Jakob and Wilhelm Grimm, *Deutsches Wörterbuch* (Leipzig: Hirzel, 1860), s.v. Lichtstubete, vol. 12, p. 893. Also see the legend of the canton Zurich that K. W. Glättli talks about in *Zürcher Sagen*, II, Oberland Nr. 46, p. 96.

6. Reinhard Eyer, *Die Armen Seelen*, radio transmission with Arthur and Leo Eggel, Radio Rotten Oberwallis Visp, October 1998.

7. Moritz Tscheinen and Peter Joseph Ruppen, *Walliser Sagen* (Zürich: Olms, 1979, reprint of the Sitten edition, 1872).

8. Josef Guntern, *Volkserzählungen aus dem Oberwallis: Sagen, Legenden, Märchen, Anekdoten aus dem deutschsprechenden Wallis* (Basel: Verlag G. Krebs, 1979).

9. A psychiatrist with Valaisan origins, Gottlieb Guntern, also reports on these effects in his book *Social Change, Stress and Mental Health in the Pearl of the Alps* (New York: Springer Verlag, 1979).

10. Beat Albrecht and Matthias Bärenfaller, *Hundert Jahr nur ein Tag: Walliser Sagen, erzählt in Walliser Mundart* (Visp: Rotten Verlag, 2002), and *Der Geiger nach dem Tod: Walliser Sagen erzählt in Hochdeutsch* (Visp: Rotten Verlag, 2003). Karl Biffiger, *Rollibock: Karl Biffiger erzählt Walliser Sagen*, 2 CDs, live recordings from the Berner

Kleintheater "Die Rampe," 1972, ROMM (Visp: Rotten Verlag, 2006). Bernhard Schmid (Gioco), *Sagen,* CD (Reckingen: Hotel Glocken). Speedy (Gilbert Jossen) and Corinne Stadler, *Saguhaft—Dr schwarz Tänzer, Walliser Sagen gesungen und vertont* (Visp: Radio Rotten Oberwallis, 2009).

11. Text *Sagenhaft* in *Geheimtip Gornergrat* (Matterhorn Gotthard Bahn: *Zuglektüre. On Board Reading*), p. 36.

12. See Louis Carlen, *Naters-Blatten-Belalp, Schweizer Heimatbücher,* no. 168 (Bern: Verlag Paul Haupt, 1973), p. 6.

13. Verein Z'Tärbinu, *Wohnen in Visperterminen und im Oberwallis 1950-1997*; Verein Z'Tärbinu, *Wohnen in Visperterminen und im Oberwallis 1900-1950, Begleitpublikation zum Wohnmuseum Visperterminen* (Visperterminen: S & Z Print, 1997), p. 39. For the term "Bozen" also see note 18.

14. Volmar Schmid, ed., *Kulturführer zur Geografie, Geschichte, Wirtschaft, Sprache und Kultur: Brig, Glis, Naters und Ried-Brig* (Brig: Verlag Wir Walser, 2001), p. 151.

15. Laudo Albrecht, *Aletsch—Eine Landschaft erzählt, Die Reichtümer der Natur im Wallis* (Visp: Rotten Verlag, 1997), p. 28.

16. "Gratzug" is a special Valaisan name for the procession of the dead.

17. Theaterverein Naters: *D'alt Schmidtja*, performance video of the play with the same title by Ernst Klingele, dialect version by Walter Zenhäusern, directed by W. Zenhäusern, 1998.

18. "Boozu" is a specifically Valaisan word and means "spirit, ghost." See Antiquarische Gesellschaft in Zürich, *Schweizerisches Idiotikon: Wörterbuch der schweizerdeutschen Sprache*, vol. 4 (Frauenfeld: J. Huber Verlag, 1901), p. 1994f., s.v. "Boz."

19. P. I. Szenographie Schweiz: *sagenhaft*, radio play of the project *sagenhaft* from Visperterminen, summer 2004, and also the DVD of the performance of "Versehen Vergehen—eine inszenierte Sesselbahnfahrt durchs Jenseits," 2007, where the same group again staged a performance with legend themes and included the whole village and the cable car.

20. See note 16.

21. Oberwalliser Spillit on CD Holliger Heinz, *Alp-Chehr*, Nr 9, *Totutanz*, "Dance of the Dead."

22. To be seen and heard in the music film *Heimatklänge*, about cheering and other chants, by Stefan Schwietert, with Erika Stucky,

Noldi Alder, Christian Zehnder, Sina, Stimmhorn, Huun Huur Tu, Paul Giger, Knut Jensen, production maximage GmbH Zürich 2007.

23. Wilhelm Ebener, *Illustrierte Walliser Sagen* (Visp: Rotten Verlag, 1995). The legends have been illustrated by various artists.

24. Some of them are exhibited in the Lötschentalermuseum at Kippel.

25. Ames perdues, Gamay 2005 AOC Valais Varone Sion, Cuvées des Métiers d'Art.

26. All of these behaviors have been suggested in the legends as being desirable; see Guntern, *Volkserzählungen aus dem Oberwallis*, pp. 341-664.

27. Quatember (from Latin, *ieiunia quattuor temporum*, "four jejune times," i.e., Lenten seasons) denominates the days of penance in the church year originally dedicated to fasting, praying, and giving alms, and taking place four times a year. The Quatember dates are approximately the same as the beginnings of the four seasons.

28. Abridged by the author after Guntern, *Volkserzählungen aus dem Oberwallis*, p. 448.

29. And that is the title of a CD with a compilation of Valaisan legends: Andreas Weissen, *Dr Ettro isch kei Lugner gsii* (in High German: Der Onkel war kein Lügner, The uncle was no liar), Andreas Weissen erzählt Walliser Sagen in Mundart (Visp: Rotten Verlag, 2005). See also Guntern, *Volkserzählungen aus dem Oberwallis*, pp. 364, 382, 393.

30. Jung, "Definitions," in *Psychological Types*, *CW* 6 (1921/1976), a revision by R. F. C. Hull of the trans. by H. G. Baynes, § 716ff.

31. For Jung the heritage of the ancestors is always linked with the archetypal dimension; see Jung, *Two Essays on Analytical Psychology*, *CW* 7 (1953), § 119-120; *The Structure and Dynamics of the Psyche*, *CW* 8 (1953), § 98, 230, 337, 570ff. ("The Psychological Foundations of the Belief in Spirits"), 712-720; *The Archetypes and the Collective Unconscious*, *CW* 9/1 (1959), § 84, 224, 227, 316, 387, 498f., 518; *Aion: Researches into the Phenomenology of the Self*, *CW* 9/2 (1959), § 50, 422; *Psychology and Alchemy*, *CW* 12 (1953), § 105, 169-171.

32. C. G. Jung, *Memories, Dreams, Reflections* (New York: Pantheon, 1973), pp. 228-231.

33. C. G. Jung, 30 November 1960: To Olga von Koenig-Fachsenfeld, in *Letters 1951-1961* (London: Routledge & Kegan Paul,

1976), pp. 611-612; Jung, *Civilization in Transition*, *CW* 10 (1953), §
701.

34. Obviously this fact, for that time, was substantiated by various
studies. See Jung, *The Symbolic Life*, *CW* 18, § 610-612. It is difficult to
say what the outcome of such studies would be today.

35. *Ibid.*, § 615.

36. *Ibid.*, § 626.

37. Biffiger must have had a similar view, as he said: "In telling a
legend the Valaisan gives away secrets from the core of his soul. But you
do not share such secrets with a stranger" (trans. H. Fehlhaber): see
Mirjam Britsch, *Wallis im Wandel*, p. 12.

38. *Ibid.*

39. Jung, *The Symbolic Life*, *CW* 18, § 632.

40. *Ibid.*, § 634ff.

41. Jung, "Definitions," *CW* 6, § 819ff.

42. Jung, *CW* 18, § 633.

43. Jung, *CW* 8, § 533.

A COLLECTIVE SYMBOLIC LIFE OF NOTHINGNESS IN POSTMODERN TIMES

BERNARD SARTORIUS

I will use the concept "collective symbol" when speaking of collective manifestations (buildings, rituals, texts such as constitutions, etc.) in which the collective, either directly or through political/economic rulers and/or power structures that are more or less supported or at least accepted by the population, has invested its main libido—usually in the form of money, labor forces, and mental efforts (institutions of learning).

By "postmodern times," I mean our present period, some fifteen to twenty-five years after the disappearance of the ideologies alive in the twentieth century (Communism, Fascism, etc.).

In every period, collective symbols of past periods are still around, but one can try to spot the most recent collective symbol, the "symbolic vanguard," so to speak, which indicates the beginning of a next step in the evolution of collective symbolism.

In the collective symbols, we can try to see how, on the collective level, psychic life is viewed and experienced. In the visible collective aspects of religion (churches, etc.), economic and political powers, collec-

Bernard Sartorius is a training and supervising analyst at ISAPZurich. His particular interests are Near-Eastern spirituality and its implications for Western culture, and for analytical psychology in particular. He travels frequently to Arabic countries and lectures widely about the meaning of Islam for the psyche of modern people.

tive works of art and monuments, etc.—wherever the collective libido is invested—we can spot essential features of the psychic life of a whole society.

Our presupposition is that collective symbolic life is of paramount importance for the psychological life of the individual, for it conditions to a large extent the way individuals experience symbols, hence the way they experience themselves, their psyche, and its symbols (dreams, etc.).

It seems to me that we are tending at present in our Western culture towards a collective symbolism of Nothingness, in the sense that there is nothing behind the realities as they appear phenomenologically, and this "nothingness" tends to dissolve the fantasy that there should be a deeper meaning to life than the just-givenness. As it compensates thousands of years of meaningfulness, Nothingness as symbol of our time tends to be nihilistic, in the sense that it tends to devaluate and destroy the reality of life, of psychic life in particular.

This present mythic constellation may result from an evolution start-ing, in fact, with the ancient Greeks, an evolution that initiated a growing number of splits, as I will try to show, in the perception of reality—a growing number of splits that, according to my hypothesis, have finally led to a gap, a "nothingness" in postmodern Western man's perception of reality, like a hole appearing in a cloth that is torn apart from all sides.

CULTURAL HISTORY AND BACKGROUND

Before looking more closely at today's collective symbols in order to understand why they are all pointing at symbolic Nothingness, I will glance at an example of collective symbols of each of the main cultural-historical periods preceding and determining ours, by paying special attention to the way the collective of each period has invested its energies.

In Old Egypt, the major collective symbolic investments were the tombs and temples. They, especially the tombs, feature an architectural element that is highly significant for our subject: the "false door." It is the sculpture of a door, not a real door, being usually part of the wall behind the sarcophagus—or the "Holy of Holies," in some temples. It is an image of an intimate connection between this life and the other life. In other words, the "concrete" experience of life and its "poetical" (religious in this case) perception are very close, though not identical; the "door" stands between two "dimensions"—the one of the living, and the one of the gods and the dead. But it is a door, so the "other side" is very close. Coming from the gods or the souls of the deceased, this "poetical" experience of life is given, not fabricated: the "spirit" or the "god" can go freely through the "door," coming from the "other side," whereas from "this side" any striving for it hits solid stone. So the "false door" can be seen as an image of the way the Old Egyptians related symbolically to life: the Mystery is very close to daily life experience, and the whole of life is an expression of a (hidden, behind the "false door") mystery. Consciousness of reality is at once consciousness of presence and absence, strangeness and familiarity, simplicity and depth, meaningfulness and not, all this being more or less this or that freely, without an ideologically compelling meaning. Many "theologies" were thus possible and did not exclude each other. One feels a similar aura in all the paintings in the Egyptian tombs: at once a presence and an absence, a strangeness and a familiarity—as in the fact that the Egyptian gods were represented as humans as well as animals. The basics ("animals") of life are "divine," i.e., are experienced "spiritually." In other words, for the Old Egyptians life was experienced as one reality, the visible and tangible and instinctual realities being themselves openings towards a "spiritual" depth, but a depth that cannot be "man-made."

With the Old Greeks we notice the beginning of a drifting apart of the two "sides" of the perception of reality as depicted by the Old Egyptian "false door." The evolution of their collective symbolism goes in two different directions. On the one hand, it moves towards more "extraverted" religious symbols, celebrating national power and wealth rather than the gods. An example of this was the twelve-meters-high gold and ivory statue of Athena put inside the Parthenon on the occasion of the victory over the Persians. On the other hand, we witness an evolution towards experience of more specific "interiority." A good illustration of this trend is the image Plato uses to describe the personality of Socrates. Seen from the outside, he resembles an ugly Silene clay statue, but he has, hidden inside, the precious and beautiful small statuette of a god, this being the image of the "daimon" inside Socrates. Despite this beginning differentiation of "outside-inside," the statuary of classical Greece (500-350 B.C.) still evokes a wholeness of life experience. The statues of the Nike of Samothrace, the Driver of Delphi, etc., seem to be alive and "soul-full," thus demonstrating that the proximity of existential experience of life and its mystery is still very present. Another example is the Parthenon, whose shape is not mathematically symmetrical. It displays a "lightness" despite its size, which lets the observer perceive in the monument, so to speak, what exists behind the "false door."

With the Hellenistic period (200 B.C.E.-0 C.E.), things begin to change. The wholeness of life experience begins seriously to split up. For instance, the Altar of Pergamon (around 200 B.C.E.) presents a cluster of soulless bodies with anatomically perfect shapes, but with no connection among them other than a destructive and bloody conflict, the battle between the Titans and the gods. This altar is in itself an image of how—with a growing momentum, as we will see—in Western collective consciousness the perception of reality becomes divided: here the "gods" (life in its depth), there man in his titanic inflation. On the other hand, having very little to do with these anatomically correct but soulless sculptures, there flourished in Hellenistic times a spiritual philosophy (Plotinus and the Neoplatonists) with esoteric features. In collective perception, this increased the distance that appeared in classical Greece, as we have noticed, between "exteriority" and "interiority," and thus added explicitly a new line of fracture between spirit and matter in the perception of reality. This led, in Hellenism, to an interiority that became in time more and more subtle, individualized, spiritualized.

For the Romans, the important collective investments were the temples, and in this way they maintained collectively a strong reference to the gods as symbols of the mystery of life. But their monumentality tended to transform them into monuments of Rome, of the Civitas and then of the Empire, taking on thereby an almost similar purpose—to glorify State and Ruler (as, for instance, the Coliseum and its bloody spectacles, the large public baths, etc.). The Roman road system covering the whole Empire (a letter from Spain to Turkey took in those days less time than nowadays!) points to the paramount importance given to practicalities, in other words, to what belongs to full extraversion. On the other hand, one notices an increasing number of small, "in-group" religious places—smallish temples, intimate gathering places, etc.—hosting a growing variety of divinities ranging from the old Roman cult of the ancestors (Lares), the Egyptian Apis, Isis, etc., to Jesus Christ and other "initiatory" cults (Mithra, Eleusis, etc.). They were places symbolizing, as such, "interiority"—introversion. The great success of those places gives the impression that the by now explicit split in collective consciousness between exteriority and interiority (the first appearance of the "private" character of religion!) resulted in an uneasy quest, pushing individuals to look for wholeness in the attempt to heal this fracture with the help of secret initiation rituals (for instance, in Eleusis, as described by Apuleius in *The Golden Ass*).

The Christian civilization that followed—its sociocultural background being already a mix of the Hellenistic (spirit/matter) and Greco-Roman (exteriority/interiority) splits—opened a further crack by taking over the Hebrew perception of life, namely, the radical separation between God and creation, or, symbolically speaking, between reality and the mystery of life, i.e., transcendence. From now on, nature is not divine anymore. This means, symbolically, that nothing is divine, not only in the creation (plants, animals, stars, etc.) but also in the nature of things. Life as it is became emptied symbolically of its transcendent secret. Revelations coming from "above" relativize the value of the "just-so" experiences of life. Furthermore, the Hebrew myth of the "chosen people of God," transferred to the church, absolutized another split in collective consciousness: humanity was imagined to be cut in two—the ontologically "good" ones (not because of their good deeds or achievements but because of God's choice), on the one hand, and the rest of humankind, on the other. Here we have the seed of the white superiority myth. But in this context, Christian collective consciousness still lives from a powerful life-unifying myth that tends symbolically towards the healing of those splits. The main message of Jesus of Nazareth ("The Kingdom of God is within —or among—you") implies that the mystery of life is here, neither "outside" nor "inside," neither "material" nor "spiritual," etc. This insight leads to the dogma of incarnation: God has become a historical man. In other words, the two sides of the "false door" are connected again. This is ritually experienced in the Mass, bread being the body of and wine the blood of Christ. This side and the other side of the "false door" come together in the sacrament.

Medieval Christianity therefore put much libido into the collective building related to this incarnation of the divine in life as the Mass reenacts it—many churches, cathedrals, monasteries. Concrete life is meaningful because it "hosts" (to pun on "*Hostia*," the Eucharist) God. But the already existing cracks tended to lift the Christian unifying myth up and away: away from matter (in the separation of spirit and matter inherited from Hellenism), away from creation (in the radical distinction of God and creation inherited from the Hebrews), away from humankind as a whole (in the distinction between church members and pagans). Hence the collective symbols of the Christian era certainly pointed at the unity of all reality, but at the same time they perpetuated and enforced (also through Christian morals) the existing dichotomies in collective consciousness of reality. And they also enforced a distinction that previously was not absolute—though perhaps it already was with the Hebrews—between truth and error, a distinction that now became a radical split between absolute truth and heresy. This crack was consistent with the separation already existing in the radical distinction between the "chosen by God"—i.e., the church— and the rest of humankind. The Inquisition and its pyres were the dramatic monuments of this crack in the medieval collective consciousness. So the Mass and the buildings related to it could not really be a restatement of the Old Egyptian collective symbol of the "false door," or the "god who is also an animal." Being lifted up away from nature and matter, there developed a need for a compensation from below; hence the growing interest in alchemy, sorcery, and astrology, all of them attempts to stay connected with an undivided consciousness. But this is not yet "Nothing," despite the splits. The collective symbols (churches, etc.) still reflected a very strong collective perception that life has its wonder, its unfathomable origin and dimensions, and its essential Oneness. But the consciousness-splitting worm was in the fruit, and the late Middle Ages saw the appearance of the first universities, where autonomous rationality, cut off from other psychic perceptions of life, would attain top priority.

With the Renaissance, the existing dichotomies in collective consciousness gathered full momentum: collective religious symbols like St. Peter's in Rome tended to become signs of power (of the Popes) and less of life as a whole; the still unknown aspects of life were seen as having to be discovered by reason (whereas earlier the unknown was seen as animating life), in parallel to the discovery of the Americas, a process fostering the dichotomy objectivity/subjectivity through the development of natural sciences, which had already appeared in Old Greece. And a new split began to manifest itself. This was the growing distance between collective and individual consciousness. This was shown in the emphasis on the value of the individual that one can spot, for instance, in Renaissance paintings, where the collective religious theme becomes a pretext for depicting the individual faces of the ruling citizens (e.g., in *The Annunciation to Zacharias*, by Domenico Ghirlandajo). And one notices also a phenomenon consistent with the gradual loss of a living collective perception of the wholeness of reality: the reduction of symbols to allegories, which thus become univocal signs. Venus stands for love, Mars for war, Jupiter for power, etc. This trend towards allegory appears in the Lutheran and Calvinistic Reformation, where the Mass—bread and wine really transformed into body and blood of Christ—becomes a mere allegory of Christ's suffering and of fellowship among the believers. In these basic tendencies, collective symbolization in the Renaissance sets the stage for modernity and its huge development of reason-based sciences and technologies ultimately geared to the happiness of the individual, who is thus more and more cut off from inner and outer nature.

The Protestant Reformation seems to be in the straight line of development from the Renaissance. The main religious issue became the salvation of the individual soul. The religious images, having been allegorized, were no longer necessary because words can say the same thing in a better way, so they were destroyed. The Scriptures were not chanted anymore (chanting a text puts it onto the poetical, i.e., the symbolical level!), but read, rationally discussed, analyzed, and preached as the centerpiece of worship. The Mass is no longer a mystery (symbol) but a sign, a memorial. So we have the emergence of a further sharp polarity in the collective reception—and in its expression of this reception—of life: the radical difference between rational and irrational, a schism that, amalgamating with the already existing polarities (exteriority/interiority, matter/spirit, God/creation, absolute truth/error), will culminate in the collective symbolism of the Enlightenment.

With the Enlightenment, we have, in addition to the usual symbols of power such as castles, the great buildings of rational learning (schools, universities) and the first museums and collections celebrating the emerging scientific curiosity. It is the last building period of churches invested symbolically by the collectivity, now in the Baroque and Rococo styles that we find, for example, in the Monastery of Einsiedeln near Zurich. At its core, it still contains a symbol of deep connection with the mystery of life: the Black Madonna. But the paintings on the ceilings display a spectacular dissociation between form and content. The content is otherworldly (e.g., the Assumption of the Holy Virgin), while the form is as realistic as possible, as if one had taken a photograph. When such dissociation between form and content appears in symbolic expressions, it usually indicates the coming end of the living symbol, since through this dissociation the symbol is becoming a sign. Thus, with the Enlightenment, the collective receptivity of the mystery of life is nearing its definitive end. The split between the collective and individual meaning of life, which already appeared during the Renaissance, now becomes common truth, and this leads straight to the radical privatization of religion, art, and other symbols in the nineteenth and twentieth centuries.

What about the Romantic period and the nineteenth century—Goethe's *Faust*, Beethoven's music, the Catholic revival ("Sacre Coeur"), etc.? And what about the large crowds flocking to those concerts and plays? On the surface, they seem to express a true connection to the depth of life, but these occasions are by now separated from daily life and produced by individuals, and not by the collectivity as a whole anymore. The great symbolic investments by the collectivities of the nineteenth century are the factories, the railroads, universities, colleges, museums, etc., all celebrating the production of goods and rational knowledge and cut off from any perception of the mystery of life. European colonialism will be justified with the help of another split existing since antiquity: it will thrive on a secularized version of the myth of the "chosen people," i.e., the belief in the superiority of Western civilization. One finds a last trace on a truly collective level of the mysterious roots of life in the preambles of some nineteenth-century national constitutions such as the Swiss one, which begins with: "In the name of God Almighty…"

In the twentieth century, the splits we have spotted on the collective level, as they appear during the history of the reception of reality in the West, are now reaching a kind of paroxysm. We have by this point in collective consciousness a clear distinction between objective reality—as symbolized in schools, universities, and their study programs—and inner subjective experience—as seen in artistic expressions and in private matters like religion (still, some church buildings, but now mostly in the private hands of associations, etc.). The experience of life in its wholeness and depth is not expressed anymore in symbols invested and carried by the collective. This leads to the objective split between purely egoistic interests (whose satisfaction becomes more and more possible thanks to scientific and technological developments, themselves resulting from the split between rationality and soul experience) and inner and outer nature. The outcome of this is fully known today: the burgeoning of the worldwide consumer society and the full-fledged, worldwide ecological crisis resulting from it. In a compensatory way to this egoistic/rationalistic evolution, the twentieth century witnessed sudden massive resurgences of collective symbolisms manifesting powerfully the irrational dimensions of life—but because of their compensatory nature and their having to break through repression, they appeared in a perverted, destructive form: first, the (in retrospect, crazy!) European nationalisms leading to World War I and its some twelve million dead; then, the nationalistic ideologies, combined with mythologies of "roots," National Socialism and Fascism (some eight million dead); and, last but not least, Marxism, as opposite pole to individualism, producing the Communist regimes and their victims (untold millions dead). In those collective, mythological enactments there was no erotic connection to life, but possession by those contents combined with power plays of groups and individuals in an almost, if not plainly (e.g., Hitler), psychotic way. (Possession also occurs in individuals when the reception of the wholeness of life experience is split into unrelated "pieces" and one of them "pops up.")

When we put the psychoanalytical movement into this context, we see that in his way Freud was right in describing the fragmented Western way of perceiving reality as being "neurotic," and in summing it up as a split between conscious and unconscious. This "neurotization" of the individual seems to be, by now, more severe than in previous periods, because there are no longer any living integrating symbols on the collective level. The attempt to experience reality as a whole has become a purely individual—and for more and more persons, an excessively heavy—task. Jung experienced and formulated adequately the fact that symbolic life is still a reality, not just nostalgic, wishful thinking. But now it has to be experienced in the—smallish?—*vas Hermeticum* of individual life. When this is illustrated by collective symbols, they have to be taken mostly from foreign civilizations, or they are local symbols dug up from former times, e.g., alchemy, etc. Is archetypal psychology a survival kit for experiencing a wholeness of life for the few who are still consciously striving for it?

THE CONTEMPORARY SCENE: THE ARCHETYPE OF THE VOID

At the beginning of this paper, I formulated a hypothesis: the more splits there are in the perception of reality—inner/outer, subjective/objective, rational/irrational, true/false, form/content, individual/collective, chosen/not chosen, conscious/unconscious, to recall a few splits we have spotted in our quick excursion through the history of Western collective perceptions of reality—the more this opens a space for true meaninglessness and fosters a psychic experience whose archetypal image would be Nothingness. Now, in present postmodern times, this seems indeed to be the collective symbol that expresses people's psychic connection to reality.

I will try to spot this contemporary nihilism where the symbolic in collective life is concerned, in the same way I tried to spot collective symbols in former periods: in the monuments in which today's collectivities are making massive new libidinal investments. I see this mainly in the field of telecommunications and in the vast acceptance of this phenomenon—the Internet, wireless phones, a multitude of TV stations, satellites, etc., and in other global telecommunication systems like publicity and public relations. The postmodern fantasy of communicating has in all its specific forms a main common feature: It can transmit any content, which amounts to the fact that collective libido does not invest in any *particular* content, which is to say, in any real content at all. The system can be filled at random by anything, as long as it satisfies opportunistic, mostly short-term, economic and political purposes.

It is fascinating to see that when we look more closely at some of these monuments among the contemporary collective libidinal investments, they incarnate in their very reality the symbolic Nothingness we spot in today's civilization as a whole. In the case of the computer, for instance, the libido goes mainly into developing and running more and more complex systems; little libido seems to be left for what is transmitted, a trend that can also be observed in the transportation systems (railroads, roads, airlines). *Where* to go tends to disappear behind the need just to *go* somewhere. Another important feature of the computer is a strict minimum of waiting time, if any, between the input and the output. In other words, no time is set aside for gestation, for growth, for a maturation process. Consistent with this lack of time for growth, a computer doesn't know a dialectical process. Its mental structure is yes or no, black or white, one or zero—never both. This itself points at a void, as all forms of real life —biological, physiological, ecological, psychological, social, etc.—are dialectical in their essence. In life, there are everywhere "opposites" that are linked to and need each other. Thus, when the value of contents has no importance, as in computers and their worldwide network; when no time is imagined and built in for organic, living growth; when opposites can only be formulated as either/or binary systems, we have indeed, so goes my hypothesis, a concrete symbol of Nothingness, of Void, of Absence of anything and anybody and above all of meaning.

The Void can be observed directly in other heavily invested postmodern collective symbolizations such as publicity. Its evolution over the last century and up to the present time is significant for our considerations. At first, and until recently, the products to be advertised were associated with symbols of life (love scenes, children, animals, nature, landscapes, clergymen (!), etc.). But in recent times, this gimmick seems to be wearing out, as if through the association with a car, an insurance company, a soup, etc., those symbols of life got themselves pulled down into the relative nothingness of the product, thereby lessening the efficiency of the advertisements. So in a more recent phase, the images became violent, very erotic, shocking—as, for instance an Italian designer displaying crippled people in his ads to sell T-shirts. But today, the nihilistic trend goes even further, as it takes into its aura the products to be advertised themselves: either they are shown with an absurd commentary (e.g., "Be yourself," commenting on a pair of underpants), or the lighting of the whole ad is very strange, almost otherworldly, making the products look surreal. An extreme illustration of this trend that affects the image of the product itself nihilistically was a recent ad for a new drink: At first there were posters proclaiming, "On day X comes X." And then the day came, and new posters went up saying: "Drink the new Cola, drink Nothing."

To give a final example, public "relations" can be a place where Nothingness can be found on the collective level. "My name is…," says the lady on the phone, apparently in an effort to be "personal," but in fact this is an empty utterance because the spirit of this personalization has nothing to do with real relatedness and is being used for purely institutional (in this case economic) purposes.

We also have explicit illustrations of the collective symbol of Nothingness, for instance, cartoons like the one showing a fellow searching for something and asking: "Who am I? Where am I going? Where is my TV remote control?" Or the drawing of a fellow looking around the frame of a mirror behind which he wants to see something different than his known mirror image of himself, and ending up by seeing nothing else than his own arse—a pathetic image of introspection ending up with nothing. And there are public exhibitions displaying real human corpses in different positions, preserved by the injection of some plastic substance. A local Swiss example was the posters announcing the "Welttheater" ("World Theater") in Einsiedeln in 2000 and 2007, one showing a skeleton running away with a baby, the other an angel hiding behind his back a bunch of already ignited dynamite sticks. I need not mention the catastrophe and doomsday movies produced lately in increasing numbers by the vanguard studios of Hollywood and elsewhere. One could find numerous other illustrations in contemporary Western literature and philosophy. All this illustrates how evidently the archetype of Nothingness seems indeed to be *the* collective symbol at the beginning of the twenty-first century.

CONCLUSION

I end with some remarks and questions. First, I observe that the collective postmodern experience of Nothingness is compensated by a regressive collective ideology preaching satisfaction through consumption. This fosters a mentality fully in accord with the present collective vicious circle, since it accelerates Nothingness through the destruction of inner (psychic) and outer (planetary) nature, leading sooner or later to its own dead end.

Having said this, we must not forget that although Nothingness is the most up-to-date way of relating collectively to life, the other former collective symbolic ways of expressing life are still around—from industrial, to rationalistic and individual romantic (Jungian individuation), to classical religious, etc., and even including some just-discovered tribe still living symbolically in the Stone Age. Since we are in one world, they may also be mysteriously and dialectically linked to the present Nothingness, contributing thus to the shape of a possible future collective symbolic life. We can have no idea of the outcome, except that present Nothingness will have to be integrated into what is still alive from former periods of our cultural history. But for the time being, we have to receive Nothingness as a "just-so" fact, without value judgment, since collective psyche is symbolically constellated in this image today. The Jungian colleague Wolfgang Giegerich does this in a very sober way: "Collective consciousness today," he writes, "leaves behind the quest for meaning (the 'precious pearl' inherent in reality) and lives only through its structures, its empty forms....To 'surf' in the World Wide Web is one of the possible subjective experiences of this new objective quality of consciousness."[1]

To this sober way of seeing the situation, I would add that, as we have seen, the death motif is present in Nothingness. It can be acted out in a concrete way when combined with political and/or psychological factors, as in the event of 9/11, amok killings in high schools all over the developed world, and normal heads of families killing themselves and their families because of existential difficulties. But Nothingness as death is also a symbolical condition for change: the old must die in order to make space for another way of seeing life. Does the collective constellation of Nothingness indicate that Western civilization is at its end ? The end of a purely ego-centered, i.e., purely anthropocentric, way of life? Is it a yet unconscious opening towards some Greater Being? If so, this would be beneficial for the survival of nature, hence also of humankind. That pure Western anthropocentricity is in its twilight could be seen in an occurrence at my daughter's primary school: in a story for which they had to invent the ending, ten out of twelve kids chose a conclusion in which animals rather than humans were saved.

There remains nothing further but to remember the graffiti along the railway tracks in our cities, whose shapes are by "sheer coincidence" so close to Arabic—i.e., Koranic—writing. Is new collective symbolic life an opening towards a never-ending Indefinite that may be pictured in those arabesques, a Meaninglessness as true meaning (while the need for conscious meaning would be, psychologically speaking, an outdated projection), a Meaninglessness implying no definite direction in which things should go? If it is so, our civilization could take its foot off the gas pedal of economic growth, psychological and other developments, and develop a greater acceptance of the just-so reality of life, thus becoming aware of what life really is—a part of a Whole whose reality surpasses in an indefinite and infinite way the transitory reality of our egos and their numerous desires. It could be the precondition for the continuation of human life on this planet, beyond the cancer of a civilization that through its own splitting dynamism has reached a perhaps salutary paroxysm: Nothingness as a chance for real change in civilization.

NOTE

1. Wolfgang Giegerich, "Das World Wide Web aus der Sicht des logischen Lebens der Seele," in *Gorgo* 39 (2000): 21; "The World Wide Web from the Point of View of the Soul's Logical Life," in Giegerich, *Technology and the Soul* (Spring Journal Books, 2007).

THE RED BOOK—*PRIMA MATERIA* OF C. G. JUNG: AN "ENTERVIEW" WITH SONU SHAMDASANI

ROBERT S. HENDERSON

SONU SHAMDASANI was born in Singapore. He is Philemon Professor of Jung History at the Wellcome Trust Centre for the History of Medicine at University College, London, and the editor of C. G. Jung, *The Red Book*. He received his PhD and Msc degrees from the Wellcome Institute for the History of Medicine at University College, London. His undergraduate work was completed at Bristol University in Bristol, England. He is the author of four books: *Le Dossier Freud: Enquête sur l'histoire de la psychanalyse*, with Mikkel Borch-Jacobsen (Le Seuil, 2006; Cambridge University Press, forthcoming); *Jung Stripped Bare by His Biographers, Even* (Karnac, 2004); *Jung and the Making of Modern Psychology: The Dream of a Science* (Cambridge University Press, 2003); and *Cult Fictions: C .G. Jung and the Founding of Analytical Psychology* (Routledge, 1998), for which he received a Gradiva Award from the National Association for the Advancement of Psychoanalysis. He is the editor of four other books: C. G. Jung, *The Psychology of Kundalini Yoga* (Princeton University Press,

Robert S. Henderson is a pastoral psychotherapist in Glastonbury, Connecticut. He and his wife, Janis, a psychotherapist, are co-authors of *Living with Jung: "Enterviews" with Jungian Analysts*, Volumes 1 and 2 (Spring Journal Books, 2006 and 2008). Volume 3 will be released in 2009. Many of their interviews with Jungian analysts have also been published in *Spring Journal*, *Quadrant*, *Psychological Perspectives*, *Harvest*, and *Jung Journal: Culture and Psyche*.

1996); Michael Fordham, *Analyst-Patient Interaction: Collected Papers on Technique* (Routledge, 1996); Theodore Flournoy, *From India to the Planet Mars: A Case of Multiple Personality with Imaginary Languages* (Princeton University Press, 1994); and, with Michael Munchow, *Speculations after Freud: Philosophy, Psychoanalysis and Culture* (Routledge, 1994).

Rob Henderson (RH): How did you become interested in Jung?

Sonu Shamdasani (SS): I first heard of Jung while visiting ashrams in India, just prior to going to university to study philosophy. The first work of his that I read was his commentary on "The Secret of the Golden Flower," which immediately struck me as offering the possibility of a mediation between Eastern and Western thought. At the same time, it initiated my interest in psychology.

(RH): Do you feel that the Jung you have come to know through your work with the unpublished writings of Jung is different from the Jung the world has known through the published writings? If so, what are some of the differences you have discovered?

(SS): I can say that the Jung I came to know through my historical researches bears little relation to what I thought I knew based on my initial reading of the published works and secondary materials. Time and time again, through my researches, I found that I was taken aback when I noticed the gulf between what I had unquestioningly taken to be the case, and what I was finding.

In retrospect, I think that I only started to comprehend his work when I began to grasp the non-Freudian contexts from which he drew, through my reconstructions of late nineteenth and early twentieth century psychology and psychiatry, and to realize that his published works were by no means either complete or fully representative, and that consequently one had to start from scratch with primary research.

How typical my initial assumptions were is hard to tell. In a number of my publications, I have tried to identify some widely held "received" ideas, account for how they arose, and indicate why I consider them to have been mistaken in the light of historical research. It is hard to characterize the differences, as I feel that the situation today is one in which there is a limitless array of conceptions, fantasies, and legends about Jung, which show no sign of receding.

(**RH**): What are some examples of the Jung you have gotten to know through your research that are contrary to what the world has come to know?

(**SS**): To address this question, I think that it is useful to consider the situation that pertained before Jung's death. It was often stated that one could not fully understand Jung's psychology without meeting Jung, on the assumption that he was the ultimate embodiment of his psychology. Whatever the validity of this statement, it is clear there were esoteric dimensions to his work that were not fully spelled out in the published volumes.

After Jung's death, the principal manner in which individuals gained knowledge of Jung's work was through his textual work. As I found through my research, this corpus was far from complete or reliable. In my view, the secondary literature in any field of scholarship can ultimately only be as good as the quality and representativeness the primary literature allows.

The *Collected Works of C. G. Jung* (Princeton University Press, Princeton, New Jersey) was not a historical critical edition, so the editorial apparatus did not present what would have been required for orientation within the numerous contexts in which Jung's work was embedded. The organization of the volumes often makes it hard to establish when Jung wrote particular statements. The English translation leaves a great deal to be desired, and there are unpublished papers that in my view (and also that of the original editors!) should have been included in it. In addition to this, there are quite a few unpublished seminars, and by far the larger share of his correspondence remains unpublished. In 2003, the Philemon Foundation was established by myself and Stephen Martin to raise the funds to enable this immense unpublished corpus to be edited and published.

Thus, before one even gets to materials such as Jung's *Red Book* and *Black Books*, there are huge gaps in primary material. When used with due caution and with additional research, one can glean a great deal from the existing corpus, as many have done. My own experience has been that the task of understanding his work is considerably easier if one studies it in a historical context, and studies the unpublished as well as the published materials. In some of my publications, I have identified what I consider to be some common misunderstandings of his work, and have tried to account for how these arose (the Freudocentric reading of Jung and the image of him as a psychotic philanderer would be examples).

(**RH**): The world reacts in many ways to change. How are you finding the world to be reacting to the changes you are proposing about who Jung is?

(**SS**): I find that one of the pleasures of writing is the unexpected responses that publications bring. I've found that my work has been very well received in historical circles. Amongst Jungian circles, the response has been more polarized: Many individuals have responded with enthusiasm, and I've been fortunate to receive a lot of lecture invitations from Jungian groups and institutions, which have facilitated and furthered my research—particularly in terms of being able to present work in progress and to see what questions are of particular interest to people. At the same time, some appear to be opposed to historical research, and some continue to write as if there has been no change in the historical landscape over the last twenty years.

(**RH**): Throughout my training as a Jungian psychotherapist, I have been told that to understand Jung, you need to understand his life and how he lived it, as that is an important basis for his psychology. How do you feel about that?

(**SS**): I think that, in important respects, there is more truth in the obverse—namely, that to understand Jung's life, you need to understand his work. In *Memories,* he stated that his life was dominated by one task, to penetrate into the secret of the personality. In my view, it is quite clear that Jung was someone who was orientated by ideas, and so he tended to live in particular ways because of how he thought.

His work was by no means simply a passive, reactive mirror of his life. Moreover, there are a number of pitfalls in attempting to proceed in the other direction, of trying to understand Jung's work on the basis of his life. On the one hand, one has a lack of reliable biographical information, which is coupled with a surfeit of gossip, rumors, and fantasies. Too much of the latter has been taken as established fact. Hence, for example, the myth of Jung as a psychotic philanderer, which I challenged in my book on the Jung biographies. On the other hand, there is a tendency to employ reductive psychobiographical interpretations, which short-circuit intellectual history, in assuming that the source of Jung's ideas can be found in putative life events rather than in complex developments in Western intellectual history from the latter half of the nineteenth century onwards.

(**RH**): You have now spent a lot of time working on the *Red Book.*

What has the experience been like for you? How much time will you have spent on it?

(SS): The sensation I had when I started to work on it was one of relief: having had my life profoundly affected by Jung and my work on him, I was relieved that I would be able to study this pivotal work, and hence understand the genesis of his work better—and thus, indirectly, understand better what I have been involved with that has so affected my life. Now, after many years' work, this initial sense has been borne out: the work was an unparalleled window into the constitution of his later work, and has transformed my understanding of it. I've been working on it, so far, for over a decade.

(RH): What importance does the *Red Book* have for understanding analytical psychology?

(SS): In *Memories, Dreams, Reflections* (recorded and edited by Aniela Jaffé, New York: Random House, 1962), Jung described his "confrontation with the unconscious"—of which the *Red Book* was the central work—as the most important period of his life, and stated that it contained the *prima materia* that he spent the rest of his life elaborating and integrating. I think that the situation is exactly as Jung described it. So the *Red Book* is the central text for understanding the constitution of Jung's later work (i.e., post-1914) from a historical perspective.

(RH): After all your research, what are your views now on Jung's autobiography, *Memories, Dreams, Reflections*?

(SS): I commenced my research on *Memories* in 1988, and by the time I had studied the Jung-Jaffé protocols in the Library of Congress and related editorial correspondence in 1991, the differences between the published version and the manuscripts had become clear. I had established, with documentation, that the work should not be considered as Jung's autobiography, but a biography by Aniela Jaffé to which he made contributions, and that he never saw the final published version, which went through considerable changes after the drafts that he had seen—and indeed, he had been highly critical of these.

The further research that I have conducted since then has confirmed and amplified these conclusions. The reception of my presentations (from 1991) and publications on this subject, and those of Alan Elms at the same time, was an eye-opener—I was really surprised at that time to see to what extent people preferred myths to historical actuality.

The one area where my understanding of *Memories* has shifted concerns his discussion, in the protocols, of his "confrontation with the unconscious." His comments are hard to understand fully without reading the *Red Book*, and it is impossible to establish a clear chronology. There is a sense in which his discussion was intended to form something like a prelude to the *Red Book* eventually being made public sometime after his death.

(RH): What will it mean for you, finally having the *Red Book* published and available to the world?

(SS): For me, personally, it will be the release of an unbearable burden.

(RH): As you worked on the *Red Book*, what are some of the impressions of Jung that came to you?

(SS): Metaphorically speaking, it is a book written with blood (and, I dare say, edited with it, too). Jung himself described it to Aniela Jaffé in the *Memories* protocols as the "numinous beginning which contains everything."

(RH): What is the most interesting experience you have had in your work with the *Red Book*?

(SS): Due to confidentiality requirements, my work on the text has been an enforced solitude for too many years. Given this, the discussions with Mark Kyburz and John Peck on the translation have been a fascinating and absorbing experience through which I have learned much, and which has brought some much-needed new wind into the sails.

(RH): Sonu, it has been wonderful to share this enterview with you. What are some of your hopes for the *Red Book* as it is published and enters the world?

(SS): I have no doubt that the publication will be a turning point in the historical understanding of Jung. I am confident that in ten years time, the discussion of Jung will be completely transformed, and people coming to Jung for the first time will start from a completely different basis.

I am less certain about the immediate response and, to be frank, apprehensive—as one sees from history, change on such a scale takes a generation, particularly as new information inevitably becomes folded back into old legends. We have already seen so much of this in Jung studies. Jung spent sixteen years directly working on the text, and then decades trying to integrate the material within cultural and intellectual history. I've now spent thirteen years in solitary confinement on the project. To read the work properly also requires rereading much of the *Collected Works* from 1914 onwards in a new light—I've read through the *Collected Works* a number of times, and rereading it after the *Red Book* was by far the most illuminating. My recommendation is that people spend at least a year immersing themselves in it before beginning to write about it or give talks about it.

THE PSYCHOLOGIST AS REPENTANCE PREACHER AND REVIVALIST

Robert Romanyshyn on the Melting of the Polar Ice*

WOLFGANG GIEGERICH

J ung opened his early major work, *Transformations and Symbols of the Libido* (later revised as *Symbols of Transformation*), with a chapter on "Two Types of Thinking." He must have felt that in order to really start upon the work of psychology one had to draw a clear dividing line between the type of thinking it required and the generally prevailing, different type of thinking. This was early in the twentieth century. But this

Wolfgang Giegerich studied at the University of Würzburg and the University of Göttingen, and obtained his PhD from the University of California at Berkeley. He received a diploma from the C. G. Jung Institute–Stuttgart. After many years in private practice in Stuttgart and later in Wörthsee, near Munich, he now lives in Berlin. He has lectured and taught in many countries (Germany, Switzerland, Austria, England, Italy, the USA, Russia, Japan, and Brazil) and before many professional societies. His more than one hundred and seventy publications in the field of psychology, in several languages, include fourteen books, among them *The Soul's Logical Life: Towards a Rigorous Notion of Psychology* (Peter Lang, 1998; 4th ed. 2007), and the three volumes of his Collected English Papers: *The Neurosis of Psychology*, *Technology and the Soul*, and *Soul-Violence* (all published by Spring Journal Books).

Editor's Note: Wolfgang Giegerich has written this article as a response to Robert Romanyshyn, "The Melting Polar Ice: Revisiting *Technology as Symptom and Dream*," in *Spring* 80 (Fall 2008), "Technology, Cyberspace, & Psyche."

clear demarcation of a particular style of thinking necessary for psychology did not once and for all settle the question of psychology's self-constitution. Obviously, psychology is a truly precarious field. Throughout his life, Jung needed to contrast the approach and thinking of psychology proper with those of theology, metaphysics, philology, the natural sciences, strictly technical and medical approaches to psychotherapy, and sociopolitical ways of thinking. Psychology is, however, not only in need of marking its borders to other fields. It also needs to draw clear dividing lines between different types of thinking that come up within its own precincts, and this, time and again. I could not help but be reminded of this latter necessity when lately becoming aware of a growing tendency in the Jungian field to advocate what has been called eco-psychology. It gives rise to my proposing another and different differentiation of "two types of thinking."

Although I don't know whether Romanyshyn would himself use the label "eco-psychology" for his work, his well-argued paper on "The Melting Polar Ice: Revisiting *Technology as Symptom and Dream*"[1] could be considered as a high-level example of it. It nicely exemplifies, and thus allows me to demonstrate, one type of thinking based on certain premises and tenets, displaying certain attitudes, and leading to certain strategic moves that I find incompatible with what I would consider psychology proper, a "psychology with soul" in the tradition of C. G. Jung.

ANXIETY

The first section of Romanyshyn's paper is entitled "Anxiety and Ice," and right at the start we are informed: "So I begin to write in this anxious state, …remembering that anxiety was also the beginning of my book, *Technology as Symptom and Dream*….The anxiety then was the imminent prospect of a nuclear winter; the anxiety now is the prospect…" of the new catastrophe of melting ice caps: anxiety as the explicit *archē* and principle of his writing and thus as the *spiritus rector* for all that follows. The author does not see this as a problem, but gives a psychological justification for beginning in this emotional state. Anxiety is ennobled as the "proper starting point for the discovery of integrity." Staying in touch with it is even claimed to be an "ethical process in which 'one's infinite obligation to the other is expressed.'" "To stay with the anxiety of the moment is to be responsible, able-to-respond, because I am listening." This is the view of the one type of thinking.

The other type of thinking would say that emotions in general inevitably make us unfree to the extent that we are under their spell. They tend to blind us. Let us hear Jung on emotion:

> And you always have emotions where you are not adapted. If you are adapted you need no emotion; an emotion is only an instinctive explosion which denotes that you have not been up to your task. When you don't know how to deal with a situation or with people, you get emotional. Since you were not adapted, you had a wrong idea of the situation....to be emotional is already on the way to a pathological condition.[2]

In quoting Jung I do not wish to suggest that because Jung said this it must be right and everyone has to accept it. In his long life, Jung said so many things that all sorts of views, at times even opposite ones, could be supported with quotations from his writings. It is the other way around. I quote his statement because it hits the nail on the head.

This passage serves here merely the purpose of showing the other type of psychological thinking. According to it, there is nothing ethical about staying with one's anxiety. On the contrary, it is the ethical obligation of any writer striving for insight to first free himself of any emotion so as to become able to study his subject *sine ira et studio*, to become "up to his task."

Also, as a therapist I know that when I have a new patient whose deeply suppressed but powerful fury uncannily fills the whole atmosphere of the consulting room, or who seems to be threatened by a psychosis, *and I become anxious*, I have ceased being his therapist, his analyst. In my fear of him or of his threatening material I can no longer do justice to him, because I am no longer free. I am not adapted to the situation, not up to my task. It is vital for the therapy that I struggle to overcome my anxiety and gain my freedom vis-à-vis what made me afraid. If I don't succeed, I cannot continue this therapy. In a very similar sense, how can I write on technology if I am under the spell of anxiety caused by the imminent prospect of a nuclear winter or the melting ice? It would be unprofessional.

Strangely, very strangely, the possibility of *overcoming* one's anxiety seems to have no place in the first type of thinking. The only way that Romanyshyn can imagine of dealing with this emotion, other than staying with it, is "numb[ing] myself against this feeling," "going to sleep, benumbing myself," entertaining a "comfortable illusion." In other words, the only other option for him would be repression, avoidance, escapism, which, psychologically, is out of the question from the start. But the possibility of truly *overcoming* one's fear, of rising above it—and this means to honestly face the threatening reality without illusions but precisely with a wakeful mind—does exist. For example, to free myself as analyst of the anxiety evoked in me by threatening aspects of my patient means anything but going to sleep, closing my eyes to what may be dangerous, or cherishing illusions. No, it means my conscious willingness to allow whatever caused the anxiety to *be*, and to show itself in the consulting room, unhindered, without my need to inwardly defend myself against it, without any resistance against it on my part (and my anxiety would be, of course, a form of resistance). I let it be and expose myself to it. In full awareness, I allow Pandora's box to be opened.

But, as Jung said, "We don't like to control our emotions because we enjoy them."[3] People relish anxieties. They thrive on them—just remember how most of America wallowed in anxiety after the terrorist attacks on the Twin Towers in New York. Hysteria. And why do we enjoy our emotions? Probably because emotions make us feel much more intensively alive than normally. They strengthen the *unio naturalis* for us. This is why Jung was right to continue by saying, it is felt to be "partial suicide when we control them," because it cuts into and dissolves our natural oneness with ourselves, and so "[w]e regret[4] ourselves; we are sorry for ourselves."

Formerly, by contrast, to control one's emotions, to overcome oneself, was generally expected of people as a matter of course—as part of being civilized, educated. And in the spirit of this latter view, the second type of psychological thinking still now believes that the first step and *sine qua non* of the psychological *opus* is the dissolution of the *unio naturalis*, and that the Work itself is an *opus contra naturam*.

In 1975, James Hillman, on the first page of his *Re-Visioning Psychology*, quoted Ortega y Gasset saying: "Why write, if this too easy activity of pushing a pen across paper is not given a certain bull-fighting risk and we do not approach dangerous, agile, and two-horned topics?" One can hardly imagine a greater difference than that between the bull-fighting spirit vis-à-vis a dangerous topic and one's purposely rooting oneself as author in one's own anxiety. With the avowal of one's anxiety one has *psychologically*, from the outset, succumbed to what is feared: no risk-taking anymore, no willingness to intellectually hold one's place vis-à-vis the feared. The mind has already given up. And so it is no surprise that

Romanyshyn's paper ends with his confession that he is writing "from this place of near despair." "The pull to go numb, to fall asleep...is strong." One is tempted to console him by saying, *requiescat in pace*. The quest for insight is drowned in emotionality, in a sinister *mood*.

I mentioned that the first section of Romanyshyn's paper is entitled "Anxiety and Ice." But this is a misnomer. There is no ice in this section. There is only the mood of anxiety. Moods are warm, emotions are hot. Psychologically the ice, the soul's icy coldness, is already melted to begin with; it is dissolved prior to the feared melting of polar ice out there. Ice is cold, hard, crystal clear, sharp-edged. And I would think that an icy mind would be needed to do justice to the topic of polar ice, since only like can know like. But in this paper what is "like" on both sides is not the ice, but the melting, the crumbling away. A mind that has some ice in it, a mind that is willing to take a certain bull-fighting risk, does not need to get hysterical or depressed over the insight that melting polar ice may have terrible, disastrous effects. For millennia, people in most parts of the world have lived with the firm belief that there would be an end of the world—apocalypse, doomsday, Ragnarök, the grand finale of the Kali yuga. What is so special about a coming doom? *Media in vita in morte sumus.* We all know that we will have to die. Is this a reason to make, *in advance*, a huge fuss and bother about it? Let's keep both feet on the ground.

This whole anxiety business is, in my opinion, a case of what Jung once termed, with a drastic, vulgar expression, *Hosenscheißerei des Ich*.

> Question: is it an object worthy of anxiety, or a poltroonery of the ego, shitting its pants [*eine Erbärmlichkeit i.e., Hosenscheißerei des Ich*]? (Compare Freud, 'The ego is the seat of anxiety,' with Job 28:28, 'The fear of the Lord, that is wisdom.') What is the 'anxiety of the ego,' this 'modestly modest' overweeningness and presumption of a little tin god, compared with the almighty shadow of the Lord, which is the fear that fills heaven and earth? The first leads to apotropaic defensive philosophy, the second to γνῶσις θεοῦ.[5]

This quote nicely contrasts the two types of thinking I am speaking about, although only in the one specific area of fear, namely, the anxiety of the ego versus "the fear that fills heaven and earth." It is a small example of the general difference between a psychology construed as ego-psychology and one construed as a psychology of soul.

A German proverb states that anxiety is not a good advisor. But the very thesis of Romanyshyn is the opposite: that staying with the anxiety is an ethical obligation and precisely connects us with the other. It makes him, he says, "responsible, able-to-respond, because I am listening." I think this is a great illusion. Of course I admit that anxiety, because it is a fear *of something*, in a literal and superficial way connects us with this something, this other. But that is psychologically absolutely irrelevant. *Psychologically*, anxiety inevitably makes us circle around ourselves; it constellates the ego that wants to survive and fears for its life. Anxiety makes one ego-centered, if not downright selfish, egoistic; it precisely does *not* open one's psychological ears to the other. To the exact same extent that anxiety rules, the other has no chance, or only a chance to the extent that one has overcome one's own anxiety and is willing, in Ortega y Gasset's sense, to face the bull. Is it not symbolic of this ego-centeredness that the first as well as the last paragraph of his paper begin with the word "I"—and, mind you, not with the "I" of the *author* who may at the beginning wish to outline what he intends to do in his paper or to present his first argument or the like, but with the private "I" of the ordinary empirical human being and his subjective inner state?

SIN

In Romanyshyn's paper, this ego-centeredness certainly does not show as selfishness or egotism, nor even as focusing on himself. No, on the level of contents he goes away from himself and indeed bases his reflections on a very interesting and substantial exploration of important objective soul events, above all that of the invention of linear perspective during the Renaissance. They are later further backed up by more or less detailed discussions of aspects of works of literature from the Romantic period. So the way the ego shows must be different in his case. It appears in the style of viewing, in the perspective with which he approaches linear perspective. His apperception and interpretation are informed by "the anxiety of the ego," and are thus guided by an ego perspective. He does not perceive the phenomena he studies from the point of view of soul— that is, as the soul's own further development, its further-determination, its advancing to new statuses of itself—but from an ego bias. Instead of merely describing and analyzing what happened, allowing the material itself to provide for him the categories and criteria by which it is to be interpreted, he interferes with a subjective moralistic judgment of his own that he brings to bear on the material from outside.

He rightly observes certain essential historical changes, but the condemnatory evaluation that these changes receive from him is his own addition. Of course, he himself denies that he condemns anything or, conversely, that he judges the condition prior to those changes as being better. "I am not arguing here that the pre-linear perspective world was a better world. On the contrary, my argument here is that while this way of dreaming the world as it moves toward the vanishing point has produced many benefits and has given us a great deal of power and control, it has exacted a price. In the face of the melting ice it is our task to know that price."[6] However, this way of putting it does not correspond to what he actually presents in his paper. The price to be paid is something different from what he is talking about. When I desire an object and buy it, then afterwards I have this object but I have less money than before, because I had to pay the price it costs. Similarly, when I leave the home of my parents in order to stand on my own feet, I acquire a certain degree of adult maturity, but have to pay for it by the loss of all the advantages of containment in a family. The price is the particular loss that is concomitant with a gain or acquisition.

But the melting polar ice caps in the twenty-first century are not the price for the invention of linear perspective in the fifteenth century. In his scheme, it is more like punishment for a crime. A criminal usually does his deed with the hope of being able to reap for himself only its benefits and, blinded by the dream of the benefits, either scotomizes his knowledge that there might be punishment or at least is pretty sure that he will escape punishment because of his clever precautions. If he nevertheless gets caught, his punishment comes to him as a later, new, separate and external event. For this reason (the external nature of a punishment), the model of crime and punishment is not completely suitable in our context either. Rather, the fantasy that Romanyshyn seems to be working in is more adequately described as that of a sin that carries its punishment—as its inherent, unintended consequence—within itself. An example might be one's starting to take drugs for the sake of an exciting experience, and later finding oneself a hopeless addict on an inevitable path to ruin. According to Romanyshyn's logic, we might say that the people who invented linear perspective gave in to an extremely promising, but sinful, temptation—he calls it "a dream"—without any idea as yet of what they were letting themselves (and all future generations) in for, and only now, six hundred years later, do we become aware of and find ourselves stuck in the disastrous consequences of the development that they set in motion.

It is in the light of those disastrous consequences that Romanyshyn apperceives the achievements of the Renaissance artists who invented linear perspective. The presently felt threat of impending disaster (climate change and melting ice) provides the gauge with which in retrospect the early beginnings are to be judged. This is how the "the anxiety of the ego" becomes the lens through which one can assess the historical phenomenology of the soul—and, of course, assess it as a terrible sin.

Romanyshyn himself generally does not speak of sin (except that he says that Coleridge's Ancient Mariner "sins against nature"). But he names the sin, and with numerous names: abandonment of the body of the earth, flight from nature, taking leave of the flesh and of the senses, breaking the erotic bonds (and freezing our feeling connection) with nature, becoming oblivious to what matters, a kind of imperialism, a forced colonization of the natural world by the light of a mind that knows no darkness, a solely masculine mind generating what it creates apart from the feminine, the despotism of an eye that sheds no tears, a consciousness without flesh, a nature dreamed as inanimate and a soul as unnatural, the broken connection between body and world, the fragmentation of the world into its divisible parts, being above and unmoved by what is experienced, and so on. The end result is: "We have all of us become trigger-happy cowboys ready to fix our gaze, not blink, and take aim at what is other to ourselves": point-blank killers.

All this he reads into the invention and cultivation of linear perspective in the art of the Renaissance, which becomes for him embodied in imaginal figures that he calls the Spectator Mind and the "despotic eye." His view is pure moralism, but I think it is also a terrible misconstrual of the historical *telos* and achievement of the invention of linear perspective, a misconstrual that needs to be contradicted (although this is not my main point and interest in my critique of his paper). Phenomenologically and historically, this evaluation is untenable. While it is true that linear perspective goes along with a distancing and a fixed, unmoved viewpoint, one must not single out this one abstract aspect, see it in isolation—completely apart from the whole context and spirit of Renaissance art, philosophy, science; apart also from the treatises of the artists themselves—and blow it up as the central or even the one and only feature. Such an interpretation does not become any better even if it is backed up by (likewise untenable) quotations from an art historian, Samuel Edgerton.

Romanyshyn and Edgerton are unable to see the dialectic of the creation of distance, the dialectic of the vanishing lines. It is as if neither of them had looked at actual paintings that were inspired by the spirit inherent in and underlying the invention of linear perspective, and had not read Nicholas of Cusa, Ficino, Pico della Mirandola, Dürer, Leonardo da Vinci, etc. Flight from nature? Taking leave of the flesh and the senses? A dream of nature as inanimate? The opposite can be seen in the work and thinking of the artists. Whereas, in earlier pre-linear perspective paintings of the Middle Ages, rather stiff figures had been depicted as abstract types, now, all of a sudden, there is an interest in the real looks of people as individuals. For the first time, painters try to capture the exact hue of the color of skin as well as the real facial expressions of people with all their emotions, as well as their wrinkles and dimples. The many nudes that were drawn and painted from then on (absolutely unthinkable during the earlier Middle Ages) show the celebration of sensuality—just think, for example, of Giorgione, Lucas Cranach, Rubens.

The painstaking attention to detail, to the individual hairs of fur, to the surface structure of materials like silk, brocade, linen, marble, wood, shows the dedication to the natural world that inspired those painters, and the numerous studies of hands, feet, faces, of trees and rocks, and even something as trivial as grass painted or drawn from nature are unmistakable evidence of a loving devotion to nature. The goal of the artist was to learn from, be taught by, nature. Whereas in the Middle Ages the depicted scenes were usually set off against a gold background that denoted the otherworldliness of divine light, i.e., not situated in our natural, earthly world, Renaissance painting shows that the soul has come down to earth and situates even sacred scenes here in the real world—such as the Annunciation in a real fifteenth-century interior equipped with all the practical items of daily life, and other scenes in real-looking landscapes or architectural sites.

By talking of a "despotic eye," Romanyshyn already smuggles his subjective value judgment, his moral condemnation, into the very designation of the phenomenon to be described, which is of course manipulative, especially because phenomenologically there is really nothing despotic about the eye in the Dürer woodcut in which Romanyshyn claims to see this despotism. All one can say phenomenologically is that the depicted artist practices a disciplined, concentrated, and controlled looking. Discipline practiced by somebody is not despotism. Yes, this eye is held fixedly in place. Yes, distance is thereby created. But in itself there is nothing wrong with that. Distance is the a priori condition of the human possibility of having a *world* and being in a "world" instead of merely being, like animals, factually involved with, and an integral part of, the *environment.*

Romanyshyn finds fault with the fact that Alberti, when painting, first draws a rectangle, a rectangle that Alberti says he regards as an open window through which the subject to be painted is seen. Although on a very different level and in a very different context, this act seems to be structurally analogous, for example, to the ancient city-building ritual of first drawing a sacred furrow in the earth around a square within which the city was to be built (as, e.g., practiced by Romulus in his founding of Rome), or to the alchemist's enclosing (even imprisoning!) in a hermetically sealed glass vessel the matter to be worked on and carefully observed. Romanyshyn seems to forget that an artist is an artist, that his work *per definitionem* is something "artificial," and that, as a matter of course, he is not living in "sensuous proximity to things," does not have an immediate but a reflected relation to the world. And is it astonishing that a painter privileges the eye as the mode of relation? After all, he's making pictures. *C'est son métier.* The musicians and poets of the time did not privilege the eye.

The vanishing point, Romanyshyn claims, "was prerequisite for taking leave of the earth." But no, the leave-taking of the earth, the longing for the beyond, and the mortification of the flesh had been the medieval soul's ardent desire for centuries prior to the Renaissance invention of linear perspective, and it was conversely now, along with this invention, that the soul for the first time truly *entered* the world; rooted itself in the earth; really, carefully opened its eyes to it in its sensuous beauty. What begins here is a *conscious* relationship to nature, instead of people's merely unconsciously living in and with it, taking it for granted (because their eyes and soul were turned upwards, to heaven, to eternity).

It is the dialectic of the vanishing lines that they go both ways. They do point to infinity, but they also show the real, natural world in unbroken, continuous contact with the infinite—the finite as permeated by the infinite and the infinite as the ultimate source of everything created. This is why the natural world had become an *explicatio dei*, as Nicholas of Cusa put it.

But Romanyshyn walks into Edgerton's trap, whom he quotes as saying, "space capsules built for zero gravity, astronomical equipment for demarcating so-called black holes, atom smashers which prove the existence of anti-matter—these are the end products of the discovered vanishing point." In other words, for Edgerton the vanishing point is, *in nuce* and *avant la lettre*, in itself already a black hole. What a lack of historical sensitivity! A clear case of a retrojection of the logic of modernity into the psychology of earlier and totally differently structured ages. A retrojection across the fundamental divide, the great historical rupture that separates all the ages in the Western tradition prior to the nineteenth century from the modern world. Through the eighteenth century, the world as a whole had been an intact order permeated by God's spirit: No broken connection. No emptiness, no nothingness at the vanishing point, and thus no vanishing in the nothingness of a black hole. Human life and all human striving ultimately had a clear *substantial* goal. The vanishing point was the symbol of the undepictable infinity and fullness of the creator God, whose spirit permeated all of the natural world and was—potentially—revealed to the *mens humana* through its (the *mens's*) *lumen naturale*. Spinoza would later even speak of *deus sive natura*.[7]

It is silly to retroject our modern godlessness, nihilism, and centerlessness, and our disjunctive logic of unbridgeable difference and *différance* way back into the invention of linear perspective by viewing the latter as the starting point of the former, and the former as the end product of the latter. A false genealogy. The "black holes" as *our modern* "vanishing points" (in quotation marks!) and the vanishing points of Renaissance paintings are totally different, unrelated things. The broken connection with nature has a fundamentally different origin. The prerequisite for the possibility of the broken connection with nature is precisely that the divine order of the world, of which linear perspective and the whole art executed in its spirit were expressive, and thus also linear perspective's vanishing point (fulfilled infinity), had absolutely crumbled away and thus left a great hole, a fundamental lack, an unbridgeable difference. It in fact happened—in the depth of the soul—around 1800 to 1830, with the transition from the handicraft mode of production to the industrial mode of production, and with the transition from the logic of the *copula* (which had prevailed throughout classical metaphysics) to the copula-less modern logic of the *function* (as it would later be called by Frege).

It is noteworthy that for Edgerton and Romanyshyn there is, on the one hand, in the depth a *historical* connection, the unbroken continuity of a dream prevailing from the fifteenth century to the present, while, on the other hand, what gives this history its continuity is for them precisely the fact that it is the history *of* the dream of a *broken connection*. The historical rupture of the connection between man and nature that occurred in the nineteenth century reappears in *their* theory, safely encapsulated, as the *content*, *project*, and *nature* of the continuous dream from the invention of linear perspective to the present. A displacement.

In the light of what I will show below, I think it likely that the deeper unconscious reason for this displacement is the ego wish to escape the painful insight that there has in fact been a real, irrevocable rupture of the connection with nature, an irreparable rupture that happened *in the soul*, truly *happened* "to us" and simply has to be endured by us (rather than its being the result of a "dream" or world design on the part of the Spectator Mind), and to substitute for it a man-made disconnection as a faulty development that we can condemn (and maybe correct). A syntactical change is reduced to a semantic one. Factually, Romanyshyn and Edgerton have to accept and endure the historical rupture, too. But psychologically, they try to rescue for themselves the old consciousness, the idea of a unity between man and nature, by moralistically rejecting the broken connection as a mere mistake or crime. "Ontologically" or logically, nothing fundamental has changed: nature, the flesh, the senses, the earth are still as real as ever; only our human views, attitudes, behavior have changed in the direction of the "Spectator Mind" and the "despotic eye." The problem is merely our human abandonment of the body of the earth, our taking leave of the flesh and the senses—in other words, our sin, not a real rupture of the *unio naturalis* itself. Instead of our having to live with a fundamental rift in the very logic of the objective soul itself, both in its own historical process and between the psychic opposites, we get a grand narrative of a history of psychological degeneration and aberration.

Interestingly enough, the second half of Romanyshyn's paper focuses on a poem by Percy Shelly, Lord Byron's *Manfred*, Mary Shelley's *Frankenstein*, and Coleridge's *The Rime of the Ancient Mariner*—all works of the early nineteenth century and as such reflective of the great severing of the *unio naturalis* that happened at that time and was sensed as a deep shock by the more creative minds of the time. It is the absolute shock, to the sensitive poetic mind, at what had happened in the depth of the soul (or the depth of the logic of the world) at the time of these writers that led to a first interpretation of this change in terms of an outrage, a crime, just as the nineteenth century is in general the time of the invention of crime and detective novels, which earlier would not have been possible because they would not have made any sense, since the "crime"—the dissociation of the soul's copula, the dissociation between the psychic opposites—had not yet happened. The unity had still been intact. Only with this poetic material from the Romantic period does Romanyshyn's thesis about our present-day situation get some sort of a phenomenological backing, since *this* material, in contrast to the linear perspective, is itself concerned with the modern dissociated condition. But instead of realizing from his own material that it is the beginning of the nineteenth century when the decisive fissure happened, he wants to see it as a continuation of what had begun in the fourteenth century. And he also interprets the event moralistically, from the point of view of the modern ego rather than of the objective soul, taking literally the early nineteenth century shock-induced misinterpretation of what had happened as a *crime* and making it his own.

Let us imagine for a moment that all he asserted about the Renaissance beginnings of the Spectator Mind and the "despotic eye"—the broken connection between body and world, the exclusion of the feminine and darkness, the dichotomy of inner and outer, the flight from the earth, the taking leave of the senses and the flesh, etc.—were true. What would justify us, insofar as we are psychologists, in condemning it? Who are we to claim that we know what is right or wrong for the soul? Does the soul have to follow our ideals, our normative ideas of health, wholeness, unity of masculine and feminine, and a feeling connection to the body and the senses? Is it we who dictate to the soul the program that it ought to follow in its history, or are we not much rather at the receiving end, and simply have to take note of how it in fact historically developed and develops, in order to take it from there? I think we have to let each new event and manifestation of soul teach us afresh what "soul" and "soulful" means. Eachness, rather than preconceived standard definitions.

There is no good reason, except our own childlike naivety (which is *not* a good reason), why the soul, at certain points in its history, could not need to become purposely one-sided and, for example, insist on abandoning the earth, divorce itself from nature, overcome the flesh and the senses, exile the feminine. Why could it not need, at times, to marginalize certain aspects? It is absurd to expect that the soul follows our modern principles of political correctness. All this insistence on a *wrong course of history* only shows, I quote Jung again, "the intensity of our prejudice against the actual development, which we obstinately want to be as we expect it. *We* decide, as if we knew."[8] Had not Pseudo-Democritus taught us already that "Nature rejoices in nature. Nature subdues nature. Nature rules over nature"—in other words, that it is inherent in the dynamic of the soul to negate and overcome itself, so that this turn against itself is part of its *soul-making*?

Furthermore, when talking about soul, do we mean the soul as something really real in this our real world, as a possibly ruthless and fearful dynamic that goes its way without concern for our human wishes and throws us at times into unexpected and undesired predicaments, the soul as the dynamic Mercurial spirit *in the actual historical development*—or do we only mean an imagined and ideal soul *apart from, above, and over against* the real development, as a second world, an ego ideal—soul as nice and sweet, morally good, with the opposites light and darkness, masculine and feminine, mind and matter always perfectly balanced in the wonderful pop-sense of "wholeness," so that any deviation from this wholeness could only be a human fault and psychologically wrong (soulless)?

We can sense a desire and great effort in Romanyshyn's paper to construe the history of the last six hundred years as a wrong development. We see this same need also in the *theologian* (not the psychologist) Jung,[9] when he charges Christianity as being one-sided, with the shadow, evil, darkness, and the feminine radically split off (which, by the way, is a sign that Jung had simply refused to follow the revolutionary logical move of Christianity beyond the psychology of paganism and not grasped what it was really about, not entered the spirit of Christianity; instead he approached it with crude pre-Christian categories—but this is not our topic here). Romanyshyn gladly cites these views of Jung's. However, the *psychologist* Jung knew that such value judgments are misplaced. Calling a historically real religion wrong or deficient is an ego-trip. In psychology the categories of good or bad, right or wrong amount to an "artificial sundering of true and false wisdom." Jung speaks of one's succumbing "to the saving delusion that *this* wisdom was good and *that* was bad."[10] He frequently attacks the old idea that *omne bonum a Deo, omne malum ab homine*, which follows the same logic. Why is it a *saving* delusion, a defense mechanism? Because by blaming a *real phenomenon* or *develop-ment* of the soul for being bad, wrong, one-sided, the ego succeeds in res-cuing *its own ideal*, its wishful thinking, its own program, value system, and categories from being refuted and sublated by the soul's actual devel-opment and *ipso facto* escapes the *psychological* challenge of the present, the psychological task that its own historical locus confronts it with.

As I pointed out, Romanyshyn stated that the development he dis-cussed had a price. But it seems to me that he does his best to avoid truly *paying* the price, where "paying" could be understood psychologically as well as literally. Psychologically, it would mean without reserve and resis-tance allowing the irrevocable rupture of the *unio naturalis* or the loss of the unifying bond between the opposites to come fully home to con-sciousness as the *soul truth* of modernity, allowing it to work on, decom-pose, and distill the inherited logical form of consciousness with its traditional expectations. This would be tantamount to giving up the nar-cissistic illusion that our situation is merely the result of a faulty devel-opment, of our outrageous aberration from soul, of our crime (*nostra culpa, nostra maxima culpa*), as well as to giving up the *unus mundus* delusion. Literally it would mean facing, for example, the melting of the ice caps without flinching,[11] and understanding that our response to this threat has to be *only* a sober pragmatic (technological, scientific, rational) one, very much down to earth, without any higher aura of having a soul meaning.

But Romanyshyn proceeds the opposite way. He starts out with the melting ice (or the prospect of a nuclear winter) and a priori apperceives it as a *corpus delicti*, evidence of a crime. In other words, his is not a psycho-logical or phenomenological, but a criminological consciousness that deals with this, and a *corpus delicti* naturally immediately incites the inter-est of consciousness in *Who dunnit?* After a careful search for the "traces" and "footprints," both "carbon and lunar," left by the perpetrator and now "leading us to the melting ice," the suspected culprit is quickly found and arrested: it is the Spectator Mind with its despotic eye that, still juve-nile during the early fifteenth century with the invention of linear per-spective, allegedly committed the first crime of a long criminal record.

A good policeman, however, would (a) not only catch the dogsbod-ies, but would try to get the brain behind the whole operation, and (b) would not arbitrarily arrest just any one of the usual suspects, but identify the actual perpetrator. As to (a), if the "crime" is the distance from earth and the appearance in history of the Spectator Mind, in order to find the "brain behind it all" a good detective would have to go way back to Adam and Eve and their original sin—to the moment of hominization, i.e., of the initial emergence of a reflecting consciousness, an emergence that is tantamount to what in mythological parlance is called the expulsion from paradise. From the very moment that *homo sapiens* became human and, as *zōion logon echon*, started to speak, he had already left the "sensuous proximity to things," had also learned to "kill at a distance," and lived, high above "the earth," in language, myth, ideas, notions. Already then, and not only from around 1400 B.C. onwards, "the world (was turned) into a double of itself so that what it [the mind] thinks about the world is what the world is." This is how it had always been. The soul is "un-natural" from the outset. If it were not "un-natural," if it were itself a piece of nature, there would not be soul at all. As Jung never tired of pointing out,[12] we are hopelessly enclosed in an exclusively psychic world; we live in images, and only see the world through them. What happened later at different times in the course of history, such as during the Renaissance, was only the further unfolding of this "original sin," *if* you want to view it as sin.[13]

To the extent that this "original sin" is the fact of hominization, "sin" in this case is not a moral category, but a logical one, man's logical (not biological) always-already having pushed off from the animal state or, in mythological terms, the expulsion from the paradise of animal existence; it is not a particular deed, but the very nature of man (as *logon echōn*), part of the logic of being human. Inherent in the very idea of original sin is that it is inescapable, has to be borne by every single human being as a fact that is absolutely out of reach for us, because it is our logical a priori.

And concerning (b), the real psychological problem of a rift in the very logic of our being-in-the-world, of the loss of a copula that connects heaven and earth, man and nature, etc., came up as late as the early nineteenth century after the conclusion of Western metaphysics and along with the Industrial Revolution, and not earlier. It is likewise inherent in the very concept of this historical rupture that it is both inescapable and out of reach for us because it is a rupture brought about by the objective soul, and thus amounts, as indicated, to a radical change in the logical constitution of our modern being-in-the-world. There is no possibility of going back behind the radical loss of *mater natura* and behind the broken connection between the psychic opposites brought by this historical rupture, and no chance of possibly undoing or correcting them. The cards of the game of life have been mixed anew for us by the soul, and they are the only cards we have. As it has always been, so it is also for us today: we have to prove ourselves in this new situation. *Hic Rhodus, hic salta*. That's all there is to it. Everything else is illicit speculation and wishful thinking.

Against the backdrop of this foil, the function and achievement of the criminological mind's moralistic condemnation of the rift (which was a *happening* in the history of the soul) as an alleged *doing* (the Spectator Mind's "dissolving" the tension between mind and nature and its "aligning itself on the side of mind split off from nature"), and of the search for the criminal responsible for this doing, becomes clear. It is the wish for the revival of what was lost or destroyed by the invention of linear perspective.

REPENTANCE

It is the task and purpose of the police to secure and restore the old order. The psychological equivalent to the police, the moralistic and criminological mind, has correspondingly the task of rescuing an obsolete consciousness. In the case of our material, moralistic condemnation has the psychological function of construing what happened as merely caused by a false attitude, false views. Inasmuch as attitudes and views are only ego perceptions or interpretations, human perspectives and ideas, they are only an overlay over reality. They happen in and belong to the ego, to the human intellect, but do not necessarily reflect the truth. Since what happened is, according to Romanyshyn, merely caused by *false* views, the underlying truth is not really affected, but only obscured, forgotten, discarded and ignored, mistaken. So in the soul, logically, the breaking of the bond between mind and matter did not really happen. In the depths, the old order, the connection, the *unus mundus* still exist intact, and all that is needed is to "radically alter our view of the world." The function of this moralism is to uphold the *dream* of paradise *not* totally lost, the dream of the unity of mind and matter, man and nature, light and darkness. For this dream to become powerful, the construal of history as a faulty and morally bad development is needed. Because only if there is sin—here the sin of the Spectator Mind's "dream" of an ideal spirituality, of power, control, and dominant mastery over the forces of the natural world, of leaving the earth, etc.—will there be need for repentance. And only in the preaching of repentance does the new dream become psychically effective, the dream that there has not been a rift in the objective logic of the world and that the world is still undissociated.

Romanyshyn's dream is a counter-dream to what he thinks was the "dream" of the Spectator Mind, of which he says, "We are the inheritors of that dream." But his is, I believe, not only a counter-dream to that earlier "dream," but also a *counter-factual* dream, an idle ego fiction without any psychological, phenomenological basis. Just wishful thinking. A new belief system or ideology.

John the Baptist preached, "Repent ye: for the kingdom of heaven is at hand." (The Greek has for "Repent ye," *metanoeite*: "About-face! Radically change your minds.") Romanyshyn preaches: We must radically alter our views, for the melting of the polar ice caps is at hand. And just as the medieval repentance preachers happily availed themselves of the terrifying plague epidemics in their time to present them as a clear sign of God's punishment for our sins and as evidence of the imminent end of the world, so Romanyshyn makes use of the melting ice as proof of the crime of the Spectator Mind and as an apocalyptic threat that gives urgency to his call for repentance.

Let us hear a bit of his sermon. "There can be no solution to this crisis without some radical change in the fixed attitudes of the Spectator Mind, no solution without…an ego-cide of sorts.…For this transformation to take place we will have to develop new rituals, which make room for what has been discarded and ignored." It is clearly the activist ego, the technological mind, that is speaking here. There is a will to change things, to solve the problem, to correct and better (if not rescue) the world. This impulse is, of course, very common (it also clearly comes out, for example, in the title, cited by Romanyshyn, of the book by Hillman and Ventura, *We've Had a Hundred Years of Psychotherapy—and the World's Getting Worse*), but it is not a psychological one; it is even incompatible with psychology and (truly psychological) psychotherapy. What is it to a psychologist—*to the extent that* he is really the representative of the standpoint of soul—whether the world is getting worse or better? The psychologist knows himself not to be the healer, the doer. He only accompanies and "attends to" the real process. He knows that *if* there is to be a healing that deserves this name, it has to come from the soul, to be the work of the soul itself.

Although Jung himself is not always free of the world-rescuer impulse, he nevertheless expressed the *psychological* attitude very clearly when he said, we "want to see the world as it is and leave things in peace. We do not want to change anything. The world is good as it is."[14] The world is good as it is *even* in view of the melting ice and other possible disasters. This statement about the goodness of the world is neither a sign of total blindness to illness, misery, dangers, to all that is wrong in the world, nor a religious dogma or a metaphysical assertion, but merely an articulation of the psychological, psychotherapeutic methodological as well as ethical principle of leaving things in peace, abstaining from meddling in the process by intruding with our own moral norms, recipes, wishes, or activism. Just as the cobbler should stick to his last, so the psychologist should let the soul do its own thing, whether it be pathologizing or healing a pathology. That Jung's maxim also applied to work in the consulting room comes out in his repeatedly stating that when asked by patients in distress what they should do, he was wont to answer that he did not know either and that the only thing to do was to look at and attend to the dreams. The psychologist is not a problem-solver, not a politician, a technician, or a social engineer, not a healer or savior, educator, or reformer, not a do-gooder. He is *only* a "careful observer" of and attendant to the products and processes of the soul, without a salvational program of his own.

Only the ego wants solutions. Only the ego can think that *we* should or could develop rituals. A psychologist knows that true rituals have to come from the soul, from the objective psyche, in order to *be* rituals in the first place. Just like gods, rituals are not of our making, not our inventions. And how could we possibly develop rituals if it is their purpose to first make room for what is the a priori condition of the very possibility of rituals, namely the missing connection? A *petitio principii*. Without the copula between the opposites, without the actual living connection between the sensible and the notional, any so-called ritual could only be an empty ego ceremony. But for Romanyshyn, *we* have to *make* this connection. "The melting ice is a symptom that calls once again for us to bridge that divide between inside and outside." But soul bridges cannot be made. They are logical bridges. And if they do not exist for us, as is the case in modernity, then all our attempts at bridging the divide are idle acrobatics at the one bank of it. A *pontifex maximus* can only build those bridges that logically already exist and allow him to be logically on both banks at once.

"We will have to," "there can be no solution without": rhetorically mild ways to express a commandment, a "Thou must." It is the ego that is speaking here; and it, this ego, with its demand of a radical change, also constellates only the ego in the reader and speaks to it; and it furthermore tries to press its own ego program upon the latter, just as it started out from an ego emotion (anxiety) and approached its theme with ego moralism. This stance is all ego, an ego completely cocooned within itself. Soul does not figure here. On all counts it is the very opposite of the stance of psychology: psychology as the careful listening to the soul's speaking to *itself* about *itself* and only for *its own* sake (*not* to us and about us or about the world and for our sake, our better). "In myths and fairytales, as in dreams, the soul speaks about itself, and the archetypes reveal themselves in their natural interplay, as 'formation, transformation / the eternal Mind's eternal recreation.'"[15]

Small wonder that a standpoint that is so exclusively steeped in ego comes up with the demand for an ego-cide. This idea would be absurd in the stance that inspired Jung's statement just quoted, because in it the ego did not figure at all, from the outset. The ego had dropped out altogether. This stance was psychological to begin with. It had taken its position on the standpoint of soul. But the fact is that the called-for ego-cide would not change anything, could not reach its goal. It would by no means bring an end to the ego and take us to the land of soul. Paradoxically, an ego-cide would only confirm and build up once more that same ego that is to be killed, because this whole fantasy is itself a desperate ego move of a technical, problem-solving mentality. You can only get to the soul if you are already in it, have begun with it, have left the ego behind.

THE EGO'S FIFTH COLUMN UNDERMINING PSYCHOLOGY FROM WITHIN

But the soul is of no concern for our author. He has no interest in that *self*-contained "interplay" that Jung, with a poetic allusion, characterized as "the eternal Mind's eternal recreation." *This* soul is *fundamentally* "absent," distant, cold. And it even requires distance. By contrast, Romanyshyn wants our *immediate* involvement with the facts of this world, the ecological crisis.

"The melting ice is, in Al Gore's term, an 'inconvenient truth' because the soul and its symptomatic speech remains an inconvenient truth." I have no difficulty with letting a politician get away with calling the melting ice "a truth," but in psychology this would be a frivolous use of the word. The melting ice is not a truth, but an external, empirical fact, a positivity. The very purpose of Romanyshyn's paper, however, is precisely to obliterate the psychological difference between soul truths and external facts of nature, as we can see from the quoted statement about the inconvenient truth, which tries to suggest that the melting ice is *the soul's* "symptomatic speech," as well as again from the very last sentences of his paper: "The collective, archetypal unconscious at the core of the melting ice is an inconvenient truth. But it is truth we cannot afford to ignore. Depth psychology has a special obligation to this truth."

A fact of nature is, just like that, an expression of the collective, archetypal unconscious, and, mind you, not due to that rare, mysterious, because by definition *acausal*, connecting principle that Jung called synchronicity, but directly and, according to the author, obviously caused by human attitudes and behavior! A positive fact of nature is here not just happening as an event, but it is also *speaking*, just as in animistic, magical, or mythological times the soul spoke through thunderbolts, trees, rivers, the flight of birds, earthquakes. Instead of viewing the melting ice as an *unintended consequence* of human behavior, it is immediately claimed for the soul as the voice of the collective, archetypal unconscious. I would call this superstition or mystification. Without any need, what is completely satisfactorily explained as a practical consequence of certain long-term actions[16] is inflated with soul importance. Here even the founder of the theory of the collective, archetypal unconscious would feel the need to apply Occam's razor (*principia non sunt multiplicanda praeter necessitatem*).

But we would misunderstand Romanyshyn if we viewed this as a slip. No, it is his program. He wants to bring down and reduce the relation between man and soul to a positivistic level, the level of the relation between inner attitude and outer fact. A telling symptom of this is his use of the idea of an *Axis Mundi*.

"The polar ice caps are the *Axis Mundi* of the world and the Polar Regions of the soul." It is odd that ice caps—broad, thick masses of ice—are said to be an "axis," which is something linear that goes through and connects, normally, two wheels or, in a figurative sense, also two regions or perhaps two poles. But it may well be that this strange mixture of images is already indicative of a tendency in Romanyshyn's paper to identify an imaginal or logical idea with, and stuff it into, the thick materiality of an external fact. The *Axis Mundi* is actually the very ancient, hallowed, and nearly universal mythological idea of a cosmic tree that went through the three regions of the cosmos—the underworld, the earth, and heaven—and that above all both connected and held apart (distanced!) heaven and earth. This tree, of course, did not exist anywhere as a positive biological reality in nature. It was exclusively the property of the mind, an *imaginal* reality that was the early mythological equivalent of the later *logical* copula that connected and held apart subject and predicate, the particular and the universal. In Romanyshyn's version, the *Axis Mundi* gets stuffed into the literal geographic or geological reality of the earth, the positively existing ice caps. The archetypes are now out there in actual things.

This positivization is the one problem. The other problem is that now the *Axis Mundi* does not hold apart and connect two *logically different* realms any more—earth versus heaven, the particular versus the universal. The whole tension is gone. The psychological difference is canceled. The polar regions of the earth are "the *Axis Mundi* of the World-Soul." The entire dimension of heaven, mind, *logos*, transcendence, God disappeared from this scheme. The *Axis Mundi* has become flat, earthly, utterly meaningless. It has no other anymore. With the loss of its function to bridge the psychic opposites, it has also lost its soul. If it still holds apart and connects two "opposites," it is the literal realities of the polar ice caps, which are twice the same thing, merely at different locations on this empirical-factual earth.

Apropos of the topic of dream interpretation, Jung once said: "[W]e see that behind the impressions of the daily life—behind the scenes— another picture looms up, covered by a thin veil of actual facts. In order to understand dreams, we must learn to think like that. We should not judge dreams from realities because in the long run that leads nowhere."[17] The same applies to all psychological interpretation. Our author, however, views the important pieces of poetry from the Romantic period to which he devotes himself, and the invention of linear perspective, precisely in the light of present-day ordinary realities, and conversely applies the poetic motifs directly to our modern empirical facts, as if "ice" in the one sense and "ice" in the other were the same thing. It is his express purpose "to bridge that divide between inside and outside," to proclaim that "the ecological problem…is a psychological problem," and his ecological anxiety is his psychopomp, his only bridge, expressly so: "in this moment of anxiety I know in a way that deepens its uneasiness that the melting ice is more than a reasonable problem." "We cannot imprison the melting ice within the confines of our technological ideas and treat it only as a problem that is out there." As we already heard, the polar ice caps ARE for him, quite literally, the polar regions of the soul. The soul is literal fact, out there. It has now been buried in *mater natura*, or no, not in the divine Mother Nature of old, but in modern physical reality. What for Jung had still been a thin veil of actual facts has completely solidified and is *tel quel*, as the *prima facie* impressions of daily life, supposed to be soul. And so the new divide to be bridged is no longer between heaven and earth, God and natural world, the universal and the particular, but, completely secularly and positivistically, between inside and outside.

As to what happened in the Renaissance over against the earlier Middle Ages, Jung wrote that the heavenly goal was exchanged for an earthly one and the vertical orientation of the Gothic style turned into the horizontal one of the discovery of the world and of nature. And he implies that this shift led, via the French Enlightenment and French Revolution, directly to our present, clearly "antichristian," condition.[18] Although I do not think that this view does justice to the *psychology* of this change, on the surface this is an adequate description, and I mention it here because it can serve us as an image for what happened to the *Axis Mundi* in the hands of Romanyshyn. It is a shift from verticality (heaven/earth) to horizontality (the poles of the earth as well as inside/outside, subject/object, consciousness/natural world).

The psychological difference is not one between inside and outside, which is solely an ego problem, a problem of personalistic psychology and also of "ecological psychology" (which is an oxymoron or even a downright contradiction in terms). How could inside/outside be a problem for a psychology based on the insight that "the soul speaks about itself, and the archetypes reveal themselves in their natural interplay, as 'formation, transformation / the eternal Mind's eternal recreation'"? For such a psychology, the entire inside/outside issue has dropped away, and along with it both inside and outside. Because "inside" is the opposite of and as such dependent on "outside," what is "inside" is itself inescapably *external* and unfit for a psychology that is defined as the discipline of interiority. An "ecological psychology" makes externality—in Jung's just-cited terms, the earthly, horizontal orientation, the banalities of everyday life—even its very principle. It exclusively celebrates the ego's interests in its own and the earth's survival, and transfigures them as if they were a *soul* interest, thereby eroding the very concept of soul. Psychology's interiority is absolute, i.e., absolved, *freed*, from the whole inside/outside opposition. It comes about through the methodological process of the absolute-negative interiorization into itself, into its concept, its soul, of any phenomenon that happens to be of psychological interest.

The soul's images therefore have everything they need within themselves. They do not refer to anything outside, but only to themselves. The psychological difference properly understood is, for example, the difference between "the thin veil of actual facts" and "the other picture that looms up behind it," or that between *aurum nostrum* and *aurum vulgi*, and so also between "*our* melting ice" and "the melting ice as an *ecological* problem."

But the new dogma is precisely: *aurum nostrum* IS *aurum vulgi* and the ecological problem IS a psychological problem (and vice versa); the melting ice IS in itself "a symptom and dream." This is the dogma of a secular but pseudo-religious doctrine of salvation, one whose sterile components are boosted up and fired solely by ego emotions and ego desires to give them the appearance of truth. Emotions: fear, despair, hope, moral condemnation, guilt feelings. Desire: that our flat, positivistic reality be "*more* than a reasonable problem," *more* than unintended consequences. The demand for MORE as a substitute for the eliminated psychological difference, for absolute-negative interiority, for the soul's verticality and for what is "behind the scenes." *More* means: what is by definition secular and systematically apperceived as an external problem ("outside") ought nevertheless to have a religious aura, and the nihilistic ought to have a depth of meaning.

The psychological response to this desire would be that the *soul* (as what is behind the impressions of daily life, behind the scenes) would make us realize that the melting ice outside is "*only* that!"—*only* one of the empirical facts or of the banalities of life that make up Jung's "thin veil."

SALVATION

The ultimate aim of Romanyshyn's paper is to cultivate the dream of the possibility of (psychological) salvation, the possibility of restoring and reviving all that was lost and destroyed by the Spectator Mind. We learn in more detail of all that can be restored, because the melting ice, we are told, is not only a terrible threat but also

> a chance to heal the split between mind and nature, a chance
> to reanimate an aesthetic sensibility that unfreezes the feeling
> connection that has been lost…, a chance to remember the
> feminine principle in the work of creation, a chance to recover
> a sense of the sacred within an integrated spirituality that
> honors the darkness in the light, and a chance to restore the
> symbolic attitude that…is able to witness in the albatross [an
> allusion to Coleridge's *The Rime of the Ancient Mariner*] the
> extraordinary in the ordinary, the miracle in the mundane,
> the numinous in nature.

New Age kitsch. All the faddish slogans of the ecological variety of pop psychology are gathered here.

So we are said to have now all these many wonderful *chances*. But what does the author have to offer to back up his huge salvational promises, other than his admonishment at the address of the ego to repent, to "radically alter our view of the world"? What does he have to show that would raise all these marvelous chances beyond mere wishful thinking and turn them into *real* chances, concrete options for which the conditions of possibility are provided? Does he say *how* we could in fact go about radically altering our view of the world and *how* we could actually achieve this? For obviously, we cannot change our views like we change our jackets. Views are deeply ingrained in us, in our institutions, and in the entire organization of social life. Jung might have said, *we* do not have those views, they have *us*.

Aside from the blame for what he considers a wrong development and aside from the call for repentance, we hear nothing that would give convincing reality to the alleged chances mentioned, unless one considers the construct of a "deep unconscious of the *unus mundus* world of soul where psyche and matter are one" as something. But this idea does not make those chances more credible. Both "the unconscious" (let alone a "deep" unconscious) and the *unus mundus* are fictions, "metaphysical" assertions without empirical or phenomenological basis, irresponsible clichés that come up here only as a *deus ex machina*. Since I am speaking as a psychologist and not a metaphysician, I would not want to claim that it might not possibly turn out, at some point in future history, that psyche and matter, in some way, are one. I simply have no knowledge about that issue either way, and it also is none of my business, since the task of psychology is to devote itself to *what actually shows itself (has shown itself) of its own accord.* But in our present situation, it is completely out of the question for me to frivolously assert the unity of psyche and matter when, in this our present situation, this idea is contrary to our actual experience and remains absolutely speculative, mere ideology, a thought-thing.[19] By relying on this spurious product of the intellect's wishful thinking, Roma-nyshyn himself precisely "align[s] [him]self on the side of mind split off from nature," split off from the real! Ego wishes for a *retour à le paradis* of absolute unity are given out as "the deep ground of existence, the deep unconscious of the *unus mundus* world of soul where psyche and matter are one." The actually existing rift is simply pasted over by an assertion, an ideological belief.

Thus his new belief-system IS his having given in to the very "pull to go numb, to fall asleep,...to grasp at...easy solutions" that he said he wanted to resist. Because the easiest "solution" is to indulge in wishful thinking and to turn it into a doctrine. It is *consciousness's* going uncon-scious.

There is one passage in his text in which he seems to give us a hint about how he possibly imagines what the healed split would look like. He speaks of what he calls the "negative gnosis of a metaphoric sensibility" which "is responsive to this de-stabilizing influence of the unconscious. It is a linguistic alchemy, which always dissolves the certitude of 'is' in the possibilities of the 'is not' and thus holds the tension between the dog-matic arrogance of the fixed mind and the cynical despair of the postmod-ern mind." This sounds to me pretty similar to the stance of Nietzsche's *last man*, who, by the way—Romanyshyn will rejoice—*blinks* (in contrast to his "despotic eye" that does not blink). The ideal here is: a little bit of this and a little bit of the opposite, of "is" and "is not," of "dogmatic arro-gance of the fixed mind" and "the cynical despair of the postmodern mind." It is the trick of switching back and forth between two discon-nected rigid stances, playing the one against the other, and thereby creat-ing the *impression* of flexibility and life. It is this "undulating" that is called by him "metaphoric sensibility."

The undulating is the expression of the fact that the I reserves itself. It does not make either position fully its own so as to be fatefully exposed to the negation coming from its own internal opposite. Rather, the I stays aloof, uncommitted, it holds its place vis-à-vis the two positions as a sepa-rate third party, which thus is free to alternate at will between them, untouched. Since the I only switches back and forth, it preserves the "is" and the "is not" in their initial form, locking them firmly in undialectical opposition, and preventing their possible clash and thus the resolution of the contradiction. The dogmatism of the fixed mind here is just as much as the postmodern cynical mind over there, preserved intact—indeed, both are (alternatingly) being subscribed to by the ego, but they are also kept abstract, I-less: not real *minds* at all but abstract theoretical positions. Since the I does not take a stand, stake itself, and own up to its dogmatism (or, conversely, to its cynicism) as its own stance, it must not and cannot die as dogmatic I (or as cynical I, respectively) and thereby become a truly psychological I. The psychological I is not dogmatic (it does, for example, not indulge in ideologies like that of an *unus mundus*) and it is not cynical (it does not just switch between positions without committing itself). It is committed, determined. *Hic Rhodus, hic salta.* But it knows the position that it takes with determination to be "*only* that!": this one mortal I's personal view today.

I mentioned that Romanyshyn's paper ends on a rather pessimistic note, "near despair." He wonders, "Is there still time to approach the melting ice at the poles of the world as a symptom and dream?" Probably not. But I think whether or not is only of subjective, *psychic* importance. Regardless of what will factually happen, all that *psychologically* counts is that he established and confirmed for himself the belief in the *unio naturalis* as a present possibility and passed over the really existing split by condemning it as false. Whether all the chances he sees will come true in real life or not makes no difference psychologically. An idea or illusion, such as the dream of the oneness with nature, is psychologically "true" inasmuch as it exists. It does not need factual corroboration. Even if this belief were to be refuted by reality and there would have to be utter despair on the *psychic* level (i.e., for the ego personality)—on the *psychological* level, for the salvation of the soul (*if* the latter happens to be so inclined), it is perfectly sufficient that the eco-psychological ideology of those chances is being *entertained* and *promoted*.

NOTES

1. Robert D. Romanyshyn, "The Melting Polar Ice: Revisiting *Technology as Symptom and Dream*," *Spring: A Journal of Archetype and Culture* 80 (Fall 2008), pp. 79-116.

2. C. G. Jung, *Nietzsche's* Zarathustra: *Notes of the Seminar Given in*

1934–1939, ed. James L. Jarrett, 2 vols. (Princeton, NJ: Princeton University Press, 1988), 2:1497f.

3. *Ibid.*, 1:158.

4. "Regret": Jung was probably thinking of German *bedauern*, which can mean both "regret" and "feel sorry for."

5. C. G. Jung to Arnold Künzli, 16 March 1943, in *C. G. Jung Letters*, 2 vols. (Princeton, NJ: Princeton University Press, 1973), 1:333.

6. I would say, to *pay* that price.

7. Much would have to be said about these things, but inasmuch as what I want to show is a different matter, I will have to leave it at these few hints.

8. C. G. Jung to Herbert Read, 2 Sept. 1960, in *Letters*, 2:591, adapted.

9. James Hillman was probably the first to make the significant distinction between Jung's theology and his psychology.

10. C. G. Jung, *The Archetypes and the Collective Unconscious*, vol. 9/1 of *The Collected Works of C. G. Jung* (Princeton, NJ: Princeton University Press, 1953-1979)(hereafter *CW*), § 31, translation modified.

11. Interestingly enough, Romanyshyn accuses the "despotic eye" of the Spectator Mind of not blinking (which, by the way, is not convincing given what we see in the Dürer woodcut; there is no reason why the depicted artist could not blink). The condemnation of "not blinking" goes well together with his not facing our situation without flinching.

12. For example, C. G. Jung, *Memories, Dreams, Reflections* (New York: Pantheon, 1973), p. 352, or *CW* 8, § 680.

13. On p. 107 of his essay, Romanyshyn writes: "My point, therefore, has not been that only with the development of linear perspective has this ability [to distance oneself from nature] arisen. On the contrary, my point has been that with that development we have transformed a possibility into a metaphysics, a condition into a method." This comment appears inserted in a discussion of the arrow motif in *The Rime of the Ancient Mariner*, after about 27 pages (out of 34) of trying to convince us that this ability did arise with the development of linear perspective. His point *has* certainly *not been* what he now all of a sudden claims, claims by way of a mere afterthought necessitated by the sudden realization that arrows and killing at a distance predate the invention of linear perspective by millennia. If it *had been* his point (and "on the contrary" so), there would have had to be some trace of it before—nay, he would have had to start out

with it and describe the "dream" of linear perspective against the backdrop of this always prevailing truth of the human condition, which would have shown it in a very different light. But he does his best to make what began with linear perspective appear as absolutely singular. And besides, distance from nature was not a "possibility" but is *the* human reality, and metaphysics is the reflection and articulation of the inner truth of the actual mode of being-in-the-world (and the logical constitution of the world) at a certain historical epoch and not something that "we" make out of a possibility.

14. Jung, *CW* 18, § 278.

15. Jung, *CW* 9/1, § 400, translation modified.

16. That the melting of the ice is caused by human actions seems at least to be what most scientists think.

17. C. G. Jung, *The Visions Seminars* (Zürich: Spring Publications, 1976), Book 1, Part 1 (Lectures October 30–November 5, 1930), p. 8.

18. Jung, *CW* 9/2, § 78.

19. The very fact that, even if we radically changed our views of the world, it would not make any difference to the melting ice points to the *really experienced* disunity of psyche and matter.

BOOK REVIEW

Thomas Moore. *Writing in the Sand: Jesus and the Soul of the Gospels.* Carlsbad, California: Hay House, 2009.

REVIEWED BY DENNIS PATRICK SLATTERY

Twisting toward the Kingdom

In my home in northern Ohio, I can remember growing up and tiptoeing past the Bible sitting on a shelf between my parents' bedroom and mine—mine and my three brothers'. The Bible was intimidating both in size and regal presence: a white naugahide cover, floppy at the corners as if too big for its size, gold leaf lettering, gilded edges to the pages. It was a book that looked like it wanted to be treasured but not read. Who would foul such an outer package by opening it and reading the deep black lettering on paper so thin it was more like a membrane? From the point of view of a ten-year-old, this was THE BOOK, the actual copy penned by God. No thank you. I returned to my X-Bar-X Boys series and read of ranching and riding horses somewhere in Montana or Texas.

Thomas Moore has more than opened that book in his new study. He has performed a community service in daring to unpeel the moralistic skin of the Gospels in order to peer beneath their "Word of God" design and to expose the humanity of a historical figure, not just through those texts the church has deemed "authoritative," but also those outside the

Dennis Patrick Slattery, PhD, is Core Faculty, Mythological Studies, at Pacifica Graduate Institute. He is the author or coeditor of twelve books, most recently, with Jennifer Selig, *Reimagining Education: Essays on Reviving the Soul of Learning* (Spring Journal Books, 2009). He is currently completing a daily meditation book on Dante's *Divine Comedy* as well as a coauthored novel, with Charles Asher, entitled *Simon's Crossing*.

canon: the Gospels of James, Mary Magdalene, and Thomas, for example. The wind blows a mite easier through this fresh exposure. I would suggest that Moore has resurrected the Gospels, as Lazarus was brought forth to live another day, perhaps in the fullness of a vision that includes the darkness of death. I could see his book just as easily named *Raising Lazarus: Jesus and the Soul of the Gospels.*

Divided into eleven chapters and buttressed by an introduction and a conclusion, the book is a selection of what we could assume are key stories, within and outside of the canonical narratives, that spoke to Moore over the years and to which he has returned for a second or third look. Having spent more than a decade in a religious order, Moore knows what the traditional communal conversation should sound like. But not only does he sidestep such rhetoric, with its often self-righteous moralistic tone, he even suggests uncoupling the stories from Christianity itself, so they can breathe freely on their own soil: the soil of soul and human life as it is lived by the majority of us.

I like his claim in the introduction: "There are two ways to be spiritually secure: One is to attach to a fixed and uncomplicated teaching of leadership, and set of moral standards. Another is to be open to life, ever deepening your understanding" (p. xvi). His goal is not just the latter, but includes as well a guide to help others crack the chrysalis of frozen prose and allow the juices of life to flow through the body of the stories. One glimpses early on that his book is concerned with the imagination of the Gospels, and especially with the subtle and profound imaginings of Christ, who is depicted by the author as more a poet than a prophet, more a mythologist than a minister, more a human being than a divine messenger. Moore reveals a new hermeneutic for reading that is psychological, mythological, and respectful of what has been written, but turned now towards the shadow of soul to illuminate in its dark light the figments of being human that moralistic pronouncements shun by too glibly simplifying.

Two themes seem to guide his explorations: "Entering the kingdom" and "metanoia," the Greek word for change of heart, and more: "You adopt an utterly unconventional point of view. You live in a different reality" (p. 27). As to the kingdom, "when you find yourself in the kingdom, you will be in a different world, though at the factual level everything will be the same. The kingdom is translucent and empty. You don't see it in itself, but you see the world altered by it" (p. 15). From my reading, everything else stems from these two "stout stakes," as Henry James called those stabilizing presences that make a story both elastic and resilient. Moreover, through these double, stout stakes, Moore calls for a "spiritual poetics" (p. 16) by which to read the Gospels, for they are poetry, from beatitude to parable.

Regarding this last word, I turn for a moment to one of the best ideas in the book: "a parable is a parabola: you go far out into a story, make a U-turn, and then come back with a surprising twist. All the Gospel parables have this twist that upsets your logic and your habits of thinking" (p. 2). This insight will upset some who read his book, for he grounds so many of the Gospel stories in twisted ways of reading them. By using this term, I mean: twist something and it will reveal itself in ways that normal handling won't yield. So, for example, in his reading of Jesus' first miracle, the transformation of water to wine at his mother's request at the Marriage Feast at Cana, Moore moves it from Jesus accommodating his mother's plea for assistance to make the festival a success to a reading that includes the Dionysian element from Greek mythology: "to live this intriguing way of the Dionysian Jesus is to say yes to life every step of the way, in spite of the possibility that you will be torn apart, judged and crucified" (p. 38).

No moralism here; rather, a deepening mythology gathers around Jesus, the dark vegetative world of Dionysus, the rapture of inebriation from wine crushed, dismembered, altered so that the best of itself can be enjoyed in communal celebration. Moralism, Moore believes, "with its companion feeling of guilt, is an aspect of life lived unconsciously" (p. 43). Moralism would seem to suggest that the reader or listener simply accept what is said, with no dialogue or imaginal engagement. Death is its shadow.

Now, Moore is no hedonist, at least in the way that word has been maligned to mean one who throws off all restraints in favor of appetites ruling one's life. But just as we all have within us, Moore affirms, a Judas, "someone to betray and spoil our virtue" (p. 50), so do we have this impulse to enjoy matter, to eat, drink, celebrate, rejoice, gather, commune, and live outside ourselves in service to others. There is less emphasis on the Ten Commandments, which indeed have their governing place in one's ethical code—but Moore wants them trumped a bit by a loving disposition, a spirit of agape, that motivates us to forgive, forego, and free others through our empathy with them in their "human frailty" (p. 54).

Heaven is not a bus stop we reach at the end of our days; "Heaven is a condition in which you live an ordinary life fully and uninhibitedly based on the idea of respect...and reverence for life" (p. 54). Heaven's stop: no waiting, please. Engage it now.

Each of the chapters reflects an often different and nuanced rhetoric. Some are more colloquial in thought, while others have a darker wisdom to them. As soon as I began reading chapter 8, "Reinventing the Ego: Spiritual Vision and Human Emotion," I felt a deeper register begin to unfold. Not long into it, I felt that this was the strongest chapter thus far—more nuanced, with more libido attached to the language and ideas. It had more heart. I was not surprised then to read: "After beginning this book, a new chapter in my life began. I discovered, to my surprise, that I have heart disease" (p. 115). I felt something unique and profound in this chapter even before the author's revelation. He wrote this chapter from deep in his own "Garden of Olives." He then continues with a beautiful and elegant account of writing and living in a deeply connected way within our mortal limits—one of those incidents that cannot be cured; only endured, enjoyed, and then relinquished. My point in focusing for a moment on the life of the author is to reveal, once again: no moralism here, no "thou shalt" or "thou shalt not." Rather, Moore finds in the metaphor of the Garden a place of suffering; it is also the place of the olives, of growth, of the shaded trees that befriend Jesus and wait with him as his disciples succumb to sleep. The Garden is less a place and more a condition, even a disposition. Such is the poetic spirituality worked by the author—throughout his excellent, liberating angle of reimagining them—to free the Gospels from the disease of religion when it suffocates the spiritual reality of soul and body.

He performs this same imaginal reading on the stories of Lazarus, Jesus' baptism in the Jordan, the mysterious relationship between Jesus and Mary Magdalene, and Jesus the fisherman. I found the story of Magdalene especially rich in the way she makes present the sexual dimensions of ourselves, not as antagonistic to, but in accord with one's spirituality. Moore writes: "A heightened awareness of the positive role of Mary Magdalene provides an opportunity to deal with a major problem in all spiritual pursuits: reconciling sexual needs and spiritual ideals" (p. 128).

What gives his way of revisiting these rich stories such a fresh inflection is his ability to reveal not what has been said but what has been avoided. Moore's courage is great—he has an indomitable heart—to wrestle with the angel of the texts in order to restore waves of understanding that have been hiding just below the surface of the waters of the Gospels. The result is a refreshing wash in words that can change the soul of the reader.

C.G. Jung Club of Orange County

Follow the Bouncing Ball
Sports & the Psyche
Presented by Bernard Michaels, LCSW
Sunday, September 27, 2009
4:00 PM ~ 6:00 PM

The Feminine Archetype Illuminated
An Examination of Women's Art & Writing
Presented by Nan Aguirre, PhD
Sunday, October 18, 2009
4:00 PM ~ 6:00 PM

World of Inner Images & the Individuation Process
Presented by Sheherezad Shashaani, MA
Sunday, November 15, 2009
3:00 PM ~ 6:30 PM

Holiday Celebration
Sunday, December 6, 2009
4:00 PM ~ 6:00 PM

Dionysos
Past & Present
Presented by Daniel Anderson, JD
Sunday, January 24, 2010
2:00 PM ~ 6:00 PM

All events are held at Chapman University, Orange, California

For more information please call (714) 964-5741

or visit our website at www.junginoc.org

WHERE DO YOUR DREAMS WANT TO LEAD YOU?

Archetypal Dreamwork

is a radical return to the core truth of *your* dream. The intention of the dream is not to learn how to manage better in your life. Rather, it is to delve into the deep well of your rich experience to reclaim all that you have lost.

Find out how we would work with your dreams

- **"Submit a Dream"** free at our website. One of our trained therapists will respond directly to your dream.
- **Join a free web seminar:** *Introduction to Archetypal Dreamwork,* August 17, September 21 or October 19   6:00-8:00 pm est

* * * *

We offer: • One-on-One Therapy (available via Phone Sessions)
• Five-Day Dreamwork Intensive Retreats
working with trained teachers in small groups with your dreams
at our Retreat Center in Northern Vermont
• Individual Retreats at our Retreat Center:
self-guided, personal time for inner reflective work
• Programs and Online Classes at
The Center for Archetypal Dreamwork
Visit our website for our Fall 2009 course schedule
w w w . n o r t h o f e d e n . c o m

Affiliate Member of International Association For the Study of the Dream

Books about Archetypal Dreamwork

The Deep Well Tapes * *The Secret of the Pomegranate* * *Hubris of the Heavens* by Marc Bregman   *   *Sex, Trauma and Conjunctio* by Marc Bregman with Christa Lancaster's *Vessel*

The History of Last Night's Dream by Roger Kamenetz
as featured on **Oprah's** Soul Series

North **Y** *of* Eden

To learn more, call Susan Marie Scavo or Bill St.Cyr ~ 802.229.4785
www.northofeden.com